Conversations with Ron Rash

Literary Conversations Series
Monika Gehlawat
General Editor

Conversations with Ron Rash

Edited by
Mae Miller Claxton and Rain Newcomb

University Press of Mississippi   Jackson

www.upress.state.ms.us

The University Press of Mississippi is a member
of the Association of American University Presses.

First printing 2017

∞

Library of Congress Cataloging-in-Publication Data

Names: Rash, Ron, 1953– interviewee. | Claxton, Mae Miller, editor. |
  Newcomb, Rain, editor.
Title: Conversations with Ron Rash / edited by Mae Miller Claxton, Rain
  Newcomb.
Description: Jackson : University Press of Mississippi, 2016. | Series:
  Literary conversations series | Includes bibliographical references and
  index.
Identifiers: LCCN 2016018261 (print) | LCCN 2016029973 (ebook) | ISBN
  9781496808967 (hardback) | ISBN 9781496808974 (epub single) | ISBN
  9781496808981 (epub institutional) | ISBN 9781496808998 (pdf single) |
  ISBN 9781496809001 (pdf institutional)
Subjects: LCSH: Rash, Ron, 1953-–Interviews. | Novelists, American—20th
  century—Interviews. | BISAC: BIOGRAPHY & AUTOBIOGRAPHY / Literary. |
  LITERARY COLLECTIONS / American / General. | LITERARY CRITICISM / American
  / General.
Classification: LCC PS3568.A698 Z46 2016 (print) | LCC PS3568.A698 (ebook) |
  DDC 813/.54 [B]—dc23
LC record available at https://lccn.loc.gov/2016018261

British Library Cataloging-in-Publication Data available

Books by Ron Rash

The Night the New Jesus Fell to Earth and Other Stories from Cliffside, North Carolina.
　　Columbia, SC: The Bench Press, 1994.

Eureka Mill. Spartanburg, SC: The Bench Press, 1998.

Casualties. Beaufort, SC: The Bench Press, 2000.

Among the Believers. Oak Ridge, TN: Iris P, 2000.

The Shark's Tooth. Columbia: University of South Carolina Press, 2001.

Raising the Dead. Oak Ridge, TN: Iris P, 2002.

One Foot in Eden. Charlotte, NC: Novello Festival Press, 2002.

Saints at the River. New York: Picador, 2004.

The World Made Straight. New York: Henry Holt and Company, 2006.

Chemistry and Other Stories. New York: Picador, 2007.

Serena: A Novel. New York: Harper Collins, 2008.

Burning Bright: Stories. New York: Harper Collins, 2010.

Waking. Spartanburg, SC: Hub City P, 2011.

The Cove. New York: Harper Collins, 2012.

Nothing Gold Can Stay. Edinburgh: Canongate, 2013.

Something Rich and Strange: Selected Stories. New York: Harper Collins, 2014.

Above the Waterfall. New York: Harper Collins, 2015.

Poems: New and Selected. New York: Harper Collins, 2016.

The Risen: A Novel. New York: Harper Collins, 2016.

Contents

Introduction

One semester several years ago, I was failing miserably in my attempts to get students in my first-year seminar in literature class interested in a poetry section. Thoroughly frustrated, I happened to see my colleague Ron Rash in the hall and asked him if he might be willing to talk about poetry with my class. He agreed to come and passed out a copy of his poem "Speckled Trout." "How many of you like to fish?" he began. The students in the class, non-English majors, soon began to realize that a poem could be about catching a fish—and nature, a quest, or an elusive mystery. A fish is never just a fish, Rash might say. There is always more to the story. The interviews collected here demonstrate Rash's profound respect for the craft of the written word and his ongoing goal to connect with his readers, whether they are freshman college students sitting in a classroom in Cullowhee, North Carolina, or international readers from France to Australia.

In his 2003 interview with Joyce Compton Brown, Rash explains that much of the raw material of his writing emerged from childhood visits to his grandmother in Watauga County, near Boone. He remembers that time in his childhood as "great preparation for a writer." His grandmother was a reader and storyteller: "She would tell me stories, stories that gave me a sense of wonder, that portrayed the world as a magical place. She was very intelligent, a very good reader herself . . ." Perhaps even more important than her encouragement of reading, Rash explains that his grandmother "also just let me run free. I would go out most mornings, after packing a lunch, with my fishing rod. And I would fish some, but mainly I just explored." The freedom to explore the natural world, unencumbered by other people's experiences and interpretations, shaped his character, just as he uses landscape to shape the characters in his writing. As Rash notes in his interview with Pam Kingsbury, he also learned that "language is magical" from his grandfather, who could not read or write. In several interviews, he describes his grandfather "reading" Dr. Seuss's *The Cat in the Hat* to him. Unlike when his mother read the book to him, Rash noticed that the story was different every time his grandfather told it.

In these interviews, spanning more than fifteen years, Rash charts the slow, deliberate progress of his writing career from his late twenties, when he first, in his own words, "wrote anything that was even remotely good," to the present when he enjoys widespread national and international acclaim. While he worked as a teacher in a high school and later at a community college, he began writing poetry, publishing in small but respected journals and achieving some recognition for his work. In a 1999 interview with Jeff Daniel Marion, Rash describes his goal to write poems that have a "surface accessibility" but also connect with his readers on a deeper level. His interest in traditional Welsh poetry "using a seven-syllable line with a lot of internal rhyme . . . [to] give a kind of sound-intense quality to his work" mirrors the sound of the huge machines in the mills and the speech of the workers in his first collection of poetry, entitled *Eureka Mill* (1998). This book of interconnected poems about mill people and mill life in the Piedmont region of the Carolinas makes the lives of his grandparents and parents, who migrated from the mountains of western North Carolina to work in the mills in South Carolina, accessible and asks the reader to consider them more deeply. In the Marion interview, Rash also explains that his motivation to write comes from these relatives who gave him and his siblings the chance to go to college, to have a better way of life. By illuminating their lives, he fulfills "a sense of obligation to people who came before [him]." Rash tells Marion, "I was the first generation where it was expected that you should go to college. And the only reason that happened was because, for two generations, my family had kind of fought to get into a situation where somebody could." Rash writes his own family story in the poems included in *Eureka Mill*, but he also writes the stories of many who moved from the Appalachian mountains to work for the steady money the mills provided.

In 1994, Rash published his first collection of short stories, *The Night the New Jesus Fell to Earth and Other Stories from Cliffside, North Carolina*. As the interviews clearly reveal, geography and place are defining themes for Rash's work, the beginning and endpoint. This collection is set in the foothills of North Carolina, similar to his hometown of Boiling Springs, North Carolina, as Brown notes in her interview. She comments, however, that each subsequent work has taken Rash deeper into the mountains where his family came from and where his roots are. In this and other interviews, Rash shows how the history, culture, and even the distinctive geographical features of Appalachia impact the art that emerges from it. He states repeatedly, "Landscape is destiny." Rash's family geography continues to inform the geography of his writing. Like his grandparents, who never felt at home in the Piedmont, Rash has always considered the mountains his "spirit country." After buying a house about three miles from Western Carolina University, where he has taught since 2003, he learned that the land had been in his family about 230 years ago. Years after his family moved south to find work, Rash completed the circle back home to discover the stories that would inspire his later work.

Significantly, Rash's next works geographically straddle the border between the foothills of South Carolina and the higher mountains of North Carolina. The works in *Casualties* (2000), a book of short stories, and *Among the Believers* (2000), a book of poetry, span time periods between the Civil War and the present, but both books begin to explore his "spirit country," western North Carolina. Rash explained to Forrest Anderson in 2007, "I grew up in the foothills. I wanted to capture that world and write about it. Then, I just kind of moved deeper into that area that I felt was really my true spirit country, the place where almost all my relatives lived. In a way, it's almost like I wanted to address the foothills first and then move deeper into my family's history and the region that I was most taken with and most identified with." His subject matter includes poems and short stories about foot washing, Pentecostalism, and the hardscrabble farms where his people came from. Rash's first novel *One Foot in Eden* (2002) and his book of poetry *Raising the Dead* (2002) explore much of the same material, the specific geographical location where a dam threatens houses and farms and the people are forced to move away from their way of life. In several passages in *One Foot in Eden*, the sheriff, the protagonist of the novel, drives up from Seneca to the mountains where his family comes from. Similarly, in the last story in *Casualties*, entitled "Return," the main character begins in Charlotte and takes a bus to Boone, where he walks the final two miles up the mountain. In their literal journeys, characters in Rash's works reflect his own ascent into the mountains in search of settings and material for his works.

The literal ascent into his "spirit country" also mirrors Rash's ascent into critical success as a writer. *One Foot in Eden* brought him, if not fame and fortune, acknowledgement as a talented Appalachian writer. In 2003, Rash obtained the Parris Chair of Appalachian Cultural Studies at Western Carolina University. In 2004, he published *Saints at the River*, set in the same region as *One Foot in Eden* but in more contemporary times. The novel explores complex themes of family, the environment, outsiders versus insiders, and the ability of art to capture reality. Water as a key symbol of nature, religion, and loss unites all of these works.

Rash cemented his categorization as an Appalachian writer with his next works, *World Made Straight* (2006), *Chemistry and Other Stories* (2007), *Serena* (2008), *Burning Bright* (2010) and *Waking* (2011), a book of poetry. In many interviews, Rash considers his identity as an Appalachian writer. Clearly, he values his subject matter, a region with an incredibly complex history and culture and a people with a rich storytelling tradition. On the other hand, he argues against a limiting view of "region," drawing inspiration from writers such as Faulkner, O'Connor, and the poet Seamus Heaney. Each of these writers employs the local and regional to write the universal. In the Brown interview, Rash notes, "Regionalism is writing that transcends the local. It's writing that is strongly grounded in a particular place, but it also transcends that place. Heaney was a writer who showed me that, and because he was a poet he had a major influence on what I wanted to do." Rash also mentions other southern and Appalachian writers who supported him during his long apprenticeship. He maintains friendships with many writers he meets at conferences and book appearances. Other writers such as Lee Smith and Robert Morgan have served as mentors who read his early work and encouraged him. He notes that one of the benefits of being part of this small group of Appalachian writers is the community and camaraderie.

In recent years, Rash has been categorized as a member of an increasingly popular sub-genre of Southern literature called "grit lit," or working class southern literature. He also identifies with writers not commonly associated with Appalachian literature such as Cormac McCarthy, William Gay, and Barry Hannah. In the 2005 interview with Robert Birnbaum, Rash explains the problem of "regionalizing" authors. He states, "Ultimately McCarthy and Hannah and Gay are great writers, and I have always been a little leery of any adjective in front of writer—whether it's Jewish writer or southern writer. Because very often there is a sense of 'just.' 'Just a southern writer.'" Rash's work has moved beyond region, increasingly receiving international attention and being translated into fourteen languages. Interviewers from outside the United States represent five of the twenty-one interviews in this book. These interviews display a broader view of Rash and his work. In his 2014 interview with Frédérique Spill, for example, Rash discusses friendships with international writers, European books he admires, and even his place in contemporary American literature.

Rash's latest works, his novel *The Cove* (2012) his collection of stories, *Nothing Gold Can Stay* (2013), and his recent novel *Above the Waterfall* (2015) have continued to bring him attention from the larger literary public, as well as readers in his home region. Scott Simon from NPR (2013) interviewed Rash about his collection *Nothing Gold Can Stay*, asking him how his ideas for short stories come to him. Rash replies, "Very often, they're not ideas at all. I actually start sometimes with a voice, usually an image, an image that won't leave me alone and I have to find out where that image will lead me." In other interviews, he explains how an image might first emerge in a poem, then move to a short story, and then become fully realized in a novel. He also discusses a very few writers who work in more than one genre and who have inspired his own work, writers such as Thomas Hardy, Wendell Berry, Robert Morgan, and Fred Chappell. Asked about how poetry influences his fiction in the Australian publication *Kill Your Darlings*, Rash replies: "I think that, in many ways, the best training I have received as a prose writer is reading and writing poetry, because it demands vividness and concision. I was actually, earlier in my career, better known as a poet. Some people have chastised me for not writing much poetry now, but I hope when readers read my novels or stories that they sense that I am a poet writing prose. A lot of the poetry gets into the prose." The result is what interviewer Robert Birnbaum calls "Rash's fluent and formidable prose."

Rash has focused much of his attention on fiction in recent years, but he plans to publish a larger collection of his poetry soon. In the interview with David O. Hoffman and Sylvia Bailey Shurbutt, he comments, "I cannot write poetry when I'm writing fiction. It's like being on two completely different frequencies. It is nice, though, to have another poetry book out. It assures my poet friends I've not gone completely over to the dark side." In Rash's world, all writing requires discipline and dedication. He notes that writing can be compared to many other jobs: "One thing I've learned about writing: it's the days that you write when you don't want to that make you a writer. It's easy when you're inspired, when you have a great idea. It's the days that you slog through and work hard and something finally comes that are most important. You have to come to work every day." In the interview with Justin Tam, Rash compares the discipline of writing to his own career as a long distance runner in high school and college. He comments, "I think what athletics did was to give a certain degree of patience. For instance, knowing that you might have to train for a year to run a good race. Also the discipline to work and train every day was very good training for writing because there are so many days I would rather stab the pencils into my eyes than write another sentence."

Teaching further informs Rash's writing process. He often mentions teachers who inspired him and discusses his own responsibilities as a teacher. His parents were teachers, and his interview with Joyce Compton Brown displays his gratitude for her role in his development as a writer. Rash further acknowledges the symbiotic relationship he has with his students and his own writing. He comments in the Mincey interview: "I hope the fact that I'm struggling with my own work every day helps me to have a sense of what my own students are going through. They know I'm writing every day and working through problems, and I hope this encourages them. One of the best things is that sometimes I'll recognize something in my student's work that will help me realize something in my own. It helps me be more aware of my own writing." Rash's students, especially at the technical college where he taught for seventeen years, also taught him. Many came from difficult situations and overcame significant challenges in order to obtain an education. Rash tells their stories in many of his works.

All of the interviews clearly display Rash's reverence for the written word. He emphasizes the need to read widely and, for this reason, decided to obtain a traditional master's degree rather than pursue a master's of fine arts degree specializing in creative writing. Although he acknowledges that the writer must pursue his or her own path, for him the need was to obtain a broad literary background. In high school, although he was a very poor student in many respects, he read Dostoevsky sitting in the back row of biology class. In his own classes, he continues to urge his students to read. He also has great respect for the reader. In the Spill interview, he describes the relationship of reader and writer as one of mutual respect: "Black and white is for politicians; they give the easy answers, the simplifications. For me, this is a matter of respecting the reader—that the reader doesn't have to be preached to or told how to feel. To me, that's insulting the reader's intelligence. I believe that a novel is an act of communion between the author and the reader; it's a shared consciousness, very intimate. The reader is taking these blotches of ink I've written and bringing them to life." In order for the reader to believe "the big lie," to immerse him or herself in this fictional world, the writer must get the details correct. Thus, Rash researches each of his books meticulously, a process which opens up new possibilities for the story, as he discusses in an interview with Marann Mincey. He also connects time to geography, completing the circle back to place as the beginning and the end of all of his works. In the 2014 Neufeld interview, he explains, "Blending time is important to me. One thing that's important in terms of placement of stories in books, I want the reader to sometimes feel unmoored from time. The reader might think, this is a contemporary story and then might realize two pages in, it's 1930. I want that." When Neufeld asks why, Rash answers, "Time is a kind of geography as well. It allows us to go into different mindsets, different cultures."

Throughout the interviews, Rash is patient and thoughtful in discussing his works, his writing process, and the communities they emerge from. In many respects, by discussing the craft of writing he is also teaching us to read his work more broadly and deeply, beyond a "surface accessibility." Rash brings his wide reading, his passion for his craft, and his respect for the reader to his work and to the discussion of his work in these interviews.

The editors wish to thank Hope Quinn, a Western Carolina University student who began this book project with an honors project, and our families for their patience and love. We also wish to thank Ron Rash, who has been our hallmate and a generous, dedicated colleague for twelve years.

MMC

Sources

Lang, John. *Understanding Ron Rash*. Columbia: University of South Carolina P, 2014.

"Ron Rash." *Contemporary Authors Online*. Detroit: Gale, 2013. *Literature Resource Center*. Web. 3 Aug. 2015.

"Ron Rash." *Marly Rusoff Literary Agency*. Marly Rusoff & Associates, 17 August 2015. Web. 20 August 2015.

Chronology

Conversations with Ron Rash

Interview with Ron Rash

Jeff Daniel Marion / 1999

From *Mossy Creek Reader* 9 (2000): 18–40. Reprinted by permission.

Jeff Daniel Marion: I am interviewing Ron Rash. It is September 29, 1999. We are on campus at Carson-Newman College in the Appalachian Center. Ron read from his poems last night and also an excerpt from the novel he is working on. Ron, I want to talk to you about the background of where you have come from and also how that background, how that place, people, culture have shaped you as a writer. So tell us a little bit about your background.
Ron Rash: I was born in Chester, South Carolina. My mother and father were Appalachian, but they had to come down to work in the textile mills. But even as a child, I can remember sensing Chester never being really home. Home was always the mountains of North Carolina. My father's family was from Buncombe County, the same section Jim Wayne Miller came from. My mother's family was from Watauga County. When I was still a small child, we moved back into Western North Carolina. I spent most of my childhood in Boiling Springs, North Carolina, which is in the foothills. What I find interesting is almost all of my poetry is about the Appalachian region—either about the people that moved out of the region, as in *Eureka Mill*, or as in the poems I've done in the last few years, set in Buncombe County or Watauga County. And I think one reason is because I spent so much time up there and also just a sense this was my families' territory. I don't do this even consciously, but it seems like for some reason my imagination always leads me back to the mountains.

JDM: Did you grow up in a situation of a family that told stories, were good talkers, so to speak, or who were not?
RR: Well, it was interesting because some of my relatives, particularly the men, were very quiet but some of the women weren't. And it was from the women that I got most of my stories. My grandmother was a very good

storyteller. And one thing that I had, I think very valuable, and I think I'm in the last generation, because this was the last generation maybe before air-conditioning, was that we really did sit on the front porch on summer evenings. I mean you had to. It was too hot inside. People talked. That was what they did. That was entertainment. I can remember sitting on the steps listening to the adults and how much fun that was and hoping if I was quiet enough, they wouldn't notice me and make me go to bed.

JDM: So this was an environment in which as a child you listened?
RR: Right.

JDM: And the adults did the talking?
RR: Yes. And one other thing that happened to me as a child, I had a speech impediment. And so I was very reluctant to talk because I was afraid people would either notice me or tease me. So I grew up listening. I think that was valuable as a writer.

JDM: Was there a particular kind of language that sort of got in your head as a child that you were listening to? I'm thinking particularly of how you draw on, in so many poems, words that we no longer hear in most parts of the Southern Appalachian region, unless you're probably in some remote, rural areas. I'm thinking particularly of words like "poke" for paper bag. I grew up hearing those words, and I realize that's a language that is fading, that is tied to the past. To what extent has that influenced you? I mean that sense of their language as opposed to the language you've learned in school.
RR: Yeah, well I think I did notice that even as a child, I would notice the differences. And I would notice there would be different words and different ways of even saying those words sometimes.

And it was kind of interesting because I would then notice that I wouldn't hear these words, even in Boiling Springs, which was in the foothills. I caught up on that, and one thing that was real interesting was that when I was in graduate school, there were several times when I was reading Shakespeare, and I would read words that I had assumed were Appalachian slang. There have been a lot of people, such as Cratis Williams, who have done so much on this subject.

JDM: I remember hearing, when I was a young adult measuring tobacco in my home county, one farmer say to me "Well I holp my friend over across the road there build his barn and he holp me build mine." Now, I have not heard that "holp," which is straight out of the middle English (if you read Chaucer, "holp, holpen, hath holpen"—help). I have not heard that since, but that was a common expression in my grandmother's time. I think maybe there's something unique in the fact that both of us here are from a generation that was at a crossroads in language and being on the edge of modern or contemporary culture and having a sense of the older culture and its traditions and yet seeing that it is going to disappear very quickly. How did that affect you?

RR: Well, I think it's probably the impetus for me for writing. I think, for instance, *Eureka Mill*. Why did I write about this mill village at this time? Well, I think because I suddenly recognized it was interesting. I actually went through a mill village one time, before I started working on the book, and I realized nobody was in these houses anymore, or at least no mill workers. The mills are shut down and suddenly this world is disappearing. I think one impetus for some types of writers, I think of people like Robert Morgan and Wendell Berry, is to preserve. There is a sense that you don't want this to be forgotten, that it had some importance. And I think that's certainly true of Appalachian culture. I think certainly some of the best poetry in the U.S. is coming out of the Appalachian mountains right now. I think there's a sense of urgency that we preserve something that we recognize as vanishing.

JDM: It seems so much of our contemporary culture is more interested in figuring out the quickest, most efficient, and cost-effective way to accomplish something and we don't think about "Well why is it important to remember these things from the past? Why is it so important to remember the sweat, tears, and blood of our parents and grandparents and uncles and aunts and all those people?" Somebody said one time that poets are usually one to two steps removed from the farm or from some sense of a connectedness to a traditional culture. And I'm wondering if many of us in Southern Appalachia sense this moving into something we're not completely convinced is better than the past. Nobody's saying here that we want to go back to kerosene lamps instead of electricity. But we should raise the question of what we're trading off. It seems to me that your poems suggest that there is an enormous loss when you move from the individually owned farms and self-sufficient life of the farms. Nobody's saying it was easy, but something significant is lost when you move into the village and become a worker at the mill. And you make the point in one poem that your mother looked forward to an eight-hour shift. Everybody knows farmwork is never finished. You can't tend it in eight hours and then move away from that. So, I'm wondering how you feel about how we honor the past.

RR: Well, I think that's true, and I think I'm close enough to know. My uncle was a tobacco farmer, and I've still got relatives who farm in the mountains. I don't sentimentalize that world. I know how hard a life that is. We talked about, yesterday, how hard it is to make it as a farmer. I find that something is really askew in our culture, in our society, when you can have people working so hard and giving us the most vital thing we can have—food, and yet they make the least money. I don't have an answer for that. I wish I did. I find such a situation tragic for the sensibility of a society. Didn't Jefferson say he felt like the backbone of the country was the small farmer? And also that sense of having people in a society who are independent or at least more independent, who are not completely dependent on everything vital in their lives being provided by someone else.

JDM: Much of the really strong poetry coming out of Southern Appalachia right now is awakening readers. I think it's a sensibility that says, "let's question." So while there may not be an overt political motive in the poetry, it is by its very nature political. In a sense it's saying, "look at what is being lost." I find your poems, particularly in *Eureka Mill*, to be very hard-edged in the sense of "let's look at what's happening here, and let's look at these lives that have been in some ways forced out of what had been a fulfilling kind of life." But let's move on to another period to talk about. You went to Gardner-Webb as an undergraduate. Can you pinpoint a time when you began to feel writing was a passion driving you? Did this happen as a college student, earlier, or—

RR: I think it probably started earlier. I think there was always a sense that I liked to imagine. I was a daydreamer, not a very good student in high school, but I was a reader. I was reading a lot, and I continued to read. When I got into college, I had made a couple attempts at short stories. It started there. I pretty much spent my twenties trying not to write. I wasn't getting any encouragement. What I was writing was terrible. It was really when I turned about thirty that I started writing some things that I thought maybe captured something in words the way I wanted. I felt like I was kind of starting to break through, but it was a slow process. But I think it began very early. I think it began with my listening as a child to people and then just taking that and using that as imagination. You know a story I often tell is about my grandfather, who could not read or write, "reading" *The Cat in the Hat* to me. What he was doing was he was making up a story because he couldn't read the words. And the next time he read it to me, it was a different story. And that was wonderful because it suddenly made words magical to me. It was like they could move on the page and rearrange themselves. So I was really disappointed when I started reading in the first grade. My words wouldn't do that, but he taught me something about imagination.

JDM: Were you read to by other people as a child? Where does this passion to read come from? You said partly listening, but were there voices that cultivated your wish to read?

RR: Yeah. I think my parents. Both of my parents were very intelligent people. My father was always a big reader, and there were always books around the house. And I think that was important. I talk to some of my students who sometimes say, "We have a Bible and that's the only book in our house." And I think that is so sad. There were always books around, and there was always a sense that they had some value, and I was encouraged to read as a child. My mother would take me to the library and say, "Well why don't you pick out some books." And she read to me as a child.

JDM: Do you remember particular books that were in your house? Were there certain books that appealed to you that you remember?

RR: One of the most memorable books was the *Jesse Stuart Reader*. I read that book so many times that I think it finally fell apart.

JDM: So you cut your teeth on that book.
RR: Yeah.

JDM: Let's talk about why that was your favorite book. What do you think it was in that book that really drew you in?

RR: I think one thing was the instant recognition of the voices with the voices of my own family.

JDM: This was home.
RR: Yeah, yeah. Those people spoke exactly the way my relatives did. I think I sensed a world that my relatives had told me about. You know, some of the stories of the mountains, some tall tales, historical tales sometimes—

JDM: So let's see how this related to your writing. You said that in your twenties that you were writing terrible stuff. Was that because you had not found the kinds of things you wanted to write about or did you begin by knowing about your subject?

RR: I had to discover it. One reason I wrote so poorly in my twenties was I was my age. I think some writers mature quicker than others such as Kurt Vonnegut. Also I had been in graduate school. I wrote a story that I still feel good about (in college), but when I went to graduate school, the writing just went all to hell because I started thinking like a theorist, and I started analyzing literature instead of responding to it with my brain but with my heart as well. I think graduate school was very valuable for me because what it allowed me to do was read a lot. But I had to almost get out of the sensibility of being a critic and go back to reading like a writer and also writing as a writer. And, you know, one thing I learned immediately (once I felt like I found my voice and started writing some things) was that everything I learned about influence in classes was not true. No writer consciously says, "Well, I'm going to write this line like William Faulkner because I read William Faulkner twenty-eight years ago." Now influences are there, but they are internalized. They're almost organic and they come out. And so that just struck me—you know, the idea that the writer will put in certain kinds of "symbolism," which is a word that I don't even want to use because it seems so untrue to what writers do. I mean none of that—I think—it's almost like I think Faulkner once said he was afraid he had read too much. I don't think that's true, but I think I know what he means by that.

JDM: Well, I think you're probably mirroring the effects of graduate school and there are a lot of writers who feel like it's oppressive to them because it is a sensibility that is so foreign to a writer who wants to synthesize so much of his past and the things that are important to him and speak to him. And graduate school teaches dissection and analysis . . .

RR: Right, that's it exactly.

JDM: . . . which we both would agree are important means of understanding literature. But when it comes to the process of writing, that's another matter. While we're staying on the idea of education and formal education, was there a particular teacher or teachers who saw possibilities in you as a writer and who in some way wanted to nurture your talent?

RR: Yeah, and one is very active in Appalachian Studies, Joyce Brown, Dr. Joyce Brown at Gardner-Webb. I don't know if you've met her, but she's a really good person. She comes from an Appalachian background. She's very interested in the region and she really encouraged me—she was the first person to encourage me to write. Now as a teacher, I understand what a saint she was with me coming up to the door saying, "You want to read my new story?" And now I get that from the other end. But, you know, it makes me take them because I remember she did this for me.

JDM: I was there not long ago thinking—yeah—

RR: And as you know, she did that for me and encouraged me as a writer and it helped me to feel like I might eventually write something worth reading, though I certainly wasn't writing it then. And at Clemson, I had a professor named Bill Koon, and he was very encouraging. Yeah, those people were important. But one thing I think I've learned was, and one thing I think was you've just got to do it yourself. You can't and shouldn't expect people to encourage your writing.

JDM: It is a matter of the self. The drive has to be in you. It can't be put there by someone else. But would you talk about what really does drive you to write? You've said it's something that's inside you, and it's not something that somebody necessarily encourages you toward, but what is its fulfillment?

RR: Well I think a lot of it's in a way what we touched on earlier, a sense of obligation to people who came before me to allow me to have a life where I was expected to go to college. I was the first generation where it was expected that you should go to college. And the only reason that happened was because, for two generations, my family had kind of fought to get into a situation where somebody could, and so I think that's a strong obligation. And also I think another thing, if I'm honest, is that I know the material I can write about my relatives is much more interesting than my life. I find their world more interesting to my imagination. I mean I could write poems about a middle-aged professor suffering over having to read yet another group of 101 freshman compositions, but that to me is not a very interesting subject matter. For some reason, I can't seem to get to what I feel like are important matters through my own life or through my . . .

JDM: Their lives and their stories free your imagination to enter into other selves, and it seems to me an absolutely fundamental aspect of the writer is this ability to enter into the life of the other person. Ultimately it is that leap of the imagination that takes us into the life of the other person. And in that sense, I think maybe writing is a fundamentally moral act. It's a way of caring for and responding to the other person. That is something I think we are sorely in need of these days. I know you don't think of a particular reader when you're writing, but how do you perceive your readers? Do you have a certain perception of the kinds of people who would be reading your work, responding to it, or not?

RR: There are certain people, certain friends, and maybe in a way, that's my ideal audience and very often other writers. I think, "Is this the kind of thing that would ring true for them?" But at the same time, I do not desire to be a writer who writes for a small audience. Now that may end up being the case as a poet, but one thing I try to do is be an accessible poet. I want people who don't necessarily even read a lot of poetry to be able to read my work and say, "I understand what's going on." For me, a writer who has had a great influence is Robert Frost because he can be accessible, but that doesn't mean he's simplistic. He's a master of that. His poetry works on a number of levels. And the writers I admire are those who are willing to risk letting us know what they're saying. There's more of a risk in that than hiding behind a kind of obscurity that I sometimes think is an attempt to be profound when you're not saying much. I'm not a big fan of writers such as John Ashbery. That writing doesn't interest me.

JDM: Let's relate this to our region. Do you feel that we have an audience for poetry in Southern Appalachia now?

RR: Well you may know more about that than I do, but I sense that there is. It may be a small audience, but I just sense there's an audience out there. I think, for instance, people such as James Still and Fred Chappell and Robert Morgan have a following in the region. I think there are people who are excited when they know a new book by these writers will be coming out. Now I'm not sure how big that audience is, but I see some good signs. For instance, the Appalachian Studies Conference. I think the one thing that we're having to deal with now is that with the death of Jim Wayne Miller there is such as huge void. There's nobody to be the central focus for this. I think he was such a great ambassador for Appalachian writers. Not only was he such an excellent poet himself, but he did a lot to promote other writers. And I'm not sure that we've got anybody who's willing, who has the kind of energy that he had to do that. What do you think?

JDM: Right. I have similar feelings that we have some absolutely first-rate writers no matter what part of the country you want to put them in. I think we spend a lot of time talking about the importance of the region to our work and shaping our lives, but in the long run, these writers can speak to anybody in any culture because what we are writing about are basic truths, universal concerns. But it does seem to me that we are lacking the unifying person or voice who will step in and fill the role, as you said, of being ambassador for poetry in Southern Appalachia right now. And maybe that's just something that was unique to Jim Wayne because, let's face it, most writers need the time and the solitude to get the writing done. And if they're being ambassadors all of the time, how much work are they going to be able to accomplish? So, we're talking about a conflict here in the nature of the role of the poet in society. It cuts both ways it seems to me and makes a basic problem for the individual writers. And think about your own case. You teach five classes and the demands of that on your time and on your energy and then as you were talking to me earlier how much work you were able to accomplish in the summer maybe because, "This is the time I've got and I've got to make the best use of it." And so ten hours a day, you would write. So it seems to me the dilemma that we're facing is of a need for a figure who can be an ambassador. But at the same time this writer will need solitude to be able to do the work that is going to nurture us in the long run. And I don't know what the solution to that is.

RR: Well, one thing that I do see that's been heartening to me is people at the Appalachian Studies Conference are getting a chance to read their work to other people. And those are the kind of settings where I would like to see more poets involved. Maybe I'm wrong, but it seems like there's more good poetry coming out of the Appalachians now than any other time. I just think there's so much good work, and I think some people know that.

JDM: I think a lot of people do know that because there are a number of anthologies published and in the making. And there's a beginning of a body of critical writing about the literature that's been published. So all of this is necessary in building that audience for the poets who are going to come along after us. All of this is in service of creating a community of readers.

RR: And also just the recognition that I just wish some of these writers should receive. Jim Wayne Miller is a writer who is incredibly underrated nationally. He's well known in the region, but when you talk about who are important writers in the second part of this century, I would say Jim Wayne Miller's got to be in there. We've got some of the best writers in the country coming out of this region, and that's really exciting. And it's had an influence on me. I mean those writers have helped me because I've learned so much from writers of the generation before my own. I think that's part of why southerners have had such a long tradition. You could get forty or fifty reasons, but I think that one reason is that you grow up in the South, you're eighteen or nineteen years old, and you say to yourself, "This is what people in my region can do." O'Connor reads Welty and Faulkner, and you get somebody like Lee Smith reading O'Connor. There's a sense that these things can continue because in this region this is something that we do.

JDM: Let's talk about that in regard to your writing fiction. I think of you as a writer in the sense that you write fiction, stories, novels, as well as poems, and the uniqueness of that in this region, and in the larger South. We can name a number of writers who are adept at a variety of genres. Can you talk a little bit about what fiction allows you to do that maybe poetry doesn't allow?

RR: I think the one thing that it really allows me to do, and that's something I do in my poetry, what Keats called "negative capability," that idea of entering another consciousness but also entering another voice. And one thing I love to do as a writer in my fiction is to try to enter another sensibility. It seems to me it's an interesting act of empathy and imagination to do it and also it frees me up to use a language that I cannot use as someone college-educated. And to create different languages and what I mean by the word "create" is that we know we can't, as writers, we can't get away with speaking exactly as people speak. Both novels I've written started off with images from poems. And it was almost like, "I wrote the poem but I still haven't gotten what I want to say," and I had to keep expanding. And one of them went into a story and I couldn't get it there. Then it went into a novel and I think, I can't explain that except it's just a sense that something has been left unsaid—that the poem can't cover this.

JDM: Many of your poems are essentially lyric poems, I think. And the lyric, by nature, is a condensation, and behind every lyric there is a story. And so the lyric is a kind of emotional response to that story. And I'm wondering if part of what you're doing is recovering the rest of that story.

RR: Yeah, I think that's it. Yeah, there's a sense that there's more here than I'm able to get in a poem—it's like being on a different frequency when I'm writing fiction as opposed to poetry. But, yeah, there's a sense of expansiveness and also a sense of wonder that I can say almost anything. It doesn't have to be in seven syllables. I think that's really just a release after writing poetry where I'm constantly questioning every word and a kind of freedom. And Robert Morgan's talked about this, feeling a kind of freedom after compression.

JDM: Right, right. Do you know that whenever you're sitting down to write and you're working on something "All right, this is moving to a story," or "This is a poem." You've mentioned there's a different feel, almost a different zone, you enter into. So you know whenever "All right, this is a poem."

RR: Well, sometimes I don't know, and one thing that is kind of interesting is that I've written several stories that were poems first. And one time I wrote a story and then I wrote a poem. So it's almost like I'm trying to—sometimes it's almost like going in and getting your eyes checked, and you're trying to get the right lens strength. Which one is going to be the clear focus? And the other thing I find really interesting, I think you kind of brought this up a minute ago, I want us to talk about this a moment just because I think it's really interesting. Why is it so many of the writers that are able to do this are Appalachian? Why is it when you look back on the history of literature, there are very few people that do this. Hardy, Lawrence, but there are very few that have been able to do what Chappell and Morgan and Still and Stuart have done.

JDM: Right.

RR: I mean Berry and Warren. And what's interesting to me is it's almost all Southern even when not Southern Appalachian.

JDM: Exactly.

RR: My theory is that it's part of—it's just that so much Southern poetry, even when it's lyric, it is still narrative. I think you'll agree with me on that.

JDM: And I think behind that whole sense of narrative and lyric is the sense of traditional culture. We're the generation that does have a knowledge of a traditional culture, and we have been shaped by a traditional culture, and I think that opens up some possibilities for us as writers. And that's one of the great things I think the South and the Southern mountains in particular have provided for several generations of us is that presence of a traditional culture. In my generation, one of the buzz words as an undergraduate was "identity crisis," "alienation." Well I didn't feel that. I knew where my home was. I had a sense of place. I had a sense of belonging. And that doesn't mean that you accept wholesale everything that your culture gives you. You can have a critical perspective on it, but nevertheless you have it as kind of a locus by which you orient yourself in the world. So I'm wondering what you feel about this in relation to what we're talking about—being able to write poetry and prose and explore fiction, even essays too. We haven't mentioned the essay, but Morgan is very adept at the essay, Chappell is very adept at the essay. So the versatility of these writers may be related to the sense of having come from a traditional culture that allows some of the opportunities that if you're alienated from that you don't attain.

RR: Yeah, I think there's something to that. Certainly you're not from a fragmented culture. So, you can encompass all of this. Maybe that's part of it.

JDM: Yeah, right. I don't know, but I'm speculating about why this phenomenon exists abundantly in our region. It seems to me that this is something the rest of the country is hungry for, and yet as you were alluding to earlier, how many of our good writers from this region are known nationally? Fred Chappell is and Bob Morgan is, but there was a day when they weren't. This is something that has come about within the last ten years. But Jim Wayne Miller, as you said, is not appreciated nationally as he should be. Were there other things that you want to mention or talk about as somebody who's engaged in the writing process?

RR: Well earlier, I think you talked a little about craft, and that's really important to me. And I think one thing that's important to me in poetry I find not as important to a lot of other writers today is sound. I'm very interested in sound in poetry and I like to—I mentioned last night I'm very influenced, at least the poems I've been doing in the past three to four years have been strongly influenced by traditional Welsh poetry with the emphasis on sound that you see in poets such as Hopkins and Thomas who learned a lot from that traditional poetry. And the reason I wanted that was because my poems, in a sense, are stories, and I felt like I wanted something to give them a more lyric intensity. And so one thing I've tried to do, in my more recent poems, is to use a lot of sound-intense poetry. Sometimes maybe I overdo that, but it's something that I feel like is important. And also in *Eureka Mill*, I try to use craft to emphasize certain things. In the early poems when people are in the mountains, the verse is more free, less restricted, and I hoped that would emphasize a certain sensibility before they go into the mill. The one poem where I don't do that, the strictest one, is the "villanelle" that I use in the poem "In a Dry Time." And I wanted to use it there because the narrator is caught in a trap where there's no way out and the poem itself becomes a kind of cage. Once again, maybe that's a little heavy-handed. And when I move into the mill, almost all of my poems are iambic because the rhythms of the mill would be so pervasive. I imagine it affecting their speech, or at least I wanted the reader to get a sense of that. I use the Anglo-Saxon split line in two poems that deal with violence, "Boundaries" and "Fighting Gamecocks," to get the sense of a primitive, tribal emphasis. And so I hoped those things would add to the book. But what I've been doing in the last few years is more of the Welsh poetry using a seven-syllable line with a lot of internal rhyme, which I hope will give a kind of sound-intense quality to my work.

JDM: One of the lines I liked in the poem "Drought" seems to me to illustrate a lot of what you're referring to. Out of desperation, they resort to "the old way," as you say, and the folk belief that if you kill a black snake and hang it on a fence that it will bring rain. You say, "Black snakes we'd shared barns with for years fleshed our barbed-wire fences." And then here are the two lines that I think just sparkle. "Their hoe-hacked heads sparkled with clots of flies." It seems to me that's such a powerful sense of sound, but the sound also mirrors the act of killing those snakes. "Hoe-hacked heads" and then "sparkled" is the brilliant word in the right place, and then we make that turn to "with clots of flies." So there is that hardness. There's a physical hardness, there's an emotional hardness, and yet there is a kind of beauty in all that, maybe even a grotesque beauty. But the "clots of flies sparkling" are the snake. So I think there is a remarkable craft throughout the poems. And that struck me as just one very small example of how it works in your poems. Are there other things you want to say about the nature of the craft? Then let's talk about maybe the nature of the revision. Can you say how many drafts a typical poem might go through?
RR: I'd say probably anywhere from twenty to forty.

JDM: And that doesn't of course count all those drafts that may be working in your head before you start to write.
RR: Yeah.

JDM: And as the pot is brewing and a poem is beginning to develop, it's that sort of urgency that will lead you to the paper.
RR: One thing I do, I've heard other poets say the same thing, I always do my first draft in pencil and on a pad. I don't want to use a word processor for a rough draft. And I think one reason is because it looks too good too quick. Once you put it on the screen and run it off, there's some kind of, maybe just a tiny bit of being reluctant to change that you might not have with just a pad and pencil. What do you do?

JDM: Well, I'm very much like you in that sense that I don't want to go to the word processor until I feel the poem is pretty much completed. But it's pen and paper, and I like to write with a fountain pen simply because of the freedom and the fluidity of shaping those letters. But I'll go through anywhere from twenty to forty drafts of something to get it to the point that it's right. I've had some poems that took a couple of days, other poems took months, or even a few poems took years before I felt like I got them right. But it seems to me that there's a necessary part to the process for anybody who's serious about writing. Once you have, say, published a poem somewhere, do you feel like, "Well, I've done the best I can by that and now I'm moving on to the next work"? Do you feel the urge to go back and tinker with those poems or once it's in print do you let it go?

RR: Well, I did with several poems in *Eureka Mill* that have been published. As I was getting ready to, I was looking at the galleys, and I suddenly realized a line I didn't really like or felt like I could improve on, so I made that change. I think there's a danger in this, though. Now Phillip Larkin has said you can never recreate the time you wrote the poem. And I think there have been some examples of people who have gone back and revised. . . . And some of Auden's poems where the revisions weren't as good as the originals—I think there's a danger in doing it. I think if it's minor, okay. And I think probably I'll continue to do that in poems, particularly when poems go from magazine or journal to book form. I don't see there's a problem there with tinkering a little bit. I think there's a danger you can lose power as well. I mean I look back on some of my early poems and there are some flaws in them but also there's a kind of youthful crudeness and energy that has a worth of its own that maybe I'm better off not trying to graft on to an older sensibility.

JDM: I like that image, "graft" on them something that is older. I was talking to a class the other day about this whole process and I said, "I am reluctant to go back to earlier poems to tinker with them because that's where I was at that particular time." Why should I now try to "graft" that on to that experience? Let it stand. That was where I was, and this is how I stand now. The interesting thing to me is the next poem I am going to write. And I would guess that's true for you because it's the imagination, and it's the journey the imagination makes, that's driving us all the time. What is our imagination going to do with this piece of experience that we have? That's the ultimate fulfillment.

RR: And another thing. Maybe a good way to sum this up is that I think that one thing I admire about just about every Appalachian writer I can think of is that there's a real effort to communicate with the audience. We talked earlier about this. I think of a quote by Brendan Galvin that says, "In poetry, clarity is the deepest mystery of all." And to me, that is very true. I think the poems I love the most, most of the poems I love the most, I would say . . . (I mean there are some poems like Dylan Thomas's I love) . . . are ones where there's this surface accessibility that then as you read and reread, you suddenly realize that there's this incredible depth to this poem. To me, that's the greatest trick. "Trick's" the wrong word, but the greatest way of doing that. Once again, I think Robert Morgan's do because they seem so simple and you come to realize there's so much there. I think of the Chinese poet. I think you're achieving that kind of clarity. I think in a way, that's the kind of Chinese tradition you want—that you have this real surface accessibility, but there's a depth underneath it. Elizabeth Bishop, her poems do this for me. I've used those writers for me as models of trying to do the same thing in my work. I would rather risk somebody saying I'm a superficial poet than an obscure one.

JDM: This relates to, again, the culture in that it's important to communicate, communicate in the most basic sense. That is, *commune* with another person through language. Language is our means to connect rather than to separate ourselves. And so in that sense, poetry maybe is an ultimate form of communication of connecting us to others.
RR: And hasn't that always been what it is? You know it's an anomaly what's happening in the 20th century.

JDM: Yeah, right. Ashbery is not the mainstream of poetry I don't think.
RR: No. And I mean you go back to the idea that people originally wrote in poetry because they wanted things to be remembered, and it was easier to remember them in a poetic way than say just a regular kind of prose way, certain rhythms or whatever. Yeah. At the end, it's an act of communication.

JDM: And if we go back to some of our earliest poets in the English tradition, it was to preserve the memories of the tribe.
RR: Yeah, exactly.

JDM: So in a sense, I think that's what so many of the Appalachian writers are doing is preserving these memories of the tribe of the communities that we have existed in. And I like what you are saying about clarity. I have often used the analogy of trout fishing connected with writing. I've said that, for me, a poem should be like a really good trout stream in that you come upon this pool that looks so clear and you think you understand the depth of it. And so you start to wade toward this particular point where you are going to cast your fly. And you step in and realize that the water is up to your waist instead of up to your knees. That is much deeper, but it had that clarity that was, in a sense, deceptive, not intentionally so, but deceptive because of its very nature. Sometimes the simplest things are really the most profound and complex, deepest.

RR: That's interesting because I actually wrote a poem where I talked about looking into water in a mountain stream and seeing, as I say, "the crawfish prancing . . ." You've seen them move.

JDM: Right.

RR: It's all beyond the reach although it appears as close to your hand. And for me, there are those wonderful moments when a poem, such as an Elizabeth Bishop poem, opens up like that, and you suddenly realize there's so much more going on. I admire that a lot. That would be what I would hope for my poetry, that at times it might do that.

JDM: Well I think it does. Thank you for talking and for the wonderful reading last night. We all look forward to what you are going to give us in your work for the future.

An Interview with Ron Rash

Jack Shuler / 2000

From Clemson University Press for *The South Carolina Review* (2000): 11-16. Reprinted by permission.

Ron Rash: I was born in Chester, South Carolina. That was in 1953. My family moved back up into western North Carolina when I was eight. Both sides of my family are from the mountains of North Carolina. My father's family had come down to work in the textile mills and then my mother, after she finished high school near Boone in Watauga County, came down and worked in the mills a few years. And then, later, my father would work a shift and then go take classes in Columbia; he'd ride a bus. He eventually got to where he was a college professor at Gardner-Webb. He got out of the mill. My mother did as well. She went back to school when she was probably about thirty-five and ended up getting a degree and teaching elementary school. She worked her way out of that world. But part of that world is something I've written about a lot. I've got a new book of poems. It's called *Eureka Mill*, named after the mill in Chester where my parents worked. It's such an ironic name because in Greek that means "I have found it." What they found there were hard times. What I'm trying to do in this book is deal with the history of the mill villages because I don't think that's been dealt with enough in either history or literature.

Jack Shuler: So how did you end up in this area of South Carolina?
RR: I grew up in North Carolina and went to Gardner-Webb as an undergraduate. I went to Brevard a year, ran track. Then I came here to get a masters. I met my wife and liked the area because this is a beautiful area. It's close to the mountains. I got a job here a Tri-County Tech. I don't like living in cities. This area is still fairly rural. So I just stayed here.

JS: When did you begin writing, and at what point did you consider yourself a writer? What was that process like for you?

RR: It was very slow. I always loved to read. I think that was the most important thing. I always liked to use my imagination, even when I was very young. But it didn't come easy for me; in fact, it came very slowly. It wasn't until I was twenty-seven, twenty-eight, that I wrote something decent. I think there are a lot of people who are in writing as kind of a hobby and then there are people who are in it for life. I think the people who are in it for life can't stop. There was always something that was drawing me back, even though there was no reason to believe I could do it. I wasn't getting published. I knew the writing wasn't that good. The one thing I was doing, all that time, was I was reading a lot. I think that's the best preparation, obviously, for anybody who wants to be a writer.

JS: You also write fiction. What is the difference between the two processes, and what do you see yourself as, a poet or a fiction writer?

RR: Well, both, but they're very different. When I write one, I can't do the other. I've been working on a novel nine months now. When I was finishing it up, towards the tail-end, I was doing some re-writing and I wanted to do some poems. I couldn't. I would have ideas that normally I would have been able to put into a poem. It's like a different frequency. You have your mind, your imagination, on a different frequency and you can't make that jump. It's a different way of thinking, perceiving language. It's hard to articulate.

JS: Is it the economy of language or the use of metaphor that changes?

RR: I think that's part of it. You know, seeing something that's going to be thirty or forty lines versus something that's going to be two-hundred pages. Part of it is that, but also it's the ability to tell stories. You are using a different voice other than your own, more often, in fiction.

JS: Do you know what you're getting into when you write a story, as opposed to a poem?

RR: Very rarely. Usually it starts off as an image. It's interesting because this novel started off as a poem. It was about an eight line poem. I realized that wasn't going to tell what I needed to tell. Then I thought it would be a short story. Suddenly the short story ended up being sixty pages. And I suddenly realized—well, you've only scratched the surface. It just evolved out of one image. A man is standing in a field and feeling trapped, and his crops are dying around him. In a sense, what happened was a process of asking why he was feeling this way? What's happened? Suddenly it turned into about two hundred pages.

JS: What are some of the important themes you see in your work?

RR: Well, I think, certainly religion. Like Flannery O'Connor, I think my work is Christ-haunted. I don't do this consciously, but a lot of my imagery is religious. I'm not saying that in a didactic way, but it just seems to be pretty central to my writing. Sometimes it's Pagan, sometimes it's Christian. You know, what I find fascinating, what I love to write about is the kind of fusion you have in the Appalachian mountains—the ritual of killing black snakes, for instance, to make it rain? I've written a poem about that called "Drought." That's kind of interesting because those farmers were Christian. But, whether consciously or not, they were also participating in a Pagan ritual. That's fascinating to me. The next book of poems is called *Among the Believers*. A friend of mine said something a few months ago when she was introducing me at a reading. I had never thought of this. She said that everything I had ever written was haunted by something. Part of this is that I tend to want to write about things that are vanishing or gone. I write a lot about the mountains and the folk-ways that have disappeared. But I also write about the cotton mills. Once again, I didn't do that consciously. This novel I'm writing is set up at Jocassee, where the reservoir is. It's set in the fifties where that lake is covered now. It's a lost world. For whatever reason, my imagination seems obsessed with images of loss, things vanishing.

JS: I was interviewing a poet in McClellanville, Sam Savage, and he said that you cannot write about the South anymore, unless you write about the South disappearing. What do you think about that?

RR: That's an interesting idea. I think a lot of that's in my writing. We're at a time where you're seeing what made the South distinctive disappear, though, I think, there's something about the South that will continue. I think it will continue to be a different region, partly because, in a way, ironically, literature is going to do that. I think the literature insists on the differentness of Southerners. I think you kind of reinforce it. I mean, think of all the Southern books, and people reading these books, like Clyde Edgerton's work, Doris Betts, Fred Chappell, Robert Morgan, and Ernest Gaines. You know, it's kind of like we want to be different. I think literature is going to be one of the ways we preserve that. At the same time, it is changing, particularly in the mountains. In Watauga County, North Carolina, fifty or sixty percent of the land is owned by people out-of-state. My family lived up there since the seventeen-hundreds; they no longer know their neighbors. People have moved in from Florida, New York, Ohio, and it's lost its distinctiveness. That bothers me.

JS: Is it that they come here for something, but in doing so, they change it?
RR: Yeah, oh, yeah. One thing that really bothers me is that they come here because they want to get away from the city. They want to leave all that behind, but they want to bring it with them. Boone is a city now. When I was growing up, it was a town. I went up to read six months ago . . . It was a nightmare, I couldn't believe it. Myrtle Beach had suddenly been transported up there. Another thing is it's getting to where my relatives are having trouble holding onto their land because the property taxes have gone up because the land's become so valuable. That's unfortunate, but you know, at the same time, I'm sure that fuels my writing. It's a high price to pay.

JS: Do you feel, along the lines of all this "Southern" talk, that you are a South Carolinian? And do you feel that South Carolina is important to your work?
RR: It's a weird thing. I've written a poem called "Between Two States" because when I grew up in Boiling Springs it was almost right on the state line, about five miles from South Carolina. And most of my relatives were in the North Carolina mountains when I was growing up. And yet, I'd been born in Chester, and my grandmother lived in Chester, and we had a few other relatives down there. I always felt I was between these two places. And it's interesting almost all my writing has been either about Chester or the North Carolina mountains. But, yeah, I think it's been important, growing up in South Carolina. I had a really strong sense, early on, of being Southern. I grew up in a story-telling culture. Actually, this is a cliché, but it's true, I grew up listening to people tell stories on the front porch. We didn't have air conditioning.

JS: Do you feel, then, that natural settings are important to your work?
RR: Yeah, I find that I write so much about the natural world. I don't write about cities. I don't write about suburbs. My work is usually set, if not in small towns, in the countryside or in the mountains. This is not an original idea. Wordsworth said the same thing, if you use natural metaphors, that's the universal language. For instance, if I compare something to a blade of grass or a waterfall, not trying [to] be trite, but if I have a reader two hundred years from now, or a reader in Venezuela, that's going to translate because nature is universal. But if you write about, say, a Radio Shack, a

hundred years from now there may not be Radio Shacks, or there may not be Radio Shacks in Venezuela. Nature is the most universal of languages. So, if you set work out in nature and you use nature metaphors and similes, I think you've got a chance of your work being more universal.

JS: Back to Radio Shack. How have changes in the natural world affected your craft? You talked about your relatives losing their land. How has that affected your work or your outlook on life, your perspective of the world?

RR: It's reinforced that sense of loss. The poet Richard Hugo, who grew up in Washington state, has a great line. He says he stopped believing that change "is paced slow enough for the blood to adjust." I think part of that is that, as human beings, our lives are fleeting, and we don't live that long, but the thing that makes it even worse is when things are changing around us so quickly. That's happened in the South so much, lately. Our population has changed. The way of life has changed. Farming has really become insignificant. Just look at South Carolina and the way it's changed. Textiles and farming, probably thirty years ago, would have involved maybe seventy-five percent in the state, and now involve probably twenty-five or thirty.

JS: South Carolina has changed for better or worse. What do you think?

RR: Well, you know, in some ways better. Economically better, because those jobs did not pay well. And, you know, one thing I try not to do as a writer, because I've known too many people who have been farmers, including my uncle who died a couple of years ago . . . That's a hard life, and it's an uncertain life. And there's something to be said for the fact that now you can work and get paid. My uncle's tobacco barn burned down when I was twelve years old. He lost his crop, a year's work. I think, though, that loss of community is real loss, the uprootedness. You know you have people that live in one place for three or four years and then move on. I think that's real bad for kids. I mean that's one reason I'll probably never leave here. I've got an eleven-year-old and a nine-year-old, and I'll probably stay here until they graduate high school, at least. I think that's hard on people living in a world where the only way you're defined is by materialistic means. There ought to be something more sustaining than the kind of shoes you wear.

JS: I guess the most important aspect to your writing is your roots?

RR: I think I realized early on that the only thing I would ever be able to write about would be the Carolinas. I mean everything I've written, almost, is set almost exclusively in the Carolinas, and that's just because that's what

I know. Eudora Welty has this great line about one place known helping us understand all other places better. One of the great things about literature—and it shouldn't work this way, but it does—the more specific the setting, the stronger the sense of place, the more universal it can be. The more believable the literature is. Faulkner's proven that, and so have Joyce and Gabriel García Márquez. When people say that writing's limited because it's set in a particular place, that's the stupidest thing, because it's got to be set somewhere! Anybody who knows anything about writing realizes you've got to ground it in a particular place. It doesn't have to be the South. It could be Upstate New York, but someplace.

JS: Oak, palmetto, or pine? Which is your favorite word?
RR: Oak, palmetto, or pine? Probably palmetto, and part of the reason is because I can remember when I was a kid thinking how pretty a word that was, and I'd never seen one because we weren't far south enough to see the palmettos. I saw a picture of one when I was six or seven, and I remember how neat it was. It looked kind of like an umbrella. And I always saw it on symbols of South Carolina, but I'd never seen one. So that's always been a kind of magical word.

JS: I think those words define regions of this state.
RR: Oh, yeah, they do.

JS: Do you see any differences between the Upstate, the Midlands, and the Lowcountry?
RR: Oh, yeah, tremendous differences. The Lowcountry sensibility is more relaxed. When you get up in the Upstate, it's mainly Scots-Irish, hard people. And if you know anything about the history of the Scots-Irish people. . . . They lived hard lives. More Presbyterians than Episcopalians. A real change there in religious views. A huge difference, even in the way the people talk.

JS: In the poem "A Preacher Who Takes Up Serpents Laments the Presence of Skeptics in His Church," I thought it was interesting, the connection between man controlling nature and religion. Elucidate this idea.
RR: You mean the line about the polluted river? I guess I kind of made him an environmentalist preacher, but he would see that as a sign of what man has done to the environment. Have you seen the Pigeon River after it goes through Canton? Not even a carp can live in it. It's a trout stream until it

gets to Canton and Champion Paper Company pours its poison in, and then it's dead water. That struck me as an evil, and I was hoping that this narrator would see that as an act of man's pride and man's wickedness to do this to the natural world, which is God's world.

JS: Do you think poetry is important?

RR: Yeah, yeah I do. I think it does things that no other art form can. The precision of it, that conciseness. It has a way of making things unforgettable. One definition of poetry is "memorable speech." When a thing is said perfectly, you never forget it. "Shall I compare thee to a summer's day." "Truth is beauty, beauty truth." When it's done right, it's the ultimate form of writing. I think writers know that poetry's important, but too often people who read novels and short stories believe poetry is too esoteric. They read a poem by John Ashbery and decide they'd rather study something less dense like quantum physics. Many excellent poets write work that is accessible—Frost, Mary Oliver, Seamus Heaney. You don't have to have a Ph.D. to understand it, but it's also intricate. I have been writing in these Welsh forms a lot in the last few years, but I try to write poetry that's very accessible. But I'm doing, I hope, interesting things with language. And also with internal rhymes and certain syllable counts. I hope that I'm doing something that is complex but also that I'm writing something that's accessible.

JS: Does a poem have to mean anything?

RR: In a way, maybe no. I think it has to have something that makes it worth your attention. That's a good question. Sometimes when I read Hopkins and Dylan Thomas, I don't understand exactly what they're saying. When Dylan Thomas said, "though I sang in my chains like the sea," I don't know what the hell he's talking about, but it's so beautiful. You know, "though I sang in my chains like the sea." Now, what he's done there is a traditional Welsh form called *cynghanedd*. What you have is sang and chain and sea. The "a" sound from sang to chain, and the "s" sound repeated, as well, in a specific order. The beauty is the sound of it; that is worthwhile to me. You know Thomas, his music in his poetry, and Hopkins too, even when I don't understand them, maybe they're not saying anything, but it's still beautiful. So I would say, "No." You've got to have something happening, though. If it's not in the language or the sound, it can be in the form. A writer can sometimes startle you with an image, saying something that makes you see something in a new way. Robert Morgan has this wonderful image of pumpkins in a patch, "submerged and rising like planets." That's beautiful.

The Power of Blood-Memory: A Conversation

Joyce Compton Brown / 2003

Recorded at the Ron Rash Literary Festival, Emory & Henry College on October 24, 2003. From *Iron Mountain Review* 20 (2004): 26–35. John Lang, editor. Joyce Compton Brown, Professor Emeritus, Gardner-Webb University. Reprinted by permission.

Joyce Compton Brown: When I got the invitation to interview Ron on this wonderful occasion, I initially panicked. But then I thought who better deserves this position than an individual who has read and graded at least 26,742 freshman themes? Here I am surrounded by the ashes of my paper-grading life, and we have rising before us the bird of creativity, Ron Rash, so flap your wings, Ron. I do appreciate this opportunity to interview Ron, who was among my students at Gardner-Webb College, one of those students who make a teacher marvel at the fact that she or he is being paid to teach. Not all those fabulous students become superb writers, as Ron has, but that early relationship, along with my continuing friendship with him over the years, is my justification for serving as interviewer this afternoon.

Ron and I both lived—and I still do—in lovely Boiling Springs, North Carolina, which is the location of Gardner-Webb, now Gardner-Webb University, a Baptist institution. The school hasn't gotten any bigger; it's just decided to become a university. Boiling Springs is a small town that reflects Appalachian out-migration, set as it is in the Appalachian foothills, not the higher mountains themselves. It's a mill town as well as a small-college town. If any of you are Baptist, you know that when these colleges were being founded the idea was to place them in towns and areas where the students would be kept safely away from the temptations of the flesh and every other possible good-time activity. Boiling Springs continues to be such a place. If you drive through, you see lots of attractive little churches with steeples and a lovely little coffee house, and you say this is a good place to bring up kids. Boiling Springs' only other claim to Appalachian success is that it is the hometown of bluegrass musician Earl Scruggs. Bluegrass is one expression of the Appalachian out-migration. If you're a millworker and you have a rare break from the job, what do you do? You stand around and you pick. So that is the location, that is the background from which Ron came. Ron's first book, *The Night the New Jesus Fell to Earth*, was set in a town very much like Boiling Springs, and each subsequent book has gone farther and deeper into the mountain experience so that he's now reached his second major novel, entitled *Saints at the River*, which will be published by Holt in August of 2004. Perhaps a good way to begin this examination of Ron's past is to ask him to give us a taste of his writing future, to have him read a brief excerpt from his new novel.

Ron Rash: I'm going to read the opening. This novel is about a twelve-year-old girl who drowns in a whitewater river, and the novel centers on the aftermath of the death, the conflict between environmentalists and the parents over whether to rescue the body, because to do that they will have to damage the river, a wild and scenic river. But I wanted to start the novel off with the girl to make her a vivid presence. This opening passage records her last moments:

> She follows the river trail downstream, leaving behind her parents and younger brother who still eat their picnic lunch. She is twelve years old and it is her school's Easter break. Her father has taken time off from his job and they have followed the Appalachian Mountains south, stopping first in Gatlinburg, then the Smokies, and finally this river. She finds a place above a falls where the water looks shallow and slow. The river is a boundary between South Carolina and Georgia, and she wants to wade into the middle and place one foot in South Carolina and one in Georgia so she can tell her friends back in Minnesota she has been in two states at the same time.
>
> She kicks off her sandals and enters, the water so much colder than she imagined, and quickly deeper, up to her kneecaps, surging under the smooth surface. She shivers. Fifty yards downstream a granite cliff rises two-hundred feet into the air to cast this section of river into shadow. She glances back to where her parents and brother sit on the blanket. It is warmer there, the sun full upon them. She thinks about going back but is almost halfway now. She takes a step and the water rises higher on her knees. Four more steps, she tells herself. Just four more and I'll turn back. She takes another step and the bottom she tries to set her foot on is no longer there and she is being shoved downstream and she does not panic because she is a good swimmer and has passed all of her Red Cross courses. The water shal-

lows and her face breaks the surface and she breathes deep. She tries to turn her body so she won't hit her head on a rock and as she thinks this for the first time she's afraid and she's suddenly back underwater and hears the rush of water against her ears. She tries to hold her breath but her knee smashes against a boulder and she gasps in pain and water pours into her mouth. Then for a few moments the water pools and slows. She rises coughing up water, gasping air, her feet dragging the bottom like an anchor trying to snag water-logged wood or rock jut and as the current quickens again she sees her family running along the shore and she knows they are shouting her name though she cannot hear them and as the current turns her she hears the falls and knows there is nothing that will keep her from it and the current quickens and quickens and another rock smashes against her knee but she hardly feels it as she snatches another breath before the river pulls her under and she feels the river fall and she falls with it as water whitens around her and she falls deep into darkness and as she rises her head scrapes against a rock ceiling and all is black and silent and she tells herself don't breathe but the need rises inside her beginning in the upper stomach then up through the chest and throat and as that need reaches her mouth, her mouth and nose open at the same time and the lungs explode in pain and then the pain is gone along with the dark as bright colors shatter around her like glass shards, and she remembers her sixth-grade science class, the gurgle of the aquarium at the back of the room that morning the teacher held a prism out the window so it might fill with color, and she has a final beautiful thought—that she is now inside the prism and knows something even the teacher does not know, that the prism's colors are voices, voices that swirl around her head like a crown, and at that moment her arms and legs she did not even know were flailing cease and she becomes part of the river.

JCB: Thank you, Ron. You often use water in your fiction and poetry. Would you mind talking about the ways in which water serves as a source of both destruction and salvation in your writing? How do these opposing perspectives come out of your own experiences?

RR: Well, I've always loved to fish, loved the outdoors. Some of my most vivid memories come from being at the spring on my grandmother's farm up in Watauga County, North Carolina, and hunting for spring lizards and crayfish. And also just being a Southern Baptist, being immersed in water literally when I was baptized, that religious symbolism of water represents for Christians both death and resurrection. For me it's a very potent symbol, one I almost don't want to analyze too much, but I do know that water is something I'm obviously obsessed with, particularly in reservoirs, how that water can annihilate any human presence.

JCB: I'm going to go back a few years, before Ron celebrated his 50th birthday, back to the time when he was a very tall kid running around the streets of Boiling Springs, dodging automobiles and sometimes redneck curses as he practiced his distance running. I thought then that that kid must have the longest legs I'd ever seen. All the Rashes are tall, but obviously Ron was obsessed with his running. He competed in high school as a runner, as Tim Peeler mentioned in his paper. I wonder, Ron, whether you see any connection between your running and your work as a writer?

RR: I believe that running was the best training I could have had to be a writer. It taught me discipline, the idea that writing is something that has to be done every day. That's the part of this process that we don't like to talk about. We always want to talk about creativity, that initial spurt, but I believe that writing is something that has to be done day in and day out so that it becomes a natural part of your life. And I learned that from running, particularly from distance running. Track tends to be a solitary sport. I would spend a lot of time out running dirt roads by myself, and I would be thinking during that time. Such running taught me discipline, and it also taught me to work in solitude, which is perfect training for a writer. It's kind of interesting to see the number of writers who have been athletes. Maxine Kumin was actually an Olympic swimmer. James Dickey was an SEC hurdles champion.

JCB: Another memory I have of Ron when he came to Gardner-Webb as a student was of Ron as a reader. He had already developed that habit of reading in high school when he realized that he could get a more intellectually fulfilling experience in some of his classes by having a book tucked under his homework assignment, a book that he could read while the teacher talked about Spanish subjects and verbs, for example. He came to Gardner-Webb because his father, Jim Rash, taught in the Art Department there. Jim was *the* art professor at the college. In between his attempts to teach students and to complete his own artistic projects, Ron's father produced ceramic bulldogs for the president of the college. The bulldog was our mascot, so the president would make gifts of these ceramic bulldogs to many would-be benefactors. Jim had the same wry sense of humor that we find in Ron, for Jim explained his work for the president by noting that many of the artists of the Renaissance had commissions, so he might just as well be commissioned to make a few bulldogs.

So when Ron came to Gardner-Webb, I knew him first as a reader rather than as someone who might just go on to become a candidate for the

Pulitzer Prize. How important to you as a writer has that habit of reading been? How has it affected your work?

RR: One thing that bothers me these days about the training of younger writers is that there is not always an emphasis on reading. There seems to be a belief that they need to be writing their own work. I'm not sure that this approach is desirable. For me it was much better that I was reading a lot and, in a sense, preparing myself to write. I think that anyone who is trying to be serious about writing has to be a voracious reader, and every writer I know who's any good is. Reading was exactly the kind of training I needed. That doesn't mean students should not be writing; they should, but they should be reading more than writing. I have a straight M.A., and I actually had a very traditional master's degree program that centered on reading literature. I didn't take any creative writing classes. For me that was good; I wasn't really ready to write. But that M.A. in literature gave me a background that was very helpful when I did begin to write.

JCB: Back in those days, what sorts of reading did you do, not just in terms of what was assigned but what you felt drawn to?

RR: I read almost anything I could get. But a couple of writers were very important to me early on. One was Jesse Stuart, an Appalachian writer from Kentucky. I read him in the fifth grade, and that was a moment of real revelation for me because suddenly I saw the language that I'd grown up hearing, both in the higher mountains and in the foothills, on the page. And Stuart showed me that there was a beauty to that language, that it was something worthy of literature, that there was a poetry in it. That was a really important moment for me. I had a copy of *The Jesse Stuart Reader*, a paperback that cost thirty-five cents, and I wore that book out. I probably read it thirty times. And then as I got a little bit older, another writer that I came upon was Seamus Heaney, the great Irish poet. That was an interesting discovery for me because you might expect that it would be a Southern writer who had that impact on me—and certainly I've been influenced by many of the Southern and southern Appalachian writers that have come before me. But there was something about reading Heaney that described the rural world I'd grown up in, although his was in Northern Ireland. And I suddenly realized that such writing can be universal; I suddenly recognized the difference between local color and regionalism. Regionalism is writing that transcends the local. It's writing that is strongly grounded in a particular place, but it also transcends that place. Heaney was a writer who showed me that, and because he was a poet he had a major influence on what I wanted to do.

JCB: I want to give the audience one other memory I have of you. It's of Ron and a bunch of other teenaged guys standing around in our backyard rubbing their chins, looking wise, joined by my husband, a biology teacher, all of them gazing into a large gunny sack that occasionally emitted a hissing noise. In that bag was a snapping turtle, which they had brought up from the river to show another of their playmates, my herpetologist husband. If you've read Ron's work, you know that he's obsessed with snakes and other reptiles and amphibians. We don't find many warm fuzzy kittens in your writing. Have you thought about the configuring of the natural world in your work, especially the animal life? Why do you seem to gravitate toward what I would call the creepy-crawlies?

RR: One thing that I got from my family in the mountains is a sense of the world being a place of mystery, a place of wonder. I've always been attracted to the part of nature that is terrifying or unsettling. I was always out hunting for timber rattlesnakes, though fortunately I didn't find any. The idea that nature is complex, that it is both consoling and terrifying, is one that has stuck with me. I learned that from James Dickey's work, too, because Dickey is a poet who took that approach to nature.

JCB: I also think of Theodore Roethke, who wrote that lovely tribute to his wife: "my lizard, my lively writher." Given the fact that you are a writer who has read deeply, that you are an athlete who has committed himself to that discipline, that you are a lover of nature who observes it with appreciation (most of us would not find a snapping turtle to be a thing of beauty), I thought that you might read one brief poem to show how strongly all of those influences come together. It's a little poem about your grandmother's springhouse.

RR: This poem is called "In a Springhouse at Night," and it does make Joyce's point about my love of water imagery. My grandmother had a springhouse that ran almost like a trough, and I've actually got a newer poem entitled "The Trout in the Springhouse." One of my uncles kept a trout in his springhouse. He would feed it, and the family would drink that water. I'm glad you picked this poem because I grew up in a world in which folklore was so intense and I heard so much of it. There were all sorts of natural portents, like writing spiders that would write their messages in their webs and the ghosts that my grandparents and uncles would tell me about. All that Appalachian folklore was important to my work, the sense of mystery it conveyed. This poem, "In a Springhouse at Night," is about going into such a mysterious place by myself:

Candle-dim flickering shadows, orange
salamanders flare across floorstone,
water troughed, held like gutterswell.
Cabbage and beets, beans and sweet corn
fill the walls. Grandmother's tall
hands lighten shelves. My fingers braille
springflow verbing: unearthed, sprung.
(*Among the Believers* 45)

I'd been reading a lot of Hopkins that week.

JCB: That's one reason that I picked out that poem because it's so clear that you have read not just in contemporary poets but also in Hopkins and other earlier writers. Like me, you're a lover of Hopkins' work, and you bring that sensibility to bear on life in Appalachia, not in an imitative way but in terms of technique, by making the lines as spare as the lives that were being led here. Why do you value the incorporation of folk belief, superstition, and folklore into your work? How do you assure that such details enhance the reading experience of your audience?

RR: I believe that an important value of art, as Francis Bacon said, is "to deepen the mystery." I find the world endlessly mysterious, and the folklore is a way to emphasize that mystery and wonder. So much of contemporary life wants to blind us to that mystery, that wonder, but it's there even if we are oblivious to it. Poetry is as good at restoring that wonder as anything I know—especially poets such as Dickinson and Hopkins. Dylan Thomas is right when he says, "A good poem is a contribution to reality." Poetry enlarges the world for us, destroys the illusion that we can grasp it.

JCB: I just love "In a Springhouse at Night," and it leads me to raise the subject of your grandmother's influence on you. I should point out that my memories of Ron do not usually extend to any summers or holidays because, as far as I could tell, he spent all such times back in the mountains at his grandmother's farm. Can you say something about your contact with your grandmother and the time you spent with her?

RR: When I look back, I see that one of the most important things that happened to me was those visits to my grandmother. Boiling Springs was not really my family's home. I was always taught that home was Buncombe County and Watauga County, in the mountains. And that was where all my relatives were. From about the time I was twelve, I would spend my summers with my grandmother on her farm near Boone. There was no car there; there was no TV. She and I would just stay there together. It was a pretty isolated farm, so we wouldn't usually see people until Sunday, when we went to church. It was great preparation for a writer. She would tell me stories, stories that gave me a sense of wonder, that portrayed the world as a magical place. She was very intelligent, a very good reader herself, but she also just let me run free. I would go out most mornings, after packing a lunch, with my fishing rod. And I would fish some, but mainly I just explored. There are not many places where you can get away with that anymore, not as a kid. But it was wonderful for me. That time did several things for me. It led me to observe the natural world carefully because I was out in it, and I think that capacity for close observation paid off later in my writing, that I was really paying attention to the physical world. But it also gave me an opportunity to just daydream and to make up stories to entertain myself. That time in the mountains also gave me my primary landscape. I find that I write only rarely about Boiling Springs; instead I write about the mountains, particularly about that farm or the area right around it. I would say that that area is my spirit country—and always will be. That's where my family is buried. My father's buried there; all my relatives. Even though my grandfather and grandmother died in Chester [South Carolina], they're buried in the mountains because for them that was home. They never had the sense of being from the piedmont; they were always mountain people, Appalachian people.

JCB: That little community is called what? Aho?
RR: Yes, Aho.

JCB: I live down the street from Ron's mom, Sue, who in many ways is an artist in her own right. She got her college degree and taught fourth grade. Ron is one of three children. But now that her children are grown, Sue has delved into quilting, and one of my favorite quilts that she has done is called Stars over Aho. It's clear that Aho is her vision of her spiritual home, too. But in addition to being your spirit country, the mountains and the natural world they contain also seem to be your primary source of analogies and images and symbols. You use such material to introduce your themes and often to begin or end your poems, as in "Speckled Trout." Would you mind reading that poem?
RR: Most people don't realize that the speckled trout is the only trout native to the eastern United States. And it's not even technically a trout; it's a char. It's a very beautiful and rare fish. We would actually catch speckled trout in

a stream on my grandmother's farm, and this poem is about a cousin who took me fishing there:

> Water-flesh gleamed like mica:
> orange fins, red flankspots, a char
> shy as ginseng, found only
> in spring-flow gaps, the thin clear
> of faraway creeks no map
> could name. My cousin showed me
> those hidden places. I loved
> how we found them, the way we
> followed no trail, just stream-sound
> tangled in rhododendron,
> to where slow water opened
> a hole to slip a line in,
> and lift as from a well bright
> shadows of another world,
> held in my hand, their color
> already starting to fade.
> (*Raising the Dead* 33)

That poem is in a seven-syllable line. One of the reasons I went to that really tight line is that for a narrative poet there's always a danger that your poetry is going to end up just being chopped-up prose. You just tell anecdotes, and you decide, well, I'm going to have a line break here. Reading Hopkins, reading the old Welsh poets and learning some of their rhyme schemes, with their use of internal rhymes and their intensity of sound, was something important for me as I tried to maintain tension in my own lines. "Speckled Trout" was one of the early poems in which I aimed for that really tight line, so I'm glad you chose that poem.

JCB: And you succeeded! Those of you who teach know that one of the great joys of teaching is that you can select from a huge anthology of your favorite works. I've taken that teacher's privilege in asking Ron to read this afternoon.

You've already mentioned that Boiling Springs rarely appears in your writing, the major exception being *The Night the New Jesus Fell to Earth*. And in that fine collection of short stories, the major emblem of the town burns and is gone. To me that burning almost seemed to say, well, I got that

out of the way and can move on. Your primary voice is clearly an Appalachian voice, a voice of the mountains. Yet you didn't spend your childhood,
as many Appalachian writers do, entirely immersed in the mountains. How
do you think that living not only in the mountains but also in the small-
town setting of Boiling Springs, a foothills town, has shaped your work?

RR: I think it was a good thing for me as a writer because it pointed out
to me significant differences. Even from the foothills of Appalachia to its
mountains there were differences in speech, differences in beliefs. I found
that mountain religion, for example, was very different from what I experienced at the Baptist church in Boiling Springs. In the mountains I saw
speaking in tongues and witnessed a kind of religious fervor that I hadn't
seen in the foothills. The contrast in settings also gave me a sense of what
made the mountains distinctive and gave me a kind of insider/outsider
identity in the mountains that enabled me to maintain a certain distance
from that life. So for me as a writer having that dual perspective was very
fortunate. I actually wrote an early poem entitled "Between Two States." It
is not a very good poem, but it addresses this issue of being both a part of
Appalachia and outside of it. I was in abeyance, but I don't think that's a bad
place for a writer to be.

JCB: You were given this Appalachian landscape with the streams and the
small farms that you clearly treasure, and you don't tend to be an author like
Ernest Hemingway who goes off to Spain or Paris or wherever. How did you
decide that *one* landscape would be yours for the majority of your work?
Why did you think that that was important? Do you think that it's important for all the best writing?

RR: I do. Most of the writing I love is intensely regional. One thing that
really interests me is how the most regional work is often the most universal. Eudora Welty says, "One place understood helps us understand all
other places better." I truly believe that the more we know of one place, the
more we're going to make that place universal, because if you go far enough
and deep enough into it, you're going to realize what its essence is, and this
essence is going to be human, to involve what it means to be a human being,
what defines us. I've learned this in part from the great precedent set by
Faulkner. Sherwood Anderson once told Faulkner, you're just a country boy;
all you'll ever know is that little postage stamp of land in north Mississippi.
But if you're good enough, Anderson added, that's all you'll need. That's a
great lesson for other writers. If you can just get that one little place right,
you can get everything you want.

JCB: The Appalachian landscape is clearly crucial to your work. What advantages beyond sheer familiarity does this landscape offer to you as a writer? How do you insure that you are not feeding the stereotypes about Appalachia and Appalachians? How does your awareness of our culture's negative stereotyping of this region affect you and your writing?

RR: The landscape is important because for two centuries almost all of my family history has been played out in the North Carolina mountains. It is the landscape that I know best, and one I want to believe I have an almost genetic connection to. I also believe that landscape becomes destiny in a lot of my work.

As for the issue of stereotypes, the best way to avoid stereotypical characters is to get to their core of being, their essence, which is where all human beings are more alike than different. If you can do that, it is difficult for the reader not to relate to the characters on a human level, no matter the cultural differences. Thus I hope my characters are complex, engaging, and recognizable to readers from a different region as neither saints nor subhumans but rather as human beings much like themselves.

JCB: I look at the women characters in your work and seem to see pronounced "feminine" qualities in some of them but not in others. Some are filled with an almost mystical understanding of fate and hold on to what must be regardless of society's opinion (for example, Amy in *One Foot in Eden*), while others are pillars of practicality, sound reason, and social and economic awareness. Could you comment on these qualities in your female characters, or do you see more continuity and less polarity than I detect?

RR: I've been surrounded by strong women all my life, so I'm sure that a good bit of what I've seen in the women in my family is reflected in my writing. But ultimately I hope that my female characters are individuals, not types, each with her own complex strengths and weaknesses.

JCB: You often depict characters whose hearts are called back to the mountains but who, because of economic circumstances, cannot go back. I think particularly of your grandfather in the milltown who is described in *Eureka Mill*, the grandfather on your father's side who couldn't read. But although he couldn't read, it seems to me that what he gave you was imagination. Why don't you read "Invocation," a poem in which you give credit to your grandfather.

RR: I'm glad you chose this poem because one thing I've tried to do in my work—perhaps most obviously in *Eureka Mill*—is to acknowledge the importance of the generations that have come before us. My grandfather couldn't read or write. My father became a college teacher, but he started off in a mill. He actually dropped out of high school and worked in a cotton mill in Chester (which is where he met my mother) after having come down there from Asheville. He worked a shift in that mill, walked a mile down the railroad tracks to the bus station, and took a 50-mile bus trip to Columbia to take night classes. He did that for several years until he finally got a degree. He was a very talented man, as Joyce knows, as brilliant a man as I've ever known, but he spent his whole life and energy getting out. He gave me the opportunity to have a pretty easy life. The struggles he had I didn't have. I was expected to go to college; I didn't have to drop out of school when I was sixteen to go work in a mill the way he did. I've always felt that one of the things that has driven me as a writer is the recognition that I've had the opportunity that he didn't and that I should do as much as possible with that opportunity. To me it's a very serious thing. The same idea applies to my grandfather. I don't want to sound melodramatic about all this, but this whole idea is very important to me. I feel very fortunate, and in this particular poem, "Invocation," there's a sense of wanting my ancestors to be able to tell their story, of needing them and acknowledging them. This is the book's first poem. Traditionally, poets invoke the Muse for help, and I'm playing off that convention here—with a little help from some North Carolina moonshine:

This late night I spread
a fraying Springmaid bedsheet
across the kitchen table.
In the almost silence
of house-creak and time's
persistent tracking of eternity,
I unscrew the mason jar,
pool the lid with moonshine,
flare the battered cigarette lighter.
A blue trembling rises from liquid
expanding finally to smoke,
all elements merging tonight,
whispering out the window,
curling northward to seep six feet
into the black bony dirt
and guide his spirit across

the declining mountains to this room,
where I sit and sip, await
a tobacco-breathed haint, shadowless shadow,
bloodless blood-kin I have summoned
to hear my measured human prayer:
>   Grandfather guide my hand
>   to weave with words a thread
>   of truth as I write down
>   your life and other lives,
>   close kin but strangers too,
>   those lives all lived as gears
>   in Springs' cotton mill
>   and let me not forget
>   your lives were more than that.

JCB: That closing line presents a powerful theme in your work: that despite all the stereotyping, the flat pictures that we get of Appalachians and so-called hillbillies and lint-heads, these were multi-faceted, complex human beings. Their lives were more than a paycheck and more than moonshine.

I've often noticed, Ron, that loss and memory intertwine in your fiction and your poetry with the idea that memory is illusory and denies the reality of that which was lost. I wonder, then, how do you as a writer who uses memory deal with the human tendency to remember just the "pretty parts" and how does all this connect with your emphasis on "blood-memory"?

RR: The best way is through awareness of that human tendency to recall only "the good parts." Thus, as far as "blood-memory" goes, part of my responsibility is to be true to lives that were often tragic and complex, to avoid sentimentalizing those lives. We live in a culture that doesn't value an understanding of the past. I find that kind of ignorance frightening. One of my favorite quotes concerning the validity of writing about the past is Kierkegaard's belief that, "This backward movement is a forward movement, in so far as going backward is going deeper into something."

JCB: I want to read just a few lines from Ron's poem "Signs," which seems to me to epitomize the power of his work, especially in its use of language and character, with the speaker's words being suggestive of but not degrading regional speech and the characters presented as mountain people who earn the reader's respect. The speaker concludes the poem by saying,

And so I learned to see the world
as language one might understand
but only when translated by
signs first forgotten or misread.
(*Among the Believers* 33)

I would ask you then to read just one piece that states your sense of your purpose as a writer.

RR: This is called "Resolution." It's a rather new poem, but it's one in which I was attempting to present a sense of my *ars poetica*. One thing I admire in poetry and that I love about Appalachian poetry in particular is that the Appalachian poet is often a poet whose writing is accessible, very concrete, and yet there's an amazing depth to it. That's the kind of poetry I love. It's the poetry I find in Robert Frost, in Seamus Heaney. It's a multi-layered poetry but with a surface accessibility. One of my favorite quotes about poetry is from Brendan Galvin, who says that in poetry clarity is the deepest mystery of all. This is a poem in which I take a few swipes at people like Jorie Graham and John Ashbery in the first couple of lines and then talk about a poetry that maybe has more depth. Here's "Resolution":

The surge and clatter of swirl-white conceals
how shallow underneath is, how quickly gone.
Leave that noise behind. Come here
where the water is slow, and clear.
Watch the crawfish prance across the sand,
the mica flash, the sculpin blend with stone.
It's all beyond your reach though it appears
near and known as your outstretched hand.

JCB: How important is audience? Who would you consider to be your audience? Would your audience differ for poetry as opposed to fiction?

RR: I don't really think a lot about audience—except that, unlike a number of contemporary poets, I don't view being intelligible as a flaw. I never have a specific audience in mind. I tend to follow my own obsessions and to hope that if I write well enough those obsessions might connect with my readers.

JCB: Let's take some questions from this audience now.

Question: Your family came to this region in the mid-1700s. Many of those early inhabitants of Appalachia came from Irish and Scottish backgrounds. Would you say something about your sense of connection to these ancestors and their heritage?

RR: My father's family came into Buncombe County in the mid-1700s. One of my ancestors founded Waynesville, which is about fifteen miles from where I teach now at Western Carolina University. My mother's family came into Watauga County in the 1700s as well, so I have very deep roots in this region. But also my family is Welsh on both sides, and I would like to believe that there is some kind of genetic link that propels my interest in Welsh poetry. Probably just wanting to believe that has intensified my interest in that poetry. Like many Appalachians, I've also got some Cherokee ancestry and some Scots-Irish, and I try to bring all those connections into my work. I feel a profound tie to the region, and I really believe, though one has to be careful of over-generalizing, that landscape must affect the way people see the world. There's a certain fatalism I've seen in my own family that I think comes in large part from being in the mountains, from a landscape that lacks that long vision, of the mountains always rising up and reminding you how small you are. Now the landscape can work in another way too, and you can see it as almost womblike and nurturing. But I think that landscape has an effect on the way that people see the world. I don't see how it cannot. And I see certain aspects of my own character that I know were shaped by my grandparents and my parents, and I think certain parts were shaped by landscape as well.

Question: Can you say something about class awareness, which sometimes seems to verge on class anger, in your work?

RR: A lot of times we think of America as being a classless society, but we know that's not true. One thing that made me really aware of the class structure was seeing my grandfather, because he couldn't read or write, being put in some very awkward situations. I also had a number of relatives who would have been considered lower class. Let me give you a specific example. When my father was in high school, my grandmother wanted him to sign up for college-prep courses. He was a sophomore and he was going to do that, but the principal came to her and said, "Your son's going to be in the mill in another year, so there's no reason for him to enroll in those classes." The most haunting thing my father ever told me, about a year before he died, was that it wasn't worth it, what he'd had to do to get out of that world of the mill village. That statement has always troubled me, and it has contributed once again to my sense of obligation. But I was always aware of class distinctions and particularly of the feudal system that operated in the mills, of that hierarchy and the places that people were supposed to occupy in it, that structure of complete control. And I also saw that once you were in that caste system, you weren't supposed to get out. I witnessed that. A number of my relatives stayed in those mills. So my class awareness, and sometimes class resentment, came out of my family's personal experience.

Question: Could you comment further on the difference between your generation and your father's in terms of the greater opportunities you've had as a writer?

RR: One of the things I believe—and I think most of the people in this room would agree—is that the best writing ever done in the Appalachian region is being done right now. This is the first generation when you have lots of authors with both the time and the opportunity to write. I think, for example, of Robert Morgan, who was the first in his family to go to college. This is the first, or at most second, generation here in the mountains with lots of people who have had that opportunity. If you're working in a tobacco field 12 hours a day, you know that, despite what the Romantics might say about living close to the soil, you're too damn tired at night to write your opus. I think that the reason the Appalachian renaissance is happening now, instead of at the time of the broader Southern renaissance of Faulkner and Porter, is that it took a little longer for these opportunities—the education, the leisure, the chance to write—to reach most mountain folk. I realize that these are large generalizations and that we need to be cautious in making them. But I also think that gratitude for those opportunities produces in Appalachian writing a real reverence for family and ancestors because there is a recognition (I see it in Morgan's work, I see it in Fred Chappell's and Lee Smith's) that it has been other people, your parents and grandparents, who made it possible for you to do more than they could. One thing I love about Appalachian people, at least those I've known, is their sense of one generation's sacrificing itself for the next generation. That's certainly true in my family. My grandmother knew that she wasn't getting out. She thought that she might be able to get my father out. It was a struggle. And then my parents knew that, whatever else they did, they were going to insure that their children had a chance to be educated—and we were.

Question: Isn't it often true that the third or fourth generation is too far removed from the first generation's experience to feel the need to write about it?

RR: That's a really good point. I look at my own children and see that they don't have the connection to that world that I had. They're middle-class kids, and they've never really seen the other side. I've tried to show it to them. We go back to family reunions. But you're right. There's something that happens with that first generation to break away, a sense of having an unusual opportunity and of needing to make good on that opportunity. I think that Danny Marion would say that, for instance; he's telling those stories of his family because there's been no one who could write them down before.

JCB: That venerable Appalachian scholar Cratis Williams said that it takes three generations to get the mountains out of the family that has left Appalachia. What you're talking about is very similar. And the heritage left behind is not something that can be shown, is it? It's something that has to be lived and experienced.

Question: Have you yourself done blue-collar work?

RR: Yes, though certainly not to the extent that my father and mother did. I've worked on the grounds crew at Gardner-Webb and done other blue-collar work on summer jobs. I also took a year off between college and graduate school and did blue-collar work that year. That experience was great because when I enrolled in graduate school I had more incentive to immerse myself in my studies. I remember one day when it was really cold I was sitting inside reading a Hemingway novel and thinking, I sure am glad that I'm in here and not outside doing what I was doing a couple of months ago. And I also did some farmwork on my grandparents' farm when I was growing up. That experience taught me several things, among them how difficult it is to grow tobacco, which is a tough, tough crop to raise.

JCB: The details that you picked up from that experience do show up in the poems. And I've seen you sweat a great deal pushing a lawnmower around the campus.

Question: Is the recent recognition that your work has gotten proving liberating for your creativity? Has it imposed new constraints on you?

RR: It's kind of a mixed blessing. I have had some really good luck lately and some attention to my work, and that's wonderful. But I'm finding that there are more demands on my time. One thing about being an Appalachian writer, though, at least in my generation, is that there are authors like Robert Morgan and Lee Smith who have shown me how to handle the recognition, how to stay balanced. They're great role models, just as James Dickey is not. What I admire about Morgan is his work ethic. Often when he's travelling, he'll take his computer with him and write in his hotel room. I'm trying to emulate that. And I think that the danger—not that I'm going to have to worry about this—is being distracted from the really important thing, the writing itself. You don't want to end up like Truman Capote, where you're not even writing anymore because you want to be a celebrity. As I say, I'm not really worried about that happening any time soon. But I do keep reminding myself that I still need to go back every day and write. It's still about getting up each morning and stringing words together, hoping through hard work or luck or whatever else I can call on that I might put something on the page I can look at and say, "That's not too bad."

Question: Would you describe your writing process? Are there rituals or mechanisms you use to prompt your writing?

RR: There's an Australian poet named Les Murray who says that writing is a merging of the waking and dreaming states. I believe that. Often what happens is like watching something in water. I'll have an image that begins to become clearer and clearer and clearer. And the one thing I don't want to do is know too much about it too soon. Particularly in poetry, I want it to begin in mystery and end in mystery. It's almost as if I shut off the intellectual part of myself to a degree. That part will come back in. But what I like is that moment when, in a sense, I don't know where the image is going; I don't even know what it means. I don't *want* to know what it means. This is in large part because I'm a Jungian. I believe in Carl Jung's idea of the collective unconscious, his idea that there are certain things that happen to us that we can't articulate but that we respond to, certain images, archetypes. That's the realm that I'm most interested in. That's why I want the image to emerge naturally during the creative process.

Question: Is there a difference in your creative process if you're writing fiction rather than poetry?

RR: Yes, to me writing poetry and writing fiction are like AM/FM. They're on a completely different frequency. I can't do them both at the same time. In fact, if I'm writing poetry, it might be a couple of weeks before I can move into fiction. They're two different activities. To me they're as different as music and painting. Poetry for me is more intuitive. A story is not; a story is something you have to articulate. Russell Edson, a poet, says that prose moves through time and poetry moves around time, and I think there's a lot to that distinction.

Question: Do you have any advice on finding a title for a poem? Do you try to create a title that reflects the meaning of the poem?

RR: Sometimes I struggle with titles. I tend to tinker with the title until I find something that just seems to fit the poem. But I rarely try to select a title by articulating what I meant in the poem. In my view, that's for the reader and the critic to determine. And also there's a part of me that's very superstitious about the poem's meaning. For me, poems are often magical. You don't know where they come from. Fred Chappell has a wonderful story in *I am One of You Forever* in which Uncle Zeno is out in the woods and it's almost as if he's simply a transmitter for the stories he tells; they just come out of nowhere. Now that sounds wacky until you start writing. Why is it that two images you've had in your head for 30 years suddenly come together on an October afternoon? I don't understand that—and I don't want to understand it. I just want it to happen.

JCB: And it has been happening, extraordinarily effectively. Although I sometimes think that your success might have come sooner had you attended a larger school than Gardner-Webb, particularly because of our lack of contact with the world of contemporary literature during those days, I'm grateful for having had the opportunity to watch your steady, obstinate determination to write, to write your heritage, and to have your creative genius recognized so beautifully here and nationwide. Your work attests to the power of the spirit of Appalachia, and to its universality.

RR: Thank you.

Language Can Be Magical:
An Interview with Ron Rash

Pam Kingsbury / 2004

From *Southern Scribe*. Reprinted by permission. Pam Kingsbury, the author of *Inner Voices, Inner Views*, teaches at the University of North Alabama.

In a soft-spoken voice, the music of language rolls off Ron Rash's tongue—bespeaking years of Appalachian heritage. In his quiet nature, a love of the environment and family is exposed. His stories of loss and redemption are poignant and complex. Ron Rash's sense of place is strong.

Pam Kingsbury: Where are you from?
Ron Rash: My family has lived in the Appalachian Mountains since the mid-1700s—both families, my mother's and my father's are from here—which is why I focus on the South Appalachians as a setting. I grew up in Boiling Springs, North Carolina. It's between Charlotte and Asheville. It's also the home of Earl Scruggs.

PM: Where did you go to college?
RR: I attended Gardner-Webb in North Carolina and Clemson. I have a B.A. and M.A. in English. I have found the intense reading I did at Clemson of great benefit.

PM: Your first works weren't novels . . .
RR: My first published work was a collection of stories (*The Night the New Jesus Fell to Earth*). Then I worked in poetry for almost a decade. I didn't consciously set out to write novels. Both started with a single image I first tried to make into a poem.

PM: After publishing three collections of poetry, earning an NEA poetry fellowship, and publishing two collections of short stories, you're "an overnight success" as a novelist . . . Discuss your transition in genres.

RR: I'm a narrative poet, which makes the transition to fiction easier. I've spent the last twenty-six years of my life writing seriously. I averaged three to five hours a day, six days a week. I'm fifty now, and I've worked for a long time. I'm glad what success I've had has come slowly, because it has allowed me to work under the radar and concentrate solely on my writing.

PM: What do your two novels—*One Foot in Eden* and *Saints at the River*—have in common?

RR: Both books are set in the same landscape, the same county, Oconee, in the most mountainous corner of South Carolina, located along the South Carolina border. Some of the same obsessions as well, especially the impact of the dead on the living, the erasure of a culture, the way landscape affects people psychologically.

PM: Earlier you mentioned that there was always "one image" in your head starting each of your works. What was the "one image" for *Saints at the River*?

RR: The first image was of a child's face looking up through water.

I wanted to write a novel about environmental issues, but one that refused simplifications. I picked a situation where I was essentially in conflict with myself, the part of me who is an environmentalist and the part of me who is a parent.

PM: What was the "one image" in *One Foot in Eden*?

RR: A farmer standing in his field, crops dying around him. He had a look of desperation on his face that transcended the drought.

PM: What do you enjoy most about book signings and readings?

RR: One thing is meeting people who've heard or read my work and found something there that has given them pleasure. I've also enjoyed meeting other writers. Particularly in the South, there's a real sense of camaraderie among writers.

PM: What's your most amusing "author event" story?

RR: My first public reading EVER was at the New York Public Library. I was thirty-two and had won the General Electric Younger Writers Award. I asked them to mail me the prize money but they said I had to come to New York and do the reading to get the money. I really needed the money so I went. I told myself I'd never see any of those people again and, besides, they'd never understand my accent. It turned out to be a wonderful experience.

PM: Does book promotion interfere with writing?
RR: I worry about the danger of getting away from writing. I travel with a laptop and try to work two to three hours every morning because I don't want to get out of the rhythm of writing.

PM: What's your next book?
RR: A novel, set in western North Carolina. It's set for a winter '06 publication with Holt.

PM: You hold the John Parris Chair in Appalachian Studies at Western Carolina University. How do you balance writing, teaching, book events, and family life?
RR: I have no real social life, except the book-promotion events. I rarely go to parties. I don't belong to the Moose Club or go out to bars. I'd rather spend time at home with my family.

PM: What advice do you give your students regarding writing?
RR: Read as much as possible and read widely. Persevere. Too many good writers give up too quickly. Perseverance is underrated in creative writing. For most of us, who are not Shakespeare or Keats, it takes work.

PM: Whose works do you include in your Appalachian Literature courses?
RR: Lee Smith, Robert Morgan, Fred Chappell, Silas House, Pam Duncan, James Still, Harriet Arnow, Jeff Daniel Marion, and many more fine writers.

PM: Who are some of the writers readers should be reading or who should be better known?
RR: Donald Harington from the Ozark Mountain region. His work is tremendously underrated; Chris Holbrook out of Kentucky; and Catherine Landis. I think she's the real deal.

PM: Have you had mentors?
RR: Lee Smith and Robert Morgan have been supportive and their work is

important to me. They are both exceptional writers and exceptional human beings.

PM: What have you been waiting for someone to ask?

RR: What is it that makes someone become a writer? I have vivid memories of my grandfather—who couldn't read or write. I asked him to read *Cat in the Hat* and he made up a story. He always "read" it differently. His stories were more entertaining than my mother's. He taught me language can be magical.

Ron Rash

Robert Birnbaum / 2005

From *The Morning News*. Copyright Robert Birnbaum/Our Man in Boston. Reprinted by permission.

Writer Ron Rash has written three books of poetry—*Eureka Mill, Among the Believers*, and *Raising the Dead*—and two collections of short stories, *The Night the New Jesus Fell to Earth* and *Casualties*. He is also author of two novels, *One Foot in Eden* and *Saints at the River*, and one children's book, *The Shark's Tooth*. His writing has been published in *Yale Review, Georgia Review, Oxford American, New England Review, Southern Review, Shenandoah* and others. Rash's awards include the Appalachian Writers Association's Book of the Year and *ForeWord Magazine*'s Gold Medal for Best Literary Novel, both for his 2002 debut novel, *One Foot in Eden*. Ron Rash's family has lived in the southern Appalachian Mountains since the eighteenth century, and the region is the primary focus of his writing. He grew up in Boiling Springs, N.C., and graduated from Gardner-Webb University and Clemson University. He is currently the Parris Distinguished Professor of Appalachian Studies at Western Carolina University.

In *Saints at the River*, the small South Carolina town of Tamassee becomes embroiled in a headline-grabbing controversy after a twelve-year-old girl drowns in the Tamassee River and her body is trapped in its depths. Maggie Glenn, a twenty-eight-year-old newspaper photographer, has been sent back to her hometown to document the escalating standoff between the girl's parents, who want to retrieve her body, and environmentalists convinced the rescue operation will damage the river and set a dangerous precedent. Maggie, who left the town ten years earlier and has done her best to avoid her father during that time, now finds herself revisiting her painful past. A budding romance with the reporter who accompanies her to cover the story is burdened by his own troubled history.

As Ron Rash reveals in the chat below, this story exhibits two of his primary concerns: children and the environment. Additionally and not surprisingly, we talk about southern writing and a host of connected and unconnected issues. It is a great pleasure to present this wonderful writer whom I discovered the old-fashioned way—serendipitously.

Robert Birnbaum: Do you get above the Mason-Dixon line often?
Ron Rash: No. Not a lot.

RB: How many times in the last year?
RR: I'd say three. About a week, total.

RB: How does it feel? Do you feel it?
RR: Oh, yeah. I can tell the difference. In large part because of the way people react to the way I talk. [chuckles] One thing that's been really exciting for me is having readers outside the South. That's what we all hope as writers, that our work transcends the region. If it's significant at all, it has to.

RB: You have been at this for a while, so perhaps you might have noticed whether mainstream America has shifted its way of accepting southern writing.
RR: In a sense, as a southern writer you are almost always fighting certain stereotypes. There are certain expectations of a southern novel. There's going to be a crazy aunt in the attic and probably a couple of bodies in the basement, and you always have these kind of bizarre characters. But at the same time, a lot of that's true. [laughs] One thing I am pretty much convinced of is that we are all kind of crazy in the world—some groups hide it better than others, maybe. Southerners seem to revel in their oddness at times.

RB: Southerners do seem to be good at telling those stories about their oddities.
RR: That is something that is positive—that people expect southerners to tell stories, and southerners are good at that. It's part of our culture.

RB: As opposed to mid-westerners? Or westerners?
RR: Well, why is it that the South has produced so few philosophers yet so many novelists? There is something—we express ourselves with story. Once again, it's not like every other culture doesn't. A number of my favorite

writers—I love Philip Roth's work. He comes from a culture that's probably the antithesis of a southern culture, at least within the United States. I grew up hearing stories, and it was a very natural part of my life.

RB: Years ago when I spoke to Reynolds Price, I was operating under the bias that southern writers were being marginalized, that the writing was quaint but not universal. So what I am trying to get at is whether there has been a change in the stature of southern writing.

RR: Yeah. Right now, as compared to the '30s and '40s, when you had an emphasis on people like O'Connor and in the '50s, Welty, Warren, and Faulkner, right now I find it interesting, that at least nationally, when I read the *New York Times Book Review,* how few southern writers are recognized as being among the greatest. I think Cormac McCarthy, Barry Hannah, William Gay are writing as well as anybody in this country and yet you hear about McCarthy but you rarely—

RB: You consider McCarthy to be a southern writer?

RR: Yeah he grew up in—

RB: I know where he grew up, but you still consider him a Southern writer? [He grew up in Knoxville, Tennessee—eds.]

RR: Oh, yeah, we claim him. [laughs]

RB: This regionalizing just seems to point to Jim Harrison's notion of geographical fascism [mentioned in the "Tracking" section of *The Summer I Didn't Die*]—suggesting some stratum of quality.

RR: I agree. Ultimately McCarthy and Hannah and Gay are great writers, and I have always been a little leery of any adjective in front of writer—whether it's Jewish writer or southern writer. Because very often there is a sense of "just." "Just a southern writer."

RB: Not exactly a compliment or a superlative.

RR: And also not getting at what matters. If the writer—if McCarthy doesn't transcend the South or Barry Hannah, they are probably not that significant anyway. I think they do.

RB: It does seem that southern readers are extremely loyal and supportive of their writers.

RR: Well, yeah, southerners like to read southern writers—it's just that tradition since Faulkner and O'Connor—there's regional pride in our writers and support of them. That's a wonderful thing.

RB: Is the South still the same?

RR: No. It's always changing. At the same time, what I find interesting is how it seems to both change and not change. Just when you think there's no such thing as a distinctive southern culture, I see something that says it will always be like this.

RB: Was *One Foot in Eden* considered a so-called breakout book for you?

RR: Yeah, it did, more so than any [other] books I have written.

RB: You're including your poetry?

RR: I've written three books of poetry and two books of short stories, but today novels just have much higher visibility than poetry.

RB: It is a pleasant surprise that short story collections seem to keep being pumped out.

RR: Well, what happened with *One Foot in Eden* was that it sold much, much more than anything I had ever written, and it got reviewed in places I had never been reviewed.

RB: Why do you think?

RR: Novels—more people buy novels and they just seem to get more attention than a book of poems.

RB: But why you, now, a writer from South Carolina? What were the reviews like?

RR: They were very positive—at least the ones I saw. Probably the best one I got was in the *Los Angeles Times*. To me that was a good sign that as "regional" as the book was, ultimately there was something in it that transcended the region.

RB: I liked the opening of *Saints at the River*, which I had picked up unaware of anything about you and never got further into it until we arranged to talk but I did for some inexplicable reason read *One Foot in Eden* and was mightily impressed with it. It was an enthralling book. When I came back to *Saints at the River*, the protagonist, the woman photographer, didn't convince me. The prose was fine and fluid and the story was interesting, but it didn't move me in the way your first novel did. What do you think? Do you look at all your children in the same way?

RR: Well, that's just it. You're being asked to choose your children—which one's your favorite. [pauses] To me, if I had to choose between those books, I would choose *One Foot in Eden* myself. Part of it is because it was the first novel I had ever written. I don't know—I have some readers who like *Saints* better. I guess it depends on what you are looking for. For me the language is more interesting in *One Foot*—which is something that's important to me as a poet.

RB: I loved that story that is included in some of the biographical notes about your grandfather reading stories to you except he couldn't read so he made them up.

RR: Oh yeah, it had an impact on me.

RB: Did you learn that much later?

RR: I figured it out pretty early. Probably in third or fourth grade. At the time it was just wonderful [laughs] that his stories could just change.

RB: Is the picture of folks sitting around telling stories and, in a sense competing, an accurate one?

RR: Oh, yeah, I did grow up with a lot of people who told stories. One thing I think was advantageous to me, two things. One, I had a speech impediment when I was four or five years old. And I didn't talk much. The other thing is I spent a lot of my time in the summers with my grandmother, just she and I on a farm up in the mountains of North Carolina. And I would be around my older relatives and there was no TV—we didn't even have a car on the farm—so we were just marooned there, in a good way. I would just listen to these stories and listen to the way these people talked. That was a great thing for somebody who wants to become a writer. I didn't know I was going to become a writer then.

RB: When did you know?

RR: It's a strange thing. I always loved to read. When I was in high school and college I was mainly an athlete. I ran track—800 meters. But the kind of obsessiveness I had in running and all that kind of stuff led into literature and the love of reading. But I didn't start writing seriously until my late twenties.

RB: What did you do?

RR: A lot of it was running track, and reading and going to school. I have a straight M.A. in English.

RB: Is there a big difference between South Carolina and North Carolina?

RR: In some ways. I live in Western South Carolina and grew up in Western North Carolina and they are very much the same.

RB: Asheville is in western North Carolina. What is in western South Carolina?

RR: Not much. Clemson University and Williamston, which is the best-known city.

RB: Most of what I know of South Carolina comes from Fox Butterfield's book *All God's Children*, which was about an African-American teenage murderer whose family was from South Carolina. In the book, Butterfield gives a brief synopsis of the state's history and it seemed to be a tough, mean-spirited, martial, hard-scrabble place. And I only know of two writers from there—Dorothy Allison and Percival Everett—and neither stayed there. Is the impression I got from the book at all true? Is North Carolina looked at as more congenial?

RR: Not within the South. South Carolina has that strong sense of manners and those kinds of things.

RB: I always saw a certain kind of courtliness as being very much a southern thing.

RR: Yeah. Particularly when you think of Charleston. But I'm on the exact opposite end of that. I am in the mountains, and it's a different culture—

RB: Is there that east-west/liberal-conservative split?

RR: Around Chapel Hill they're more liberal than the rest of the state, but for the most part it's pretty conservative.

RB: I think I read in the indefatigable Dan Wickett's interview with you that you don't know when you start to write what form you are working in—so what determines whether it ends up a short story, novel, poem?

RR: I usually start off with an image—an image that essentially I obsess over. That I can't get out of my head. *One Foot in Eden*, it started with an image of a young farmer standing in his field. *Saints* started with an image of a child looking up through water. The new novel that is coming out in April starts out with a trout in water. They start with images and I just follow them. Sometimes I have a vague sense of the story already, but mainly it's just following the images.

RB: Do you still write stories and poems?
RR: Oh yeah.

RB: So it is still a real possibility that when you start what you write could be anything?
RR: *One Foot in Eden* started as a poem and then a short story and then a novel. And *Saints* did that. And this new novel was a short story that won an O. Henry and now is part of this novel.

RB: What section?
RR: The opening. I added a good bit but the first chapter is essentially the story.

RB: What's the world or community of literature like in the South? Is there congenial camaraderie?
RR: There is a sense of camaraderie. Very often, a lot of us don't live close together but we keep in touch and there is a strong sense of camaraderie and also a real sense of an older generation helping the younger writers. I find that to be a very wonderful thing. Robert Morgan and Lee Smith both have been very kind to me and supportive, particularly a few years ago, and there is a real sense of trying to help each other out.

RB: Oxford, Mississippi, has a book festival; Sonny Brewer has something in Fairhope, Alabama; and there is an annual convocation in Nashville. I assume you go to some of these, but what happens when you go outside the South?
RR: I did the *Chicago Tribune Printers Row [Book Fair]*; I have gone on tour out West, and those are great. The fun thing for me is that when I go to ones like in Nashville and Oxford, I get to see friends. This is where southern writers will get together—we're spread out. It's not like Boston, where you have fifty writers within two miles of each other.

RB: I think of North Carolina and Vermont and Boston, Cambridge, as really densely populated with writers.

RR: Oxford, Mississippi, is really close. There are some good writers in that town.

RB: Who is there?
RR: Barry Hannah. Tom Franklin.

RB: The ghost of Larry Brown.
RR: The ghosts of Welty and Faulkner.

RB: Are there black Southern writers?
RR: Oh yeah. Percival Everett. I love his work. Ernest Gaines, Alice Walker. Let's see, let me think. Marilyn Nelson.

RB: A.J. Verdelle?
RR: I don't know her. Dori Sanders, from South Carolina, wrote a book called *Clover* that did well. Yusef Komunyakaa, the poet, grew up in Mississippi. Edward Jones—

RB: Considered a southern writer? He grew up in D.C. and went to school in Worcester, Massachusetts.
RR: In his first book of stories, I got the sense that his family is very southern.

RB: Do you think that when people think of southern writers they include blacks?
RR: I do. Instantly I think of Ernest Gaines, who is very southern to me.

RB: Is there a state that is underrepresented in southern writing?
RR: In the South?

RB: Yeah, do people write about Kentucky besides Barbara Kingsolver?
RR: Wendell Berry. Silas House, a good young writer. Some states seem to do more than others. North Carolina and Mississippi are the two, you turn over a rock and—

RB: Probably it's the water. Lee Smith has a significant body of work and is always mentioned by other southern writers, and yet her visibility nationally is very low.

RR: I don't understand that. That disturbs me, that someone like Lee Smith or Barry Hannah doesn't get his or her due nationally. They're good enough. They're major writers.

RB: Why don't they?
RR: When I see something like what happened with the [2004] National Book Awards, where you had five finalists, all were from New York City—there's a provincialism there. That's pretty hard to deny.

RB: The worst part of that was the writers were being held responsible for it—
RR: No, it's not their fault.

RB: It still seems to me that none of the women were really New York writers—they just happened to live in New York—their subject matter wasn't New York-centric. So why not nominate them?
RR: I thought there were better books that should have been considered.

RB: That's a whole other issue. That's the inherent problem in awards—whittling down a list of four hundred books to five and then to one. What were some of the books that you thought were better?
RR: There was a great novel that got no attention by Donald Harington, called *With*. And it's marvelous.

RB: He's written a bunch of books and he never gets attention.
RR: When I read it, I thought, "This book cannot miss."

RB: The title is too simple. Who wants to read a book with such a simple title? [both laugh] Was it your intention to teach after you got your master's degree?
RR: I was writing by then, but yeah, I had to get a job and I didn't have a trust fund, so I spent a good part of my twenties trying not to write.

RB: Because?
RR: Getting serious and growing up. But as I got into my late twenties I felt, "If I don't give it a shot, a serious shot, I will always be haunted by 'What could I have done?'"

RB: Was there family pressure to "get serious"?
RR: No that was me. I'm sure it's part of my culture that I should be responsible and get a job. I just felt like it was right.

RB: Tell me about your students.
RR: I taught two years of high school at a very small rural high school right in the South Carolina mountains, near where *One Foot in Eden* is set, as a matter of fact. And then I taught at a technical college for seventeen years. And that was a good thing. A lot of my students were lower middle class, middle class first generation [to go to college]. I taught classes for welders, and that was good because one thing I don't like is the novel about the middle-aged academic who has a nervous breakdown—to me that's tedious and when you are in that kind of rarified air, sometimes, it can be a problem.

RB: Teaching English meant teaching grammar and such or literature?
RR: I taught it all. I was teaching five or six classes at the technical school—freshman composition, British literature, and I
did teach surveys in that. Which I loved doing.

RB: Starting with *Beowulf*?
RR: *Beowulf* to Milton and then Milton to contemporary.

RB: And who were your contemporary choices?
RR: Seamus Heaney, Geoffrey Hill—as far as poets, Derek Walcott. I didn't go much farther up than people like Graham Greene.

RB: What is life like where you live?
RR: I spend half the week at Clemson and half the week in North Carolina. It's very rural. Probably very slow paced, at least to most people who are not from the region. Very pleasant. It's a great place to live.

RB: Circling back to where we began, do you notice anything here in contrast to life where you live?
RR: One thing I noticed that is very positive that I get from walking around is the sense of history.

RB: I had in mind my own experience in Boston, now that I live in New Hampshire. I noticed quickly that you rarely hear a car horn. And they have a respect for pedestrians. [laughs] When you are in a car and someone is crossing the street, you, as a matter of course, let them do it.

RR: I don't spend much time in cities, but I do notice the pace. I have always lived in rural areas.

RB: But you use a computer and have ATMs which I am convinced are accelerants in their own right. You see people waiting in ATM lines, and they are super fidgety.

RR: When I see people like that I am reminded of Chaucer's quote in *Canterbury Tales*, "Though there was nowhere one so busy as he, he was less busy than he seemed to be." That's true of a lot of people I see today.

RB: What are the problems or issues that occupy you? Imperatives or values that you want to write about, or is it just as you said, an image comes up and you respond?

RR: One thing I think has been clear in my work that I didn't realize consciously, really, until *Saints at the River*, is that I am very preoccupied with children. And I am sure that's because I have children, the kind of fear that parents have that something can happen. I never really noticed it but looking back at my work I see it again and again. And I am certainly concerned with environmental issues, but at the same time you have to be very careful because if you are didactic that can kill a novel.

RB: There are novels that deal with really bad things happening to kids. I start them but usually can't go far. Stephen Dixon's *Interstate* comes to mind and John Burnham Schwartz's *Reservation Road*.

RR: Russell Banks's *The Sweet Hereafter*, which is one of those grim ones—

RB: Siri Hustvedt's *What I Loved* is very much like that—I was reading it and in the middle this thing happens and I am on the verge of tears. I wonder how one can write that kind of situation. To me, that's the grimmest possible thing to write about.

RR: In a way, it can be almost cathartic in the sense that you are almost confronting your worst fears. Also, if I make it up and put it in a story, it can't come true. There is almost that kind of feeling about it.

RB: In *Saints*, early on you are clear that a young girl is a goner and you accept it—it seems not to be as harrowing as if it came later.

RR: Yeah, that's right.

RB: Is where you live at risk from industrial assault?
RR: We have to worry about that more than anything, particularly in the mountains because so many people are moving there—

RB: Really?
RR: Particularly North Carolina mountains—retirement communities are springing up. A lot of the rivers and streams are being polluted and just so much pressure because of more building.

RB: What about environmental protection agencies and groups?
RR: There are but it's private land and particularly the Chattooga River, which I care a lot about. There has been a lot of building near it, and what happens is the sediment will get into the river and it really has an effect.

RB: What happens?
RR: Kills the trout and fish populations. A beautiful river becomes less pristine and ultimately destroyed.

RB: What's the local response?
RR: There's a real movement toward conserving these rivers. There are several groups, and on some level I'm involved with these groups that are trying to protect these rivers and protect these streams.

RB: Are rural southerners joiners? I'd guess not.
RR: That's probably true.

RB: So is environmental protection a cause for which people would overcome their hesitation to join groups?
RR: They have, at least where I live. It's a minority but I have two friends who have dedicated their lives to protecting this river. They are barely scraping by economically but they love this river so much that they are doing everything they can.

RB: I imagine it's less expensive to live in your neck of the woods.
RR: Oh yeah.

RB: So when you say "barely scraping by," how low is their life style?
RR: I don't know exactly but I would guess $15,000 a year.

RB: What is the work? There's still farming?

RR: Still agriculture. Some manufacturing. Tourism is really big.

RB: That would cut both ways. As exhibited in *Saints at the River*, good for local economies and burden on the environment. Any of that land protected as parkland?

RR: The Chattooga is actually a "wild and scenic river," which means it's protected and there's a certain buffer zone and all of that. And there is a lot of national parkland and where I teach is only thirty miles from the Great Smoky Mountains National Park.

RB: Your position at Western Carolina University is distinguished professor of Appalachian studies. What does that involve?

RR: It's a study of that culture—the music, the geology, and history and literature and an emphasis on that particular culture.

RB: Are there many departments like that in the South?

RR: No.

RB: Would that be the only one?

RR: It might be. One good thing for me—I mean, there are many things but one thing in particular, and it is especially true for my younger students: A lot of them come from there and there are all these popular culture negative stereotypes about Appalachian people—*Deliverance, The Dukes of Hazzard,* the hillbilly stereotype, and at the same time you don't want to sentimentalize, but there are positive aspects of this culture as well.

RB: Your accent is not Southern. It is more what would seem to be Appalachian?

RR: It is.

RB: And you study the differences in dialect?

RR: There have been studies done.

RB: How does one describe the difference in accents?

RR: With particularly the more coastal accents in the South, more like Mississippi, it's much softer.

RB: Can you talk like southern, imitate one? [laughs]
RR: Almost softer and whispering, maybe more nasal.

RB: Which part of your mouth do you use?
RR: Back, deep, more guttural. But it's different. When you go from western South Carolina to Charleston, you will hear big differences as you go across the state.

RB: How integrated—are there black people in western South Carolina?
RR: Not as many as in Charleston, because there were no plantations. The land was not [used] that way. There are and were black people. I went to schools that were completely integrated and you may have this view of the South as being a very segregated culture; even today I have friends who come from other regions and their schools were very segregated. But the schools I went to and my children went to are completely integrated.

RB: When I talked to Reynolds Price, he observed that one distinctive part of southern culture was the great familiarity between blacks and whites. I grew up in Chicago, and there were no black people in the schools in neighborhoods until the '70s, and Chicago was deeply segregated and still is. Is your view of your work as a career, as in "career arc"?
RR: I have never thought of it as that. I'll be fifty two in a month, and I have been writing seriously for about twenty-five years now, and most of that time I have been publishing in small journals and nothing really happened, no career, and I just do this because I love it.

RB: Do you pay attention to the attendant stuff, trade magazines? *New York Times Book Review*, book industry gossip?
RR: I'm human. It's wonderful to know that my books are selling. I don't want to obsess over it. And I also—the one thing I don't want to happen is that I get so concerned with that that I get where I am not focusing on the writing. I am a writer and I don't want to get to the point of whatever that other thing is—I just want to write.

RB: Well, you seem to have chosen a sensible path.
RR: I have a job now, so I don't have to write. I do it because I want to.

RB: Do people actually graduate with MFAs expecting to make a living?
RR: I don't think so. There may be a few, but the vast majority realize—

RB: The reality is too crushing. Why do you think there are these constant complaints that suggest otherwise—that somehow writers should, in the main, be supported?

RR: I don't know. All you have to do is look around and see how many writers can make a living.

RB: Do you think literary fiction is at risk?

RR: There may never be a huge number of people who read it, just as with poetry, but it won't disappear. The people who love serious literature and love poetry, they are going to care so much they won't allow it.

RB: Yet it's an ongoing debate. Civilization is always ending and literature is always disappearing.

RR: You go back and look at John Donne, who was passing his poems around at court to about thirty people—there was not much of a readership there, either.

RB: Yet in the nineteenth-century, someone like Dickens was hugely read.

RR: It was popular entertainment in a sense that was Nintendo and TV and all that rolled into one. That was the primary source of entertainment. Now people have more alternatives. I would like to think—and I do—that there will continue to be people who want serious fiction. And what disturbs me is the rise of theory in universities and colleges. Which is anti-literature.

RB: All that passed me by. I was out of school by the time critical theory was the big thing. I have not read one book by Foucault, Derrida, and such. When I studied philosophy it was Wittgenstein and the ordinary language and logical positivist movements. When I talked with Camille Paglia recently she is vociferous in her disdain for the theory, which she blames for destroying academia and everything else.

RR: I like her writing a lot and what she has to say.

RB: A book is coming out next year. What have you been doing since you finished it?

RR: I have been writing some stories in the last couple of months. I had a backlog. I finished *One Foot in Eden* and started on *Saints* before I got *One Foot in Eden* published. These novels are all taking me two to three years but they were stockpiled; I'll have another book of stories coming out in about a year and a half and they are already written.

RB: You write them serially but not with the idea that they will be in a book together?

RR: I just write them as they happen.

RB: Do you think of other kinds of writing that are more collaborative—librettos or screenplays?

RR: Probably not. I just wouldn't have the confidence to do it. I have just never thought about it.

RB: Arliss Howard and Debra Winger did a wonderful job with making Larry Brown's *Big Bad Love* into a film.

RR: It could happen. Russell Banks has been very fortunate in the way people have done his movies. They have done good treatments of his novels. So it can happen.

RB: *Affliction* was so powerful, and it seemed like an unlikely story to make.

RR: That's the one I'm thinking of.

RB: I think he is still working on *Book of Jamaica* and *Continental Drift*.

RR: He's a writer I admire.

RB: Why?

RR: He writes about tough issues to write about and in a truthful and honest way. He goes to the heart of things. And another writer I love a lot is Robert Stone—I like his ambitiousness. A book like *A Flag for Sunrise*, that is a big landscape novel. He and McCarthy are two of the most disturbing writers I know. I read those guys and they really shake me up.

RB: You can't read a Robert Stone book without knowing that there will be people in trouble—

RR: And it's only going to get worse. [both laugh] It starts off bad and gets worse.

RB: I picked up *Blood Meridian* again recently, and I thought the opening chapters were funny.

RR: The preacher, oh yeah.

RB: Any more writers like Donald Harington that you think are deserving of greater or, as in his case, some attention?

RR: I liked *Saturday* by Ian McEwan, and it got mixed reviews but I like its ambition. I read Harington's *The Pitcher Shower*—I thought that was good. I go back and reread Dostoyevsky pretty regularly. In a way *One Foot in Eden* is my *Crime and Punishment*. That book had a huge impact on me when I was a teenager. I read it when I was about fifteen, and it has always stayed with me. Another book I recently reread was Percival Everett's *Erasure*. That's a funny book.

RB: It sure is. Why did you reread it?
RR: I had been thinking about it. I read it when it came out and I wanted to go back. One reason was because I wondered why the book didn't get more attention.

RB: The perpetual question. I wonder about the complaints that so much crap is being published that fails to acknowledge that lots of wonderful writing is being published that readers miss.
RR: A good thing about the Internet is that these books will get attention that they might not get otherwise—someone like Donald Harington.

RB: My pick hit of the moment is Don Winslow's *The Power of the Dog*.
RR: Don't know it. [both laugh] That's your point, right?

RB: I pointed it out to a few people who were equally impressed. And that's a wonderful feeling. It's the joyful part of all this.
RR: That's right.

Ron Rash Speaks with Karen Spears Zacharias

Karen Spears Zacharias / 2006

From Southern Independent Booksellers Alliance. Karen Spears Zacharias is the author of *Burdy* and *Mother of Rain* (Mercer University Press). Reprinted by permission.

When Ron Rash visited Portland, Oregon in April 2006, he sat down in the stately Benson Hotel for an Author-2-Author interview with author Karen Spears Zacharias. Rash and Zacharias share a common Appalachian ancestry. His people come from Western North Carolina. Her people hail from East Tennessee.

Rash's latest novel, *The World Made Straight*, follows Travis Shelton, a high school dropout, as he gets caught, literally in a bear trap, while stealing marijuana plants from Carlton Toomey, a menacing tobacco-farmer-turned-drug dealer. Disgusted by his son's waywardness, Travis's father kicks him out and Travis takes up residence with Leonard Schuler, a half-assed drug dealer and former schoolteacher. Leonard and the boy bond over books and a shared fascination over a local Civil War incident—the Shelton Laurel massacre—that divided their town.

Karen Spears Zacharias: Do you think storytelling is something you're born to or can just anyone cultivate the craft?
Ron Rash: I think some people have a gift for it. That's been my experience, but, obviously, you can get better. But I think the intuitive sense of drama and how to move a story along is a natural thing.

Zacharias: When did you discover you wanted to be a storyteller?
Rash: As a kid, I spent a lot of time by myself in the woods, daydreaming. I

would make up narratives, telling stories to myself. It was either storytelling or a kind of madness. [laughing]

Zacharias: Why did you spend so much time alone?
Rash: I spent a lot of time with my grandmother, a widow woman. She lived on a marvelous place, in many ways beyond technology. No car or truck.

I spent my time out in the woods, and with my older relatives, who were all great storytellers. I grew up hearing an Appalachian dialect that you don't often hear today.

Zacharias: Your previous novels, *Saints at the River* and *One Foot in Eden*, especially, capture the old-timey language of mountain people. Do you grieve the loss of that talk?
Rash: There's a part of me that grieves. A part of what art does, I believe, is keep alive what is disappearing. So I'm trying to capture the language I heard as a boy and preserve it as art. To create a portrait of the beauty of it. It's a beautiful language.

Zacharias: When I visited Vietnam in 2003, I was struck by how much the Central Highlands reminded me of East Tennessee and my father's people. The mountains. The subsistence way of life.
Rash: Something interesting happened to me while I was reading at a community college in western North Carolina. A number of Hmongs came out to hear me. They were very responsive to the reading and approached me afterwards. They said that they understood the part of the world I was writing about. I was fascinated by that.

Zacharias: I guess mountain people are mountain people, no matter where they're from.
Rash: A lot of my new novel, *The World Made Straight*, deals with landscape as destiny. How where you were born affects how you see the world and how you see yourself. I think because of that people born in the mountains respond to the world in a different way.

Zacharias: Your writings carry a message about our connectedness to and stewardship of the earth. Do you consider yourself an environmental champion?
Rash: It's an important issue to me. We are inextricably linked to the natural

world. If it dies, we die with it. I think it is stupid and shortsighted not to recognize this fact.

Zacharias: What about the writing life appeals to you?
Rash: The difficult joy of writing. Doing something that you feel compelled to do. Of the actual writing, for me the best thing is when I feel the story or poem start to come together. There's a joy in having the characters and place come alive.

I enjoy meeting other writers. Writers are the most interesting people I know to talk to. It's kind of like being a member of a cult.

Zacharias: So much of a writer's life is internalized. Do you fret over being too self-absorbed?
Rash: That's why we have families and children. [chuckles] They won't allow us to do that, at least too much. But there's always that danger that you'll get too self-absorbed.

Zacharias: Where does the title of your latest novel, *The World Made Straight*, originate?
Rash: It comes from Handel's *Messiah*. There's a line about the crookedness of the world made straight. It's about having this injustice—the Shelton Laurel Massacre, a civil war massacre—and trying to set it right. Leonard is trying to help Travis become a man. They are both trying to do something redemptive.

Zacharias: There's none of the young Ron Rash in Travis is there?
Rash: I think we write about the lives we might have had, if they had gone another way. Most males experience a certain amount of recklessness when they go through adolescence, I think. Travis is a smart kid. He just doesn't have a lot of possibilities. He's never encouraged. I was a poor student in high school. Very poor. I liked the forestry and shop classes. [laughs] I wasn't taking any advanced placement courses. I barely got out of high school. Travis is a reader. He just doesn't want to read what's being assigned in class. I was like that. The kid sitting in the back of the class, reading *Crime & Punishment*, and failing French.

Zacharias: Do all the boys and girls growing up in North Carolina learn about the Shelton Laurel Massacre? How did you learn of it?
Rash: It's not taught as much. It was so traumatic and the feelings so deep,

people tended not to talk about it for fear of bringing up those old feelings and old hatreds. I didn't even know my own connection to it—I had ancestors on both sides of it. I never heard much about it until I was twelve.

In the past, bragging about such things could get a fellow killed in Western North Carolina. I think that's the reason why a lot of people kept silent.

Zacharias: Then why did you pick the massacre to focus on?

Rash: I think it's a meditation on violence. I've always been horrified and fascinated over people, who live in close proximity to each other, turning on one another. During Pol Pot's reign in Cambodia. In Bosnia. Rwanda. It's unsettling to see people fall back into a tribal mentality. To me it's horrifying and one of the most depressing things humans can do to each other. The hope is that there will always be people who fight against it. People like Bonhoeffer in Germany.

Zacharias: What truths have you learned about yourself from writing?

Rash: I've learned to follow my obsessions. I've certainly done that. I'm obsessed with history and landscape. A quote about my work that pleased me was when a critic said landscape was a major character in my novels.

Zacharias: That is a great compliment.

Rash: Nature is our most universal language. If you live in Rwanda, you know what a river looks like, and you certainly know what it smells like. No matter where you go, a waterfall is a waterfall. When you use the natural world in your writing, you're using the most universal references there are. We are all surrounded by nature. Even if you live in the city, you can get to nature pretty quick.

Zacharias: What's next for you?

Rash: I've got a collection of short stories coming out April 2007 with Picador, and I'm working on a new novel about timber barons in the North Carolina mountains, set in the 1930s.

"The Natural World is the Most Universal of Languages": An Interview with Ron Rash

Thomas Ærvold Bjerre / 2006

Interview conducted May 16, 2006. First appeared in *Appalachian Journal* 34.2 (2007), 216–227. Copyright by *Appalachian Journal* and Appalachian State University. Reprinted by permission.

This interview took place at a hotel in the small town of Mars Hill, in Madison County, North Carolina. The day after the interview, Ron Rash took Bjerre and a North Carolina journalist to Shelton Laurel. A small marker stands next to the meadow where "Thirteen men and boys, suspected of Unionism, were killed by Confederate soldiers in early 1863."

Thomas Ærvold Bjerre: Congratulations on your new novel. What has the reception been like?

Ron Rash: Thank you. Very good, so far, particularly among other writers. That means a lot. It just got probably the best review I could hope for from Donald Harington, a writer from Arkansas I really admire. His review in the *Atlanta Constitution* (14 May 2006) meant a lot to me. And it's actually sold out its first printing, so that's good.

TB: And you've been on a tour for how long?
RR: This is actually the fifth week. I went out to Portland, Los Angeles, Boston. Those are the farthest places I went. The rest were mainly in the South.

TB: The novel revolves around a Civil War massacre that has separated Madison County, North Carolina, ever since. Today, almost 150 years later,

Southern fiction is still haunted by that war. In fact, Cold Mountain is just around the corner from where your novel takes place. Why is that conflict so hard to let go of, even today?

RR: Well, for several reasons. One, almost all the battles were fought in the South, so I think that had something to do with it. And the losers tend to remember longer than the winners—though obviously African Americans and many Appalachians saw themselves as being on the winning side. It's hard to know which is the cause and which is the effect—but my sense of Southerners among Americans is that they have the deepest sense of history. They seem to, in a way, be more European that way. So I think those things all come together.

For me, one of the interesting things about writing this book was that I could show a side of that war that is not as well known: the fact that, particularly in the mountains, you had many Union sympathizers. A lot of times people think the South was monolithic as far as the Civil War goes, but that really wasn't the case, particularly up here, and in my own family. A lot of my family fought for the Union.

TB: You mentioned this sense of history. The book is also about obtaining that sense of history. Do young people today have that sense of history?

RR: Not as much, I think. It's always dangerous to make generalizations. But I was in Atlanta last night, and I was talking to a woman and her daughter who are from this county. Her grandmother was a Shelton, and she grew up hearing about that massacre. And she had obviously passed it on to her child. So at least in some instances, it is carried on, but probably not as strong as it has been.

TB: Was it important for you to set the novel in the 1970s rather than today?

RR: Yes, you hope that a novel can resonate more than just one way, and one thing I wanted to try to get at was the time I perceived as the end of that agrarian lifestyle. You just had this moment in the '70s—I saw it with my own uncle who was a tobacco farmer—where it was clear the next generation was not going to make a living this way. So what do you do?

Also at the same time in the '70s, the drug culture was first coming into the Appalachians in a big way. Not that people weren't already using drugs, or particularly, cultivating marijuana, though some of that had happened in the '60s. But in the '70s you really saw it explode, and it's led ultimately to something much more sinister, and that is meth, the use of methamphetamine, which is really rampant in a lot of rural areas in the United States, and definitely in Appalachia. So it seemed to me a turning point, because you start asking questions if you can't make a living as a farmer. When this lifestyle that in a sense your whole culture is built on suddenly is obsolete, what do you do? Do you go into drugs? Do you leave? That's what many young people have done. So it struck me as a pivotal moment, the '70s.

TB: The Civil War has haunted your writing, your poetry as well, for many years. How did *The World Made Straight* begin, and how long did you work on it?

RR: I'd been thinking about that for years. I'd grown up hearing those stories about my family's involvement with the Union pretty early. I've always been interested in the Civil War. Then as I got into my twenties, I started reading more about it and finding out more about the differences between the mountains and the rest of the country, the rest of the South. So it was kind of incubating the whole time. And then in the 1970s and 1980s, I started writing some poems about Shelton Laurel and got more and more interested in it. About three years ago, I suddenly realized I was going to be writing about it. And I actually went up to Shelton Laurel, to the burial site. So it had been fermenting a long time, and I knew on some level that I'd write it eventually. But I wasn't quite ready.

TB: Do you have a certain writing process once you get started on a project?

RR: Well, once I get into it, I tend to write maniacally for as long as I can until I just collapse, because I think it's important to get a first draft. I try not to worry about how good it is or how many holes are in it because to me it's like a potter having some clay, something to work with. I never outline, never really know where it's going, and I think that's probably a good thing, for me at least.

TB: So it's second, third, fourth draft from there?

RR: Yeah, it's a process of draft after draft. I'll do ten or twelve drafts on every novel. The first draft of this novel was maybe 150 pages. It doubles that length before it's over. The characters start to flesh out.

TB: What about the Civil War journals, the doctor's journals? Are those all made up?

RR: Yes, they were. I did a lot of research and studied some doctors' journals from that period. I studied nineteenth-century medicine and also military medicine. I enjoy doing that kind of research, and I did have an ancestor that actually was a country doctor at that time, but I didn't have any access to anything that he kept.

TB: Education also plays a big part in the novel. Could you elaborate on the role of education in Appalachia? It's a subject that another Appalachian writer, Kentucky-born Chris Offutt, also deals with extensively.
RR: I wanted to deal with that because I think education's the way you get out. Any minority culture knows that. And Lori, maybe even more so than Travis, represents a type of young person I've seen, usually a woman, who knows that she cannot make any mistakes in her life. She has this very tight, narrow way she can get out.

But there's another thing I wanted to do: with Appalachia in particular, there are pervasive stereotypes about no one being able to read, no one having an education, and that's obviously not true. But you don't want to go the other way and pretend everyone has a college education. In my family, my grandfather on my father's side couldn't read or write, but my mother's mother was a schoolteacher for a while and was educated at what was then called the Appalachian Training School for Teachers, which is now Appalachian State University. And she loved to read. So I wanted to show what, to me, was the reality, that there are people like this in the region. Not everybody is illiterate.

TB: Speaking of stereotypes, in *Saints at the River*, Maggie Glen falls prey to some of these prejudices from her editor. Have you experienced these prejudices yourself?
RR: Yes. I actually had someone from outside the region ask me, "Has anybody in your family ever read anything you've written?" The assumption was that they couldn't read, or even if they could, that they would not be remotely interested in it. And that struck me as remarkable, particularly from someone who would probably have considered himself very liberal and open-minded. I was kind of stunned, really, that someone would make that kind of broad assumption.

TB: I guess the popular media doesn't help. They did a remake of *The Dukes of Hazzard*. It's still so easy to poke fun at.
RR: It is. There are pockets of poverty in the region. You don't want to go the other way and turn away from reality—certainly, there are people who have done very well. As many intelligent people have come out of these mountains as from any other region.

TB: One of the leitmotifs in your fiction is the troubled relationship between parents and children, often father and child, which also figures in *The World Made Straight*. Is that a deliberate driving force?

RR: I think it's probably not deliberate. It's interesting to me how it comes out, and I'm not sure why. But those relationships are always so complex. I'm a parent myself, and it's such a complex situation. My father died pretty young; maybe that has a little bit to do with it. But as for having really rebellious or awful situations with my own parents, it's not autobiographical.

TB: From a literary point of view, the way I see these conflicts is that they mirror this clash, as you talked about it, between traditional Appalachian Agrarian ideals and the New South: the tobacco farmer and the children moving away into town.

RR: Yes, that's the way I want it to work. One thing I am very interested in—and maybe it's because I come from poetry—is a sense of mirroring in my work and resonance, so that these things are constantly interwoven. And I think it's there, certainly.

TB: It's interesting, especially in *One Foot in Eden*. There's a very sad atmosphere that reverberates throughout that novel, of this lost culture. The High Sheriff makes a vow to himself to serve out his term and then move back on the family farm. But at the end of the novel, which is several years later, he is still sheriff. So I guess you're not that much of an idealist.

RR: Yes, well, that's the reality. I've known enough people who farm, including my own family, not to sentimentalize that life. It's a hard life. And the Sheriff, I think, understands that. It's a little too easy to idealize it. It's a tough, tough life, and one I obviously didn't choose.

TB: But still, in all your novels you have these "wayward" characters, the ones who've left, returning home to face these unsettled issues, their unsettled pasts.

RR: That's something my generation has had to deal with in the sense that I've lived in a culture that's changed so rapidly that I feel displaced even when I'm in the same place. That's an inevitable part of change in any culture, but it's probably been more dramatic here than in a lot of places, particularly around where my grandmother's farm was. There was a time when I was a child, there was a two-mile dirt road up to her house, and I was either kin or knew personally everybody on that road. Now, I probably know three families out of sixty or seventy. And that place is gone. The accent's gone. A lot of the culture is disappearing. Once again, I don't want to sentimentalize it, but I think that something valuable there is being lost too, and a lot of it is just a matter of knowing who you are, where you come from.

TB: I guess that's progress for you, or just time.

RR: But there's something in us as human beings that—we know our lives are transitory, but we want something not to be transitory, something to endure, whether it's a landscape or a place. I think we sometimes sense that's being lost; particularly in *One Foot in Eden*, the mother actually says that. There's a sense that if it was just still here, I could deal with my own passing from this landscape, this place. And I think that's a pretty universal feeling.

TB: That situation of having to uproot your home, your existence, because of a state-controlled flooding seems, to me, unimaginable. Did you know people in that situation?

RR: Oh yes. My family lost land to the Blue Ridge Parkway. You had no choice. I've interviewed people who had to move out of Jocassee, out of that valley, and they're still bitter about it. But what's interesting to me, though, is how that novel (*One Foot in Eden*) and that situation have resonated in all parts of the United States. I've had letters from Colorado and New York State but also Australia. I've had some response from Australians who've had that happen. And obviously that's what's happening in China now, which is probably the greatest displacement in human history, to make the Three Gorges Dam. So, this has happened in a lot of places with devastating effect. There is something about that kind of annihilation of a place that's even worse than seeing development transform it.

TB: Your books, both poetry and novels, carry titles with obvious religious connotations. Are you a religious man?

RR: Yes, and I come out of a religious culture. Actually, I have a character early in this last book, whose wife says to him, "They got to you early." I grew up in a culture where belief was just a given; not having it was almost beyond imagination. That doesn't mean I haven't gone through periods of skepticism—it seems I do every day, but it's still definitely a part of my work and part of the way I perceive the world, although, at the same time, I'm more in Kierkegaard's camp than Jerry Falwell's—let's put it that way.

TB: As a European, I constantly hear skeptical talk of the United States as a religious country. But as you said, there are obvious differences between the know-it-all line and the more personal.

RR: Yes, I find people like Falwell frightening. Didn't Kierkegaard say that it would be the preachers and the ministers who would destroy faith?

TB: Given how religious a region the South is, there is not much religion in contemporary Southern fiction, is there?

RR: Because of people like Falwell and that kind of strident fundamentalism, I think a lot of Southern writers shy away from it because they don't want to be grouped or just suddenly viewed as, "Okay, here comes another religious crank." There's an interesting book (by Susan Ketchin) called *The Christ-Haunted Landscape* (1994), where it's like these writers are being outed. Larry Brown and Lee Smith, among others, said, "Yeah, I am a believer." But as I say, it doesn't come to the forefront of their work. The one exception, the most recent exception, would be someone like Walker Percy. But he's a believer, I think, more in the European tradition, like Kierkegaard and Gabriel Marcel.

TB: And when it does come out, it's more like in Barry Hannah's fiction, where the religious nuts really get it.

RR: Yes, and yet Hannah is a believer, so there you go. But I think that he probably shares the same kind of frustration that almost any religious writer does. You see people who go against the very thing they believe.

TB: In both *One Foot in Eden* and *Saints at the River*, you use female narrators. Is it more difficult to write from a woman's perspective? Do you put more thought into it?

RR: It wasn't a conscious decision in either situation. It wasn't that I wanted to prove that I could write like a woman. In *Saints at the River*, I started off with Allen the journalist telling the story. I wrote about forty pages, and I knew it wasn't working. By then, I knew Maggie well enough to know that there was some kind of mirroring or connection between the drowned girl and Maggie. I didn't really understand it completely, and I still don't think I do. But I knew that the story had to be Maggie's, so I just had to start over again. At the same time, I like that challenge of entering a sensibility different from my own. I'm really not much interested in writers who limit themselves to a single sensibility. The trait I prize is the one that Keats prized in

Shakespeare: negative capability. That, to me, is the greatest literary artistry, where you can be anyone, anything.

TB: In *Saints at the River*, there are some passages dealing with the differences between writing and photography, and photography comes out on top. That's perhaps surprising coming from a writer. Are you a photographer yourself?

RR: No. Once again, negative capability. I hope it was convincing. I tried to see the world the way I thought a photographer would, somebody who is really serious about it. Maggie is so rigid in many ways that it just felt like photography fit her, the sense that you can frame a scene, and there it is. She would be much more comfortable with that. I'm not saying that photographs can't be complex, but there is, to her, something about that, yet the irony, of course, is that the photograph she takes is very complex.

TB: And she doesn't really understand the power of that one picture she takes.

RR: Right. And it's been interesting, because some readers have said that there are aspects of Maggie's character that don't seem very positive. And I say, well, yes, she is human, not some idealized being.

TB: You are obviously very connected to the land, and many of your characters, the ones you want the reader to sympathize with, seem to have an almost mystical connection to nature. What's your own experience?

RR: I was very lucky in that I grew up in a rural area. But also I spent a lot of time, pretty much spent my summers, with my grandmother on her farm (in Watauga County, N.C.). There was no car there, and I was just allowed to roam these mountains. She would fix me a sandwich in the mornings. I'd eat a big breakfast, she'd give me a sandwich, and I'd take off. I'd come back at five o'clock. She just let me go. It was a different kind of world, but what it did for me, you know, I was just out in that world, and I observed it. But it wasn't even a conscious thing, it wasn't like I was self-consciously identifying trees or anything, but I was just in it, and I felt very comfortable there. I probably felt more comfortable there than I did around other human beings.

The other thing that happened up there was that, particularly with a lot of my older relatives, you got this sense of the world, there's almost a kind of shimmering sentience in the land. I can remember, for instance, as a child, I'd like to catch salamanders in the springhouse, and my grandmother would tell me that I wasn't supposed to do that. What was going on there was this idea that those salamanders were like guardian spirits of the purity of that water. All this folklore that I grew up with made for a very mysterious world, and also a world that was very alive, almost Wordsworthian. I think that had a lot to do with it.

I think writers who write about a rural landscape are often viewed as being provincial, but to me the natural world is the most universal of languages. I mean, if I write about mountains, a reader in Kenya or Scandinavia is going to understand what I'm talking about. Or if I write about water, describe the way a river moves, that's more universal than anything I can think of.

TB: It's also a link back to the past.

RR: Yes, that's part of it, too. And again, I try not to be didactic, but I don't see how you can ignore your connection to the natural world. You ignore it at your own peril and your society's peril, because if you think you can destroy it and it's not going to affect you, you're deluded. One thing that really distresses me now is that I think we live in a country where many political leaders don't even acknowledge that connection. And that's terrifying.

TB: You mentioned water before. It plays a huge part in all of your work. Any special reason?

RR: Certainly, I think the religious upbringing I had, and knowing the Bible in the sense of water being rebirth, but also the Flood—all that complexity of the symbolism and the imagery of it. It's like the Dylan Thomas poem "The Force That Through the Green Fuse Drives the Flower"—that kind of complexity. But the other thing I'm interested in that really played a part in *Saints at the River*, but it's always been on my mind, is that a lot of my ancestry is Welsh. Rash is actually a Welsh name, and in Welsh and Celtic folklore, water is a conduit between the living and the dead. That's something that I am very interested in, that kind of passageway between these worlds.

TB: The conflict that you describe in *Saints at the River*, was that based on any actual events?

RR: There had been some drownings like that where bodies had gotten stuck. Actually, on the Chattooga, the river near where I live, they actually used a portable dam like this, without success. But I made up all the characters. I didn't want to be too close to any actual drowning. I've never heard of a child that young drowning up there.

TB: Nature itself also plays an active role in your work: the water that floods the valley in *One Foot in Eden*, and the river that divides an entire community in *Saints at the River*. It seems you're setting up a conflict between man and nature, one in which we are bound to lose. In *Saints*, you have the two opposite sides, but in the end, it's really the river that has the last word. If you had chosen sides, the novel would be too didactic.

RR: Yes, and I didn't want that to happen. I don't feel like it's my job to tell people how to think about something. In a way, that's insulting your audience. I belong to organizations that keep rivers clean, but that is not the part of me that is an artist. I think you have to have enough faith in your audience to put it out there, and they're going to figure it out on their own, or at least think about these things seriously.

TB: Did you have any angry responses to that novel?

RR: Not really. I had a few people who said, "Why did you make the environmentalists so unlikable?" I think what they wanted was some kind of stellar champion who was pure of heart. But to me that is not an interesting character. The thing that I really liked was the fact that many readers recognized that I hadn't taken the easy way with any group.

TB: Do you see yourself writing in an Agrarian tradition?

RR: I'm very aware of that tradition, and I read *I'll Take My Stand* (1930) when I was in my early twenties. I certainly read people like Wendell Berry and Andrew Lytle and (Allen) Tate and (John Crowe) Ransom. I read all those people.

TB: When reading parts of *I'll Take My Stand* today, some of the environmental essays seem very relevant.

RR: Oh yeah. They said some things that are still relevant today. What bothered me then and now is the not-so-subtle racism.

TB: Their world was for the white elite only?

RR: Yes, it was very aristocratic. That was a kind of paternalism. You're right, though. I actually went back a few years ago and read a couple of those essays, and what they said was going to happen, it's happened.

TB: *One Foot in Eden* made me think of Madison Jones' *A Buried Land* (1963). Is there a deliberate allusion to that novel?

RR: I knew that book. It wasn't something that I did consciously, because I was so aware of what happened at Jocassee. During my first teaching job, I was actually teaching at a high school about five miles from Jocassee, and I was teaching students whose families had been displaced. But I read that book and admired it and continue to admire it. I think Jones is a writer who has been unjustly neglected in the United States. I think it's interesting that Jan Gretlund did a book on him (*Madison Jones' Garden of Innocence*. Univ. Press of Southern Denmark, 2005). I haven't seen that book, but I'd like to see it because it sounds very interesting. *A Cry of Absence* (1971) is a very good novel, and *A Buried Land* (1963, both by Madison Jones). I've read a number of his books, and I'm sure I'm a better writer for having read him.

TB: Do you feel yourself writing within a Southern tradition? And what do you think of this pigeonholing?

RR: Yes, I do see myself as working in this tradition, but "Southern Appalachian." The world I depict is very different from Welty's Delta. But, of course, the best Southern writing transcends the region; it has to. I like what Eudora Welty said: "One place understood helps us understand all other places better." To me, the tradition I want to follow, and I'm not comparing myself to them, is the tradition of O'Connor and Faulkner and Welty, because those are writers who achieved great regard and a wonderful readership outside the region, not just inside it. I would not want to be a writer who would only be read within the region and people would only understand inside the region. The one thing that bothers me about that term "Southern writer" is that, particularly in the U.S. outside the South, it means that's all you are. Your work doesn't transcend the South. It's mere local color. But to me, it's like drilling for water. The really good ones—Faulkner, O'Connor—they're going to go so deep that they're going to get past the local color, and they're going to go into that collective unconscious, into the Jungian realm. That's where I want to be. Outside the United States, from my sense of it, Southern Literature is held in higher regard. Fred Chappell is probably better known in France than he is in New York. He's won some major awards in France. Hannah is well known in France and in Britain. And he should be. I got an email a month and a half ago from a woman in the Czech Republic who is teaching my book to Czech graduate students. That heartens me. But I think it's a weird time to be a Southern writer in the United States, as far as getting acknowledged outside the region. *The New York Times* will rarely review Southern writers. Part of it is almost a sense of "it's not fair. You dominated the '20s, '30s, and '40s. You had Faulkner. You can't keep producing the best writers. It's not fair." But I really believe that the best writing coming out of the United States right now is coming from the South. I know there's nobody writing better than Cormac McCarthy—and Hannah, nobody uses language the way Hannah does. It's amazing how many good writers are working right now, especially in the Southern Appalachians. We can hold our own with any region or sub-region in the US

TB: Your novels have all had a touch of crime-fiction or thriller to them. Have any of them been optioned for movie rights?

RR: Yes, both *Saints* and *One Foot in Eden*. Nothing's happened with them, and I don't know that it will. That's something that I don't even keep up with. If something happens, it happens. But it's a long shot.

TB: You wouldn't feel that your "baby" was being corrupted?

RR: I would defer to Harry Crews on that point. Somebody asked that question to Harry Crews, if he wasn't worried what they were going to do to his book. He said, "They're not going to do anything to my book." He said it in much more colorful language, but he said that the book is a thing itself. Having said that, I'm human, and I think if they did some awful thing with space aliens coming down to rescue Billy or Amy or something like that, I would probably be horrified, but that's the devil's bargain you make if you allow somebody to option the movie.

TB: Now that you've had success as a novelist, do you think you'll return to short fiction and poetry?

RR: Oh yes. My next book is going to be a book of stories (*Chemistry & Other Stories*). It's going to be out in April (2007). Picador is going to do it. And I'm finishing up a book of poems. I'll always write poetry and stories, I think. What I've tended to do with my life is to move into one form and settle there a while, and when I feel like I've gotten to a point where I know I've exhausted what I can do, at least for the time being, I move on. It's almost like a radio, where you get a different frequency and stay on it a while. I will say that the novels are the things I find hardest to do. There are days when I'm writing novels where I'd rather just stick the pencils right in my eyeballs than try to write another sentence. They're grim, horrible things to create. Every time I finish one, I swear I'll never do another. But I am finishing up one right now, so I guess I'll never learn.

Words with Ron Rash

Jesse Graves and Randall Wilhelm / 2007

From "Interview: Words with Ron Rash." *Grist: The Journal for Writers* 1 (2008): 214–40. Copyright Jesse Graves and Randall Wilhelm. Reprinted by permission.

Ron Rash (b. Chester, SC 1953) grew up in Boiling Springs, North Carolina, and traces his Welsh ancestry to the hardscrabble mountain farms of Madison and Watauga counties where his family settled in the mid-1700s, an Appalachian landscape that provides the scene for much of his writing. Rash earned degrees from Gardner-Webb College and Clemson University before settling down to write professionally. From the beginning his work has been characterized by a knowledge of and reverence for the Southern Appalachian Mountain region, for its customs, folklore, superstitions and familial and communal histories. His first collection of stories, *The Night the New Jesus Fell to Earth* (1994), is a sequence of tales told by three narrators all coping with the loss by fire of the only café in Cliffside, North Carolina. Rash won an NEA Poetry Fellowship (1994) and the Sherwood Anderson Prize (1996), before publishing *Eureka Mill* to critical acclaim in 1998. Using traditional Welsh forms and a seven-syllable line, Rash's poetry is highly narrative, driven through the use of intricate rhythms, precise images and evocative metaphors, structured through multiple speakers capturing the disjunction, isolation and anger of Appalachian farmers bereft of their land and forced into mill towns out of economic necessity. *Among the Believers* (2000) features speakers from western North Carolina whose experiences embody the harsh beauty and violent past of the region. Ceremonial rites such as foot washing, baptisms and serpent handling blend with Civil War-era violence and a host of bodies strewn throughout, victims of flood, matricide, bad luck, murder and even of the wilderness itself. In *Raising the Dead* (2002), Rash stakes claim to the Appalachian underwater world of Jocassee Valley (the Cherokee word for "place of the lost") in northwestern South Carolina, which was flooded for hydroelectric power in the 1960s. In these evocative poems, mountain residents speak with dignity of a lost world, a place of intense belonging filled with mystery, beauty and death.

Rash published the short story collection *Casualties* in 2000, but with the enthusiastic reception of his first novel *One Foot in Eden* (2002) he gained widespread recognition, winning the Novello Literary/Award, *ForeWord Magazine's* Gold Medal in Literary Fiction, and the Appalachian Book of the Year. Set in Jocassee Valley and told in five sections each narrated by a different character, *One Foot in Eden* tells the story of Billy Holcombe and his wife, Amy, who, unable to produce a child, commit crimes in their desperation and find themselves enmeshed in a fateful web of seduction and murder. His second novel *Saints at the River* (2004) won the Weatherford Prize and the Southern Book Critics' Circle Award and tells the story of Maggie Glenn's return to her mountain home in Tamassee, South Carolina to photograph the battle of forces surrounding the drowning of a young girl in one of the most sensitive ecological areas in the region. In *The World Made Straight* (2006), Rash returns to themes originally explored in his poetry, specifically the Civil War massacre of "Bloody Madison" County, where members of a Confederate force massacred thirteen Union sympathizers. In this novel, past and present, victim and victimizer, family and country, duty and survival—all cohere in a poetic intensity that evokes Rash's larger concerns regarding the preciousness of hope, the fragility of dreams, and the moral responsibility we all must face. Rash's most recent work, *Chemistry and Other Stories*, collects thirteen of his best tales, including the giant fish story "Their Ancient, Glittering Eyes," the O. Henry Prize winner, "Speckle Trout" (2005), and "Pemberton's Bride," a story culled from his upcoming novel, *Serena*, to be published by Harper Collins (Ecco Press) in fall 2008. Rash continues to collect honors, winning the James Still Award from the Fellowship of Southern Writers in 2005. He currently holds the Parris Chair of Appalachian Studies at Western Carolina University.

Randall Wilhelm: It's good to see you, Ron, and thanks for talking with us this morning. Often, interviewers ask you about your preparation for becoming a writer, a question which you have answered by saying that you loved to read and that "reading a lot" is the best preparation. With so much material out there these days, which writers do you most admire and what advice can you offer young writers on how to select their reading material?
Ron Rash: Gosh, that's a good question. Sometimes you can read interviews of writers or essays that they've written and you're going to find out, I think, who writers are reading and I'd trust them over the literary critics right now.

Writers I admire. Well, certainly there are O'Connor and Faulkner. I read them young. And I think they did two things for me. One was just how great they were as writers, but also the sense that the kind of world I came out of, a rural world, and particularly a Southern rural world, that writing can have very much a sense of place but also be universal at the same time, and they have been exemplars to me of what I want to try to do.

RW: They each create a unique "spirit world," you might say, of their own, and you have done the same.

RR: Yeah, I'm also a great admirer of writers I came to later in life such as (Philip) Roth, (Cormac) McCarthy and (William) Gay. But at the same time I think it's important to read writers from other cultures as well. I've really responded to Dostoyevsky and continue to.

RW: Have any of his books besides *Crime and Punishment* affected you?

RR: Reading *The Possessed* just amazed me at how prescient he is. He always is, in the sense of a worldview that you see in the twentieth century and also going into the twenty-first. You see it in that book. He performed something a lot of writers today I don't think would attempt to do, and that is in a sense to be almost prophetic, to be what Pound said, "the antennae of the race," to pick up on things before anybody else does.

Jesse Graves: When did you first come to these books and how did you find out what your influences were going to be?

RR: Well, it wasn't really conscious, but as a kid I would kind of wander the library. I remember we would get this list of classic books and I would just pick up the books that were on that list. I was always ambitious that way, and a lot of times I would read books that I know I didn't get all of what was going on. Certainly, *Crime and Punishment*. I read that when I was fourteen. It was more just to prove to myself I could read it. But I got enough. [Laughs] What were considered Great Books, I tried to go out and read them. Now some I didn't get through. I think I accidentally picked up a Henry James novel [laughter] at fifteen or sixteen and I didn't get through that one. But reading people such as Hemingway, Fitzgerald, and Willa Cather, who is also a writer I admire, helped me immensely.

JG: Bob (Robert) Morgan tells a story about going to the BookMobile when he was in grade school and getting *War and Peace* since he heard it was the greatest novel ever written. He thought, "If this is the best book ever written, I better start there." [Laughter]

RW: Well, that's an interesting education. A lot of your interviewers play up the young tyke roaming around the mountains, reveling in his own imagination and the natural world but this information shows us the young boy in the library as attuned to culture as nature.

RR: Yeah. One thing my mother did that was really important was she would take me and my brother and sister to the library. And there were always books, even around my grandmother's house in the mountains where I spent so much time. She was a voracious reader. She was a farmwife but she loved to read, and there were good novels there. It was a great world because there wasn't a TV. I *would* roam around all day in the woods and then I'd come in in the evening and read. I mean, there really wasn't that much else to do. We were so isolated. It wasn't like I could walk down to the mall. There wasn't a store within probably five miles of that farm.

RW: Did she try to shape your reading?

RR: No, just by example. The fact that it was important to her, that she thought this was something worth doing. And also, as I got older, I realized that this is a woman who didn't have a lot of money and yet these books were important enough to buy. With money that would have not been so easy to obtain.

JG: Was that a working farm when you were there? Was somebody raising crops or tending livestock?

RR: It was until my grandfather died. It continued to be in the sense that she kept cattle until I was about fifteen or sixteen. But by then she was in her late sixties. What she did was actually make bedspreads, very elaborate, beautiful bedspreads, and she would make those and sell them to the tourists. So that's how she made money.

JG: So you didn't have a lot of farm work, didn't have a lot of chores?

RR: I did some. I'd go get the cow and milk it, that kind of thing. She had a milk cow. And I spent some time with my uncle who was a tobacco farmer. No, I wasn't out there behind a plow and all.

JG: You lucked out then. You got the best of both worlds.

RR: Yeah. [Laughter] My aunt one time said—and she was right—she was talking about tobacco, and hanging tobacco, which is a nasty job, and cutting it like that, she said, "It's a lot easier to write about it." [Laughter] And she's right.

JG: I know you are a great admirer of Thomas Hardy. I wonder if you could say something about that.

RR: I've actually been going back and re-reading Hardy's novels recently, and what I love about those novels is how landscape plays such a vital role. He's so good at drawing landscape and putting his characters in that place. His interest in a world that was fading away, for instance in *Tess*, how he just gives you a real sense of what Faulkner called "a last look back." Faulkner talks about how in a sense what he was doing was recording a world that was vanishing. Not necessarily that it was good or bad but just acknowledging its existence. And I think what Hardy does just puts the reader into that place. He's a writer that, as I get older, I respond to more. The end of *Tess*, the last fifty pages or so, is about as good as any novel I've ever read. I don't see how you could write a better ending than that. He does such an amazing thing with the landscape, the way the landscape is a character and I really admire that. I guess he's the greatest that's ever been in English, at least as far as being able to work in two genres, or three actually, including his short stories.

JG: Are there other writers of Hardy's era that you especially admire?

RR: Hopkins definitely, because I think once again Hopkins just seems to be so contemporary and what he did was so vitally new. I mean no one had written the way Hopkins did. To me, what he was doing was bringing this incredible, ultimately religious, intensity into the use of sound, just as Van Gogh was doing it with color. I mean the fact that it's just so *thick*. In both. It's just working at this kind of ecstatic level that few artists can attain.

RW: Both sound and image encapsulating emotion to an extreme degree . . .

RR: Yeah. And I've always found it interesting that they were working at about the same time, and they were both so similar as far as being a kind of failed priest, and found this kind of outlet in art.

RW: *Starry Night* is poetry in many ways . . .

RR: Oh, yes. I don't know that anybody has ever written about that but to me that's a fascinating connection, these two. I think that spiritual intensity that both Hopkins and Van Gogh had is reflected in their work so well.

JG: I was wondering also about Conrad, if there isn't perhaps an echo of him in your work?

RR: Oh yeah, I read a lot of Conrad when I was in my twenties. *Nostromo* stays with me. Certainly *Heart of Darkness*. I was very aware of that book. Conrad is a writer I've learned from, and I tell my students that's the way to do it. You just read these writers, and in a way it's kind of haphazard, you just kind of stumble into their world and you stay there awhile. It's not that you're consciously trying to imitate them but you're absorbing information. You're learning your craft, and who better to learn from than people such as Conrad and Hardy.

RW: Place is obviously extremely important in your writing. A story such as "Last Rite," with the mother determined to mark the very spot of her son's death, is a brilliant narrative that foregrounds the depth of feeling associated with the land. Your work is loaded with specific place names and, unlike say Faulkner who many times changed the actual name, from Oxford to Jefferson, for instance, you seem to foreground these places as fundamental to your identity as a writer. Are you aware of any conscious system when it comes to using landscape in your work?

RR: No, not really. The names of the places I think are so beautiful very often and so vivid and render the place so well. I mention Aho or Middlefork Creek and it is a kind of conjuring as a word. You're conjuring up the place and I think the names evoke that so well. There's a wonderful term the Welsh use, *cynefin* (pronounced kun-ev'in), for a primal, fierce attachment to a part of the landscape. They say it's so fierce that when sheep are sold they have to sell the land along with the flock or the transplanted sheep will wander, impossible to herd. If you have that kind of intimacy with the land, you can bring the place more intensely to the reader's mind. The kind of writing I want to do, I feel like it brings the reader to that place in a kind of intense way that allows the reader to enter the dream that is a story more fully. There are writers who are constantly reminding you that this is a construct, this is a novel, and they'll tell you that in the novel: "This did not really happen." Okay, we know that. It's a nice little trick, but after you do it one time . . . It's also to me insulting to the reader, as if the reader cannot simultaneously live in the dream and realize at the same time that it's not reality. Fitzgerald says the sign of a first rate intelligence is to hold two contradictory ideas in the head at the same time and still be able to function. And I make that assumption with my readers. Place names are often so beautiful but sometimes I do change names a little bit. I did with *Saints at the River*. I essentially made up a river, the Tamassee River, so I do a little bit of that, but you're right. For me, you have to make that place intensely felt, your characters must have this landscape affect them and at the same time you have to be able to transcend that particular landscape in the sense of the universality of the characters and their concerns. And that's what Hardy does so well.

JG: Do you keep a running journal, some place to jot down these names?
RR: I use simple wire-bound notebooks. What I put in there sometimes is a really striking line that a writer has written that I admire, an idea or something that I may want to do later. Lines that come to me, that in a sense are not in a particular poem, or something I overhear someone say that I think is interesting. All sorts of things like that. Sometimes place names. It's good to go back and look at those and they'll trigger a poem or a story. Sometimes if I have a really good line that I have to cut out of a poem because it doesn't work in that poem, I'll take it out and see if I can use it somewhere else.

JG: Do you keep other work that you come across?
RR: Yeah. There's a wonderful Edith Wharton line I read a couple of years ago, "The hard considerations of the poor." That's a wonderful line. I wrote it down and then eventually used it in a story. I think I used it in "Honesty," a short story in this new book (*Chemistry and Other Stories*).

RW: That's an interesting story, and an interesting character. Are there any hidden self-portraits in your work that you're consciously aware of? The husband in "Honesty," for instance, is an English professor writing—or more correctly—*not* writing a book on Robert Frost. And there's the character in "White Trash Fishing" that can't wait to get out of the office, the coat and tie, and get back out to the woods, chigger bites and all.
RR: No, not consciously. Not so much in "Honesty," but maybe in the other one. Maybe there's something to that, the fear that to a degree you become so insulated in the academic world that you have no sense of how most people live their lives.

RW: The character in "White Trash Fishing" seems more like you. I can see that being you.
RR: Yeah, that one I would agree would be more Ron Rash. [Laughter]

JG: You mentioned last night during your reading that you lead the most boring life in the world, sitting at your computer for five hours a day. This explains why you've been called "one of the hardest working writers in America." Can you tell us a bit about your composing process?

RR: I try to write every morning, six mornings a week usually, and I try to get in at least five hours every day. But when I'm doing first drafts of short stories, novels, and sometimes poems I'll go up to twelve hours, really like twenty-four hours because I'm getting up in the middle of the night to write because I'll have trouble sleeping. I'll be dreaming about it, and I'll get up two or three times a night and write something, sometimes just for five minutes, sometimes an hour, and then go back to sleep. I'll write less on the weekends but I'm still writing some. It's almost like, for some reason, stories and novels come to me full blown. It's like a frantic race to get it all down before it evaporates, so when I'm writing first drafts I just pretty much go into a zone, and it's incredibly tiring, but also exhilarating. I really do wish I were one of those writers who could just write a certain amount every day. Graham Greene would write up to a certain number of words and he would stop in mid-sentence. Flannery O'Connor, I think, wrote two hours every morning, but I'm just not one of those writers.

JG: So you try to get the first draft down and then you go back and revise or do you revise as you go?
RR: To me, the hard part is the first draft. Once you get that draft, particularly with a novel, you know at least you got enough there that you can create a novel. That's always the scary part, I think, in writing a novel, is the fear that there's not enough there.

JG: Do your poems go through multiple revisions as well?
RR: I think with a poem you are almost always able to write a draft in at most several days. It may be a rough draft but you're going to have a sense of the whole thing. Now, it may change radically but I think particularly with a novel it's like this huge thing you're trying to get a draft of. Unfortunately, I approach it as I would getting a first draft of a poem or short story. But it's the same way with a novel or a poem, once that seizes you, you are obsessed but you're also afraid you're going to lose it if you don't get it down on paper. I'm so afraid it's going to evaporate that I have to get it down.

RW: A little anxiety producing . . .
RR: Yeah, sure. Adrenaline. But also a kind of excitement.

JG: Yeah. There's that feeling like you see it here and now, and then you go answer the phone or take out the garbage and it's not going to be there when you get back. There's a finite moment to get a poem. Do you see poems? I wonder if the poems come to you as a whole.

RR: Yeah, even if it's just some sounds strung together. Usually those things are almost like two wires crossing that spark something. I don't know what kind of poem it's going to be necessarily or what the subject matter will be, I just know it is a poem. Or, the possibility of a poem is there. And in a way there can be a vague sense of where it's going.

JG: Do you think it comes through as an image first, as a sound first, or is it different every time?

RR: Sometimes an image, sometimes a certain line or a sound. The main thing is to just wait for the poem.

JG: Be ready?

RR: Yes. The same thing can happen with the novel. Two years ago with *Serena*, I knew immediately it was a novel. It was exactly this time two years ago. In a way I kind of went into a funk, even with the excitement, because I knew it was going to be a longer book than I had ever written. I knew it was going to have to be. It's over four hundred pages now. And I'm still working on it. But it's kind of exhilarating too. But I just feel so much better when I get that first draft because then I know I can do it. I think with a novel that's always the scary thing that you don't know if you've deluded yourself, that you think there's a book here and maybe thirty to forty pages in, it just dies. And almost every time I write a novel there's a moment where it seems like it's just stuck, like where is this going?

RW: What do you do then? Stare into space? Plumb the well?

RR: Yeah, come on back to the desk and make yourself keep trying. Reread what you've written. Just say "what if?" and run with it. There are all kinds of internal games that you play with yourself. My belief, particularly when I'm stuck, is like Michelangelo's belief that the finished statue was already inside the block of marble, and I believe that if I'm so obsessed with a story or an image or whatever that it pulls me into writing a novel that somewhere that novel's there and it's just a matter of finding it, the same way as Michelangelo knew his statue was there. And on one hand I know that's ridiculous, but it's a great thing to believe. If you can make yourself believe that it's really out there, you know, it's just a matter of finding it. I think it can help you through those periods when you feel lost. It's the most comforting lie I have as a writer.

RW: There are stories of Picasso just painting away as rival girlfriends screamed and fought over his affections, and there's the anecdote where Faulkner would go into his room and remove the doorknob so no one could get in and bother him. Can you work with other people around or do you need solitude?

RR: I need solitude. Some writers don't but, yeah, I need silence and solitude. Certain rituals I go through before I start writing, I think are good for me. It's like being an athlete, I think, before you get ready to perform. If you go through certain rituals it leads you in to what you're going to do.

RW: You read from *The World Made Straight* last night, and there's that wonderful scene where Leonard takes Travis to Shelton Laurel and present and past merge. You were just saying how all of your novels tend to reach a sticking point and I was wondering what the solution was for this novel.

RR: Oh, it was when I discovered Leonard's ancestor's medical journals, the notes he takes when he's traveling with the Confederate army.

RW: Did you do a lot of research to get that information?

RR: Yeah, I did a huge amount of research on doctors and nineteenth-century medicine, but I made up all the journals from what I read. But that was it, because I realized the true structure of the novel which was in some ways a little bit like *Absalom, Absalom!* and *All the King's Men* where you got two stories kind of intertwining and playing off each other, resonating off one another. But it took me a long time to figure that out for this novel.

RW: Yes, but it's very effective. The italics and the space around it really register a different time zone and provide an eerie lynchpin between past and present. We were wondering, is there an ideal Ron Rash reader?

RR: Well, two of them are right here. [Laughter]

JG: There were definitely a bunch of them at Laurel Theater last night, I think.

RR: Gosh, I don't know . . .

RW: If so, what would be his or her characteristics, what they look for, what they "get" that other readers might not get?

RR: Well, I'll tell you, the reader I would hope for would be the reader, who when he or she comes to my work the second time—novel or poem—, finds there's even more there, and someone who's willing to maybe even read it a third time, that the novels reward re-reading.

RW: Yeah, I think they do offer a rich reward. The more one rereads your work, the more parallels and echoes one tends to discover. They're very intricately patterned books.

RR: Well, also my ideal reader is someone who loves literature for language. It would be somebody who doesn't need black and white answers.

JG: The poet Anthony Hecht has described you as a master of form. Could you tell us more about the particular Welsh form you use so often and how you came upon it?

RR: I've always been attracted to Welsh poetry for its sound qualities. Hopkins, Thomas, Vaughn. And I knew a lot of my background was Welsh so that attracted me to it as well. But I've always loved sound in poetry. I've always thought that a lot of contemporary poetry has eschewed that. To me, it's almost like having stereo speakers and unplugging one of them. In the poems I love the most, the sound gives a pleasure just in itself that makes it worthwhile just to hear, to read. And then you've got meaning or language, and the poets I love most are always working stereo.

JG: I read in an interview that discovering (Seamus) Heaney opened up discoveries in your own work.

RR: Yeah, because he was a great reminder to me that by grounding your work in a particular place, as Heaney has so often, that once again you achieve the universal. And there was something significant about him not being a Southerner because there's that idea that, oh okay, Southerners and the sense of place, blah blah blah. But it's not just about being a Southerner—it's about being a writer. The way to make great poetry is to use place as a conduit into the universal. Philip Roth has said that all great American novels are regional. Roth's work, especially *American Pastoral*, has an incredible sense of place. You read his novels and you get a sense of what New Jersey is and what it was, but it's also a gateway into the universal.

JG: Let me ask you more about poets you like. If we consider contemporary American poetry as beginning with (Elizabeth) Bishop, (Robert) Lowell and (Theodore) Roethke and moving up from there, are there any influences out of that group or the group right after?

RR: I think certainly reading (Robert) Morgan opened up possibilities. Anthony Hecht was always a poet I was drawn to because of his toughness and the way he could use rather eloquent language and at the same time a kind of earthiness dealing with as disturbing matters as there are in the world. I've never really gotten O'Hara or the New York School. Maybe that's just a gap in my sensibilities but I've never really understood why people consider him so significant. Poets I've tended to really love, particularly after 1950, have tended to be outside the United States.

JG: It's been a great fifty years for international poetry. Have you ever attempted a poem like, say Morgan's "Mockingbird," that sort of exploration of the self?

RR: No I haven't, and to me that's a great poem. One of my very favorites. He's just an amazing poet. I wish I could do that, but I've never been able to.

RW: You keep a lot of yourself out of your poetry and your fiction.

RR: Yeah, but a writer's obsessions are always going to show up in his or her work. I'm always leery of the kind of poetry and fiction where it's about lives that are essentially pretty boring. I've never been a fan of Confessional poetry because I don't think it's half as interesting as the poet thinks it is. I greatly admire (Sylvia) Plath, though, because she was great with craft. That's what makes her a great poet.

JG: That is a big difference between Sylvia Plath and Anne Sexton.

RR: Yeah.

JG: They're often compared, and not necessarily for the best reasons.

RR: Yeah. I think Plath is magnificent. Another post-50s poet I love is (Philip) Larkin. He's another writer who's had a big influence on me. That's what I love. Even with Thomas, even if it's nonsense, I still love it. And with Larkin, you just realize "I am really enjoying reading this. I'm really enjoying re-reading this." And it's also just incredibly memorable. I still think that the best test of a good poem is if it is memorable speech. Does the language stay with you? Do you read it one time and are never able to forget it? Larkin does that so often, though: "Our almost instinct, almost true, what will survive of us is love." It lingers.

RW: Even though you do keep a lot of yourself out of your work, your novels seem to foreground family troubles, how the family—the father in particular—can stunt a child's growth by warping them emotionally and/or physically. We can only imagine Isaac's suffering as he works out the complicated mess of his life following the events of his learning of Billy's killing of his father, Holland. Maggie Glenn's final resolution with her father is tainted by its very brevity, while Travis Shelton's anger towards his father remains unabated at novel's end. Why so much trouble with the father in your fiction?

RR: Well, I really don't think it's autobiographical. I'm sure some Freudian would say it is. But I think it's because it's just such a primal, elemental conflict, the father and the son, or, in Maggie's case, father and daughter. A universal problem, the conflict between generations, the conflict within family, how family hurts us and saves us, and all those complexities lend themselves to literature. The feelings, the motivations of people, particularly in families. But sometimes people are impressed that I *don't* write about myself, some people who are obviously like me, and to me that's always the greater challenge. Coleridge talked about—and once again I'm not using the word "genius" for myself—but he says there's two levels of genius. One can render one's own consciousness in a beautiful, artistic way, but the greater genius— I think he calls it the "secondary genius"—is what Shakespeare did, where the writer's not even there. You can't even say this is what Shakespeare thinks or that he "thinks" everything in every character. That's what Keats calls "negative capability," at least part of what that means, the idea of being amorphous, almost being completely outside your own consciousness.

RW: Your poetry tends toward the more personal, though, doesn't it? Especially *Eureka Mill*, and the other volumes also seem to reveal more details about, if not you, then certainly the Rash clan as a whole.

RR: Yeah, in my poetry I have used first person and certain forms that are more personal but in my fiction I've always tended to go away from characters resembling myself, at least on the surface. I think that, like any writing, you're going to bring part of yourself into the characters.

RW: What part of you seeped into *Serena* do you think?

RR: Well, I think that almost fanatical will, that drivenness.

JG: I have a couple of questions about your sense of yourself as an artist. I read that your father was a sculptor and an art professor and your mother was a quiltmaker and a teacher. I wonder if you had an early sense of yourself as an artist or had a sense of creative prospects.

RR: I'm going to answer this in a roundabout way. I was always aware of how hard my parents had worked to get where they were. They met in a cotton mill. Father a high school dropout, mother finished high school at sixteen, left the mountains. There was always this awareness of the importance of what they did—my father, an art teacher, how important that must have been to him to have done what he did. Which was, in part, to essentially turn away from the family, the culture, the class, he was born into. I know that haunted him all his life. One of the last things he said to me—he died when I was twenty-four—was it wasn't worth it. The price was so heavy to get out, so I knew that. But going back to your question—when I was a kid I never thought of myself as an artist or as having an artistic temperament. I just thought I was weird. [Laughter] Really. I went to a county high school and although my parents were teachers, almost all my relatives, including my uncles who I spent a lot of time with, were blue collar guys who never went to college. I would never have pulled out a book in front of one of my uncles and started reading. But, at the same time, I was certainly reading those books up in my room.

JG: Let me ask you about your development. You've published so many books in such a short period of time, but you didn't publish early. Your first book wasn't the second year of college kind of novel, it was later on. I was wondering if you were writing all that time?

RR: Yeah, I was. Kind of slowly learning my craft. I think that was a blessing. I don't envy a writer who achieves a degree of recognition early. Once that happens, so many things that are not part of the writing begin to intrude. I think writers are like athletes in the sense that some of them hit their stride later than others, and I'm one of those writers who hit it late. I didn't write anything good until I was twenty-nine or thirty.

JG: How did you keep yourself going all those years?

RR: Well, Joan Acocella has written an interesting piece on that, where she says that [Rash reads from a notebook on his desk] "We know the seductive alchemy of art can transform private anguish into a narrative of truth, if not beauty. To make sense where there was none, to bring order out of chaos, these are the promises that art makes. Fulfilling them requires something else entirely, an attribute closer to blindness than inspiration, a refusal to give up when the odds predict defeat." I think there's a lot to that. And also that "Art, beneath its intoxicating surface, art makes singularly unglamorous demands—integrity, sacrifice and discipline." I had a certain stubbornness, but you also need a certain amount of faith in yourself that ultimately you're going to find your work. I had several friends in graduate school who were writing better than me at the time but they just gave up. There I was, not writing anything worthwhile, and yet I was the one who kept writing.

RW: Many descriptions of your writing use words such as "tragic," "mournful," "heartbreaking," "wistful" and "dark" to describe the tone of your work. There's the comment by a woman at a recent conference who said, "That Ron Rash, he's a handsome devil—if only he would smile." While your work has been aptly described as a "veritable garden of earthly disquiet," there is also subtle humor in many of the works, particularly in "Their Ancient, Glittering Eyes." How important is humor for you in your writing? Was the big fish story a conscious attempt at interjecting more humor into your work?

RR: I admire humor and, actually, *Serena* has more humor in it than any of my novels. I've got kind of a chorus of loggers who witness Serena out hunting with this enormous eagle. What's funny about the scene that comes after that is that the second time the eagle goes out it catches a huge timber rattlesnake but those workers don't know it's out hunting. One of the characters, McIntyre, has been quoting passages from Revelation. He's obnoxious like that and telling the rest of the workers that these are all signs of the end of time and they'd better straighten up their lives because he's gonna be gone when it happens, and then he makes this prophecy. He says there's gonna be scorpions and snakes falling from the sky. So, Serena's eagle ends up dropping the rattler out of the heavens at his feet and he falls over and collapses and has to go into the state mental hospital for a month because he thinks the Apocalypse has come. So, you know, to me there's some funny stuff in it. But one thing I love about humor is that you can't fake it.

RW: And it breaks up some of the darkness and gloom.

RR: Yeah, I think you have to do that. I think Shakespeare in *Macbeth*, that "Knocking at the Gates" scene is so good because it breaks this horrific, probably the most horrific act imaginable to his society, the killing of a king. It becomes so unbearable that you have to break it, and then let it build again.

RW: It also serves as a jarring contrast.

RR: Yeah. And I love Marlowe because he does the same thing in *Faustus*. One thing I've tried to do with *Serena* is to give a sense of it being a novel but at the same time being like a play. There are four sections, and essentially a chorus and a comic interlude in each section. In a sense I want to bring in the kind of effects that you get out of a play.

RW: We get to see a little of Serena in your short story "Pemberton's Bride," but can you tell us more about her, especially since she takes over the novel that bears her name. Where did this woman come from?

RR: Like most of my novels, I just had an image of her, almost a vision. I saw this woman sitting astride a large white horse and the sun was breaking through the trees and her hair was a burnished gold. I didn't know who she was or what the image meant. It was a very intense feeling because the more I wrote, the more Serena's world became more real than the world we're in. It was almost like *Alice in Wonderland*. It's never been that intense before. *One Foot in Eden* was the same way.

RW: Another vision spawned that first book, right, the farmer standing in his field?

RR: Yeah. And one reason I found Serena compelling to write about is that I don't think there are a lot of powerful female characters, particularly in American fiction, powerful in a sense not within a family, but having control over hundreds of people, a captain of industry. And I think, particularly at the time, the 1930s, what would that have been like? I just found her intriguing.

JG: Especially in the South.

RR: Yeah, in the South, in a very rural culture, in an almost utterly male world in every possible way. Almost all the workers in the timber camp are men, sometimes a women in the kitchen, if that, and in this most masculine of occupations. Suddenly, you have this woman who understands that world and is better suited to it than the men.

RW: How does this novel differ from your other ones?

RR: Well, I think it's a much more ambitious book in the range of character, what I'm trying to do structurally, and also with tone.

RW: Yeah, it's a grand canvas with an epic sweep.

RR: Well, I hope so. That will be up to the reader to decide.

JG: Can you tell us more about the tone, what you're trying to do?

RR: I'm trying to work on a book that moves from the comic to the tragic. I guess what I'm attempting is to write an Elizabethan novel. I'm also working with using iambic pentameter for one character's dialogue and I hope the reader just assimilates it as they read without being distracted by it. I just love those Marlowe and Shakespeare characters who have such strong wills.

JG: Well, it's hard to climb any higher than Marlowe and Shakespeare, so maybe we should close there, and let you get on the road.

RW: Good luck on your trip to New York and thank you for taking the time to talk with us.

RR: I really enjoyed it. Thank you all for having me over to Knoxville.

Twisting the Radio Dial: An Interview with Ron Rash

Forrest Anderson / 2007

From *The Southeast Review* 25.2 (2007): 104–117. Reprinted by permission.

I recently had the opportunity to interview Rash on the telephone. Through a cheap speakerphone from Radio Shack, we discussed the migration of farmers to cotton mills, distance running, ancestry, and storytelling.

Forrest Anderson: Ron, when I first met you in South Carolina, you came to Columbia to do a poetry reading with Nikky Finney, which was right around the time *Raising the Dead* was published in 2002. I knew you first as a poet, and I wanted to start our conversation by talking about your poetry and early work. You mentioned at that reading that you didn't really start writing until your late twenties. Why such a late start?

Ron Rash: Well, I was trying to write, but mainly what I was doing was preparing to write. I was reading a lot, an immense amount. I was writing some, but I was really more of a dilettante. It wasn't until I got into my late twenties that I really got serious about writing. And, for whatever reason, I think I was just ready. There are certain writers who write very early on, for instance Keats and Faulkner. Some writers go slower, and I'm one of the slower ones so I got off to a late start. I was almost twenty-eight before I wrote anything that was even remotely good.

FA: Was it during this time when you started working on the poems that became *Eureka Mill* and the stories for *The Night the New Jesus Fell to Earth and Other Stories from Cliffside, North Carolina*?

RR: Yeah. I think the first story was "My Father's Cadillacs," which is in *The Night the New Jesus*. I pretty much simultaneously started writing short stories and poems. And I've found that short stories are much closer to poems than short stories are to novels. I think because in a really good short story every word counts. With a novel, you can ramble and be sloppy at times, meander. But with poems and short stories there's an incredible tightness. Also, I think what happens a lot of times with stories is you get resonance, certain images return. A great example of that is when you look at "A Good Man is Hard to Find" and how . . . The Misfit's never quite out of the story . . . there's this kind of return to things that are set up. I mean structurally.

FA: *Eureka Mill* focuses on your family's move from the farms of North Carolina to the mills of South Carolina. Can you tell me a little about that story and how you worked it into your poems?

RR: The people that migrated from Appalachia—particularly in the early twentieth century—tended to migrate either north to the coalmining region or to the automobile factories to work or they sometimes migrated east and south to work in the cotton mills. My family tended to migrate into the cotton mills. They were just one of the many, and that was one reason I thought the material was interesting. It transcended a single family and was pretty indicative of a whole movement of people.

FA: Was your family used to help focus the larger scale of the book?

RR: Yeah. I did a lot of research for that book on mill life so in a sense it's more than just a family history, but there is family history.

FA: The people in *The Night the New Jesus Fell to Earth* populate the foothills of the mountains. Towns, in my mind, that are similar to Morganton, Tryon, and your hometown, Boiling Springs. How come both your first book of poems and your first collection of short stories occur outside of the North Carolina mountains—the region of the rest of your work?

RR: I grew up in the foothills. I wanted to capture that world and write about it. Then, I just kind of moved deeper into that area that I felt was really my true spirit country, the place where almost all my relatives lived. In a way, it's almost like I wanted to address the foothills first and then move deeper into my family's history and the region that I was most taken with and most identified with.

FA: *Among the Believers* is the first book that takes place in the mountains. The title seems ambivalent. Is this a sign of your hesitancy to write about your ancestors' mountains?

RR: Not as much that as a sense of being in some ways part of them and then not being part of them. Being outside and inside simultaneously.

FA: In the short story collection *Casualties*, a number of the stories are told from the perspective of a young narrator. I'm thinking of "Chemistry" and "My Father Like A River," which are stories where a father takes his son back to his native mountains. Was this a way for you to feel more comfortable writing about the mountains?

RR: You know I haven't thought of it this way, but now that we're talking about it . . . It is almost like I just gradually moved into that territory— maybe a little tentatively at first—but moving deeper and deeper into it with each book.

FA: In *Among the Believers* you started writing your poems in Welsh verse. How did you come across this form of poetry?

RR: My ancestry, at least on my father's side, is Welsh so I had an interest there, but I've always been interested in poets who were very sound-intense. Hopkins. Thomas. And those poets are both influenced greatly by traditional Welsh poetics. In Welsh poetry sound is as important as sense. I've always been drawn to sound. You might argue a little bit of it's genetic, but also it's just the poets that I've tended to admire are poets who are very interested in sound. Traditional Welsh poetics is very sound-intense. It's a seven-syllable line and it also tends to have internal rhyming.

FA: You said something interesting there. You said your interest in sound might be genetic. Didn't Welsh people settle in the North Carolina mountains?

RR: Yes, they did. I think we tend to think only Scots-Irish, but obviously there were early settlers from Germany, Wales, and other countries as well.

FA: The Welsh verse you picked up. Is other traditional Appalachian poetry in Welsh verse?

RR: Not that I know of.

FA: I was wondering if maybe the Welsh verse was a way to reclaim your ancestry or your family tradition or even the cadence of your grandparents' voices?

RR: Well, I think what it did for me . . . I tend to be a narrative poet and there's a danger when you're a narrative poet that you just end up writing chopped up anecdotes, stories with line breaks. What I wanted was something to intensify my lines, and that form did it for me.

FA: Do you find yourself doing that in your fiction, too, paying attention to the rhythm of the line?
RR: I do to a lesser degree, but I'm very interested in how something sounds and rhythms. My hope is that I've brought what I've learned from poetry—at least some of it—into my fiction.

FA: Let me ask you again about your poetry. Your interest in narrative poems continued into *Raising the Dead*, which tells the story of Duke Power flooding the Jocassee Valley and displacing hundreds of people from their homes. Can you tell me a little bit about the premise for the book and how you stumbled across the idea?
RR: I've always been haunted by manmade lakes because I always wondered who lived there, what was lost when this lake came about—whether it's Santee Cooper or Jocassee—and that idea of a lost world. There's a kind of horrific finality to a place that has been completely flooded; not even place names survive. And that particular valley, Jocassee, many people say it was the most beautiful in South Carolina. What I wanted to do was to try to resurrect it, at least imaginatively, to remind people what had been lost.

FA: Is that a personal draw to family and traditions lost like in *Eureka Mill*?
RR: Well, this was less personal in the sense that I didn't have any family in Jocassee Valley. To me, it worked because those lakes represent a broader annihilation of a culture, particularly the Appalachian culture.

FA: You went to Gardner-Webb University on a track scholarship. What event did you run there?
RR: 800 meters.

FA: Is it true you held some school records?
RR: No big records. I ran a 1:53. That was my best time. I did pretty well.

FA: You mentioned to me once that you have a certain theory, which is that people who excelled in running make good writers. I think Ron Carlson used to be a big-time runner.
RR: And George Singleton.

FA: Why do you think running is such good preparation for writing?

RR: It teaches discipline. I think with running, particularly distance running, you're having to push yourself. It tends to attract people who are already pretty obsessive. You have to be kind of driven to want to run, to be any good at it. I think all those elements, working in solitude, going out for those long runs by yourself—at least that's the way I trained—I think all those things are very similar to what we do as writers.

FA: Another sort of preparation you had for the writing life was to have the good fortune to be living near Clemson, South Carolina, at the same time as George Singleton and Dale Ray Phillips. Can you tell me about that time?

RR: We know each other. George was living about twenty miles away, but he would come over a lot. Dale, George, and I on Friday afternoons would go out together and talk literature. That was a good time; just being around each other made us all want to write more and better.

FA: Is it fun to look back on this time and see that all three of you have become successful?

RR: Yeah. They're just great friendships. I think that's the best thing. It was just kind of a nice dynamic. We all write differently. We would talk about what we were reading, more than what we were writing. We'd teach each other. Dale would mention maybe a short story I hadn't read. George might the next time. I might mention something to them. It was a good time.

FA: I'm curious about the time in your life when you started to break into the literary world. You started out winning a number of awards—the Academy of American Poets Prize in 1986, the General Electric Foundation Award for Younger Writers in 1987, an NEA Poetry Fellowship in 1994, the Sherwood Anderson Prize in 1996. How important were these prizes to you in the development of your career?

RR: They were a good affirmation. I never took a creative writing class when I was in college or graduate school. I didn't get an MFA. I had a straight MA. I think I really never had much outside confirmation or encouragement that I was doing anything well the way you might get in an MFA program. I wasn't even letting people know. My brother didn't even know I was writing. Those awards at least gave me a sense that maybe I'm doing okay, maybe I might finally get to where I can write a few things that might be decent. At the same time I knew once I got into my late twenties, I was going to write anyway. I don't think anything could have stopped me. And I think sometimes there's a danger in wanting to get patted on the shoulder. We can't count on that. We just have to keep writing and do the best we can.

FA: Your first two collections of stories were published on the Bench Press out of Beaufort, South Carolina, and your first novel *One Foot in Eden* won the 2002 Novello Literary Award. I've heard that major publishers accepted *One Foot in Eden*, but you declined to publish with them.

RR: I would say a noted publisher. They wanted me to make it into a single point of view, and I felt like that would ruin the book so I just declined to change it.

FA: In some ways, you really had to hustle your own books in the beginning. What did that do for you as a writer?

RR: I didn't really worry too much about it. The books were out there. I didn't really try to promote them much. My goal was to keep writing and try to make each book better. I was glad to have the books published even though the publishers were small. It was just something slow. I was sending work out to journals. I think the way my career has gone has been pretty typical. George and Dale Ray, for instance, I think all three of us have followed the same trajectory. Publishing in journals, getting small notice, and finally finding somebody in New York who was interested.

FA: How did you come into contact with Lee Smith, Robert Morgan, and Anthony Hecht? How important were these people in your development as a writer?

RR: Morgan, Smith, and Hecht had read my work and liked it. They were kind enough to let me know that and they let other people know it. That was their generosity. Also, all three of those writers inspired me by their example. By that I mean the writing always came first for those writers. They weren't big self-promoters. They just did their work as well as they could.

FA: Were these people your writing program? Your affirmation?

RR: They gave me that affirmation which was important. That was great because those are writers that I admired. What can be better than to have people whose work you admire find some merit in your work?

FA: Do you have people now who you trust to read your work?

RR: My brother. He's my first editor, and he's excellent because he's tough and honest.

FA: He didn't even know you were writing at first.

RR: Right. He's very smart, a lot smarter than I am. Not only is he a good editor, but he knows what I'm trying to do. And he also, as I say, spots when I'm being lazy.

FA: Did he do the artwork for *Casualties*?

RR: No. That was my father. My father sketched that. He's been dead a long time, but that was a sketch he made when he was young.

FA: Was he an artist?

RR: Yeah. He actually lived an interesting life. He was a high school dropout and was working at a cotton mill. Then, he went back and got a GED, went back again and got an undergraduate degree and later a masters and became a teacher. He was an art teacher, eventually.

FA: Did he give you an interest in painting?

RR: He did. I have no talent for it, just an interest in art and admiration for those who do it well.

FA: We were talking about discipline from running earlier. Maybe your discipline came from your father.

RR: What he did was incredible. I think his inspiration at how far he came, from where he came, has always inspired me.

FA: Your grandfather also inspired you. There's the story of him reading you *The Cat in the Hat* . . .

RR: My grandfather couldn't read or write. And when I was five years old, I asked him to read *The Cat in the Hat,* not knowing he couldn't read. He turned the pages and made up a story. It was a different story from the one my mother had read from the book, which was fascinating. But then, the next time I asked him to read it the story was different. The cat got into more trouble. It just kind of gave me this moment where words seemed like they were magical—almost like they were fluttering around and changing places. That idea of language kind of being this magical thing has stayed with me all my life.

FA: Can we talk a little bit about your writing process? There's a debate that goes on between writers occasionally about whether it's better to write every day or write when you feel like you can. Are you a daily writer?

RR: Yeah. At the same time, every writer has to find what's right for him or her. For me, I like the idea of structure. Once again this kind of goes back to being an athlete, the idea that you do it every day. Obviously, there are going to be days when you don't write as well or you don't get as much done. At the same time, I think there's something important in trying to write six days a week as I do. Very often I'll come in not wanting to write, but if I just put a pen on paper something will come unexpectedly.

FA: Like in running, the days you don't want to go usually turn out to be your best days.
RR: Yeah. Sometimes you think you know you're not going to be able to write or run, but you may be fooling yourself.

FA: You live in South Carolina, but work in North Carolina. What are your days like?
RR: I teach in the afternoons so I tend to write most mornings. I write from 8:00 until 12:00, and then I take a break. I like to go exercise some, get lunch, come back and work maybe a little more. Sometimes when I'm writing a first draft, though, I'll go ten hours a day.

FA: When you sit down to write or when you have that initial cusp of an idea, do you know if it's going to turn into a poem, a short story, or a novel?
RR: No, I never know. Every novel I've written has either been a short story or poem at first, usually a poem.

FA: Examples of that would be your poem "The Price" turning into the short story "My Father Like A River" or your O'Henry Award-winning story "Speckle Trout" becoming the novel *The World Made Straight.* Can you tell about the move from poems to short stories to novels?
RR: It's almost like twisting a radio dial. You're trying to find what comes in the clearest, the right frequency. You try one and can't quite get it in or it doesn't quite work. Then, you go on to the next one. Sometimes it might be a year or two later. The best example I know is with *One Foot in Eden.* I woke up one morning and had an image of a farmer standing in a field, his crops dying around him. I went in my office and wrote a fourteen-line poem. I knew that whatever that image was compelling me to say I hadn't gotten it right. So then I wrote about a fifteen-page short story and that didn't get it. Eventually, I realized that if I was going to tell this story I was going to have to write a novel.

FA: I'd heard that about *One Foot in Eden*. I believe the majority of your work is based in images. I've heard you talk about how your novel *Saints at the River* stemmed from the image of a child's face looking up through water. At the South Carolina Book Festival, though, you mentioned that the novel really may have come from when your son was hit by a car.

RR: That had happened six months earlier. My son had been hit by the car. He's fine. I think what happened was the accident was the undercurrent. I didn't realize until I pretty much finished that book that a lot of what I was writing about was my own fears as a parent. It's almost like I had somehow not wanted to know that because it's so obvious now. But the actual book started with the image of a child's face looking up through water.

FA: Was there an image for *The World Made Straight*?

RR: A trout's back wavering in fast water.

FA: Did you follow that image from poem to short story to novel?

RR: I guess so because I'd written a poem called "Speckled Trout" first and then the short story.

FA: This may have been one of the things you've brought from poetry to fiction writing.

RR: I feel like poetry's where it starts for me.

FA: Are you surprised by these changes in form?

RR: I'm always caught off guard. I never outline. I've never said, "You know here's a good idea for a novel." It's never worked that way for me, and not for a poem either. I might see something that's compelling, but usually it just happens. And I think probably that's not a bad thing.

FA: In *The World Made Straight*, the main character, Travis Shelton, becomes interested in the Civil War. This book seemed to require a lot of research, too. What sort of research do you undertake for your books?

RR: I do as much as I can. I love doing research. Several things can happen. One is that you'll find something utterly amazing that you might not have found otherwise that you can put into the book. For instance, doing research on the name Jocassee for *Raising the Dead*, I found out it means "place of the lost" in Cherokee. What could be more apt? So that can happen. Plus, I think it just gives you a familiarity with the world you're writing about. Very often for the reader to buy the big lie you have to get the small details right.

FA: Are there any dangers in research?

RR: Sometimes you can end up writing more of a history book. And sometimes you can see writers kind of stretching. You sense that okay this person's done research and wants to make sure we know it. I think you have to be careful about that. That you don't in a sense let the research overwhelm the story.

FA: I'm a little wary about asking this next question, but I feel compelled since your last novel featured two characters—Travis Shelton and Leonard Shuler—who were almost obsessed with the Civil War. Do you ever consciously think about being a Southern writer?

RR: No. What makes this a complex situation is that it's almost damned if you do and damned if you don't. On one hand, I think the greatest literary tradition this country has had is Southern literature. I think more good writing has come out of the South than any other region. Yet, there's this kind of easy pigeonholing that's very often done—I think more outside the region than in—where you're labeled a Southern writer and the implication is that's all you are.

How often do you hear Philip Roth described as a New Jersey writer? I think it's always seen or very often perceived as a limitation. If my writing only has importance in what it says about the South then it's not very good. It's just local color.

FA: In my experience (my small amount of experience), the only real benefit I've seen to being a writer from the South is that there's a camaraderie I feel with other writers from the region. We're more apt to congregate, talk literature, and give affirmation about each other's work.

RR: There does seem to be more of that. Yeah . . . I'm just becoming increasingly wary of how I think outsiders—as I say outside the South—have almost turned the term into a negative. And that's pretty hard to imagine. The best of Southern writing has always been universal—the region merely a starting point, not an ending point.

FA: I saw on Amazon.com that Picador has a book of stories, *Chemistry and Other Stories*, set to be released in April. Is this a reissue of some of the stories in *Casualties* and *The Night the New Jesus Fell to Earth*?

RR: I think there are five older stories and seven new ones. One's "Speckled Trout," which led to *The World Made Straight.*

FA: Should we be looking for anything else from you?
RR: I have stories coming out in *Tin House* and *The Sewanee Review.* I just finished up a new novel. That's what I've been working on the last year and a half.

FA: Do you have a title for it?
RR: *Serena.* It's set in 1930 and deals with the fight between timber companies and people trying to create the Great Smoky Mountains National Park.

FA: Have you read any good books lately?
RR: I think the best novel of our new century is Cormac McCarthy's *The Road.* Incredible. That's a great book. That's the best thing I've read.

FA: Thank you for your time.
RR: Thank you.

An Interview with Ron Rash

Marann Mincey / 2008

From *The Pedestal Magazine*. Reprinted by permission.

In researching his latest novel, *Serena*, Ron Rash sought out a raptor expert so involved in his field he knew of a pair of Mongolian Eagles who attacked a Snow Leopard. Rash advocates seeking out such fanatics to not only enhance the authenticity of the story, but also because the details they share can open new possibilities for story. After speaking with Rash, I also suspect his attraction stems from being somewhat of a fanatical breed himself: characterized by extreme zeal. He writes with unwavering consistency and dedication, adhering to his daily writing sessions as ardently as some folks to their morning coffee. He produces an ever-growing amount of material, across the forms of poetry, short story, and novel. His work tends to be rich with place, honoring his Appalachian roots while exploring themes of loss and redemption common to humanity. Rash has produced three other novels: *One Foot in Eden* (2002), *Saints at the River* (2004), and *The World Made Straight* (2006). He's published three volumes of poetry and three short story collections as well as a children's book. His short story "Speckle Trout" was included in the 2005 O. Henry Prize Stories, and *Chemistry and Other Stories* (2007) was a finalist for the PEN/Faulkner Award. *The New Yorker* noted *Serena* and stated, "Rash's evocative rendering of the blighted landscape and the tough characters who inhabit it recalls both John Steinbeck and Cormac McCarthy."

Marann Mincey: Some people consider the forms of poetry and prose exclusive, yet you publish both. How do the genres complement each other? Are you still writing poetry?

Ron Rash: Writing poetry, I hope, makes my prose more vivid and concise. I think it teaches concision of language, and writing prose is helpful because it helps ground my poetry. Poetry can get sometimes too esoteric, but there are elements that we have in fiction, particularly narrative, that can work in poetry as well.

I haven't written any new poems recently, but I do have another book of poetry I'm working on. I've definitely been more focused on fiction the last three years.

MM: You are often characterized as an Appalachian writer. In what ways is this appropriate? Is it limiting?

RR: It's certainly appropriate. My family has lived in the North Carolina Mountains for about two hundred and fifty years, so I am of the region and the region is my spirit country, I guess you could say. But though there is no doubt I'm very proud to be Appalachian, I am sometimes worried that when we put adjectives in front of "writer" there's a sense that he or she is *only* that. If my work only appeals to people in the region, then I've failed as a writer because I think what we want to do is what Eudora Welty said: "One place understood helps us understand all other places better." So by writing about a particular place, I also hope I'm writing about all other places as well.

MM: You often speak of your sustained work ethic, writing not only for many, many years, but also for long periods of time each day. How is this important to your success as an author? How do you do it?

RR: I think it is crucial to make writing a natural part of the rhythm of the day. Days when I don't write I feel, not necessarily guilty, but just a little unsettled because it is a part of my day the same way I might feel if I didn't exercise or didn't have my coffee. One thing I've learned about writing: it's the days that you write when you don't want to that make you a writer. It's easy when you're inspired, when you have a great idea. It's the days that you slog through and work hard and something finally comes that are most important. You have to come to work every day. I definitely have certain rituals. I sharpen several pencils and put them beside my desk, I get a huge cup of tea that I'll sip on. That sense of ritual does help, but also there are days when not much comes. I might feel that I'm not up to it. I'll work for thirty to forty minutes and finally something will come. Maybe even just a sentence or an image. There are days when I don't get much written down, but I'm still thinking about what I'm working on and thinking some things through.

MM: At a recent conference (North Carolina Writers' Network in Raleigh, NC) you spoke of seeking out fanatics in your research. Explain this, and how it enhances your writing.

RR: When I do research, I want to give the reader a sense, or at least the illusion, that I know what I'm talking about. Anytime we write about something we don't know that well ourselves, we are going to miss a few things but I want to miss as few as possible. What I've found particularly with people who are fanatical about a particular area, whether it's hunting with an eagle or the history of train engines, they will always give you something more than you would have ever thought to ask. It might be an anecdote that you would not have even imagined possible. For example, when I was doing my research for *Serena*, I talked to a guy because I wanted Serena to have an eagle to hunt with. He told me a story about a pair of eagles in Mongolia attacking a Snow Leopard and that just really stunned me, brought home the possibilities of what I could do with that eagle.

MM: So your research actually created new possibilities for your novel?

RR: Exactly. It opened up possibilities that I would never have thought of, and that was wonderful because I need all the help I can get and am grateful for anybody who can help me out.

MM: *Serena* has been called an epic, Macbeth-like. How is it relevant in contemporary society?

RR: Oh, I think it's very much about the kinds of questions we are asking today around environmental issues: whether we want to drill in the Arctic, the questions of power and who has it and what can be done with it. Because it's about the Smoky Mountains National Park, it reflects a common fight between people as far as how land should be used. Actually, when I started writing the book three years ago, I felt I was writing more about today than 1929 or 1930.

MM: You describe your writing process as usually beginning with an image. For *Serena*, you visualized an almost ethereal, bold woman on a white horse. Explain how that single image evolved into a work of *Serena*'s depth.

RR: It's mysterious to me. With every novel I've written I've had what I'd call a compelling image. It's an image that comes to me and I can't get rid of it. It becomes almost like something that solidifies inside of me. I can't forget about it; I think about it constantly. Ultimately, I think about it enough that a story in a sense starts to take place around that image. I get a lot of images, obviously, but what's interesting to me is I can tell when it's one of these; it's almost like getting a fever.

MM: Well, I've wondered about that because some of your short stories, like "Speckled Trout" and "Pemberton's Bride," have become parts of a novel. Do they begin in your mind as short stories and evolve, or do you think of them all along as pieces of a longer work?

RR: I've done both. "Pemberton's Bride" I took out of *Serena* as I was working on it. I cut out a chunk and wanted it to work as a story. "Speckled Trout" continued to evolve. What has happened several times is that I would get that image and think, well this is a poem, and I'd actually write the poem. I did that with *One Foot in Eden*. But then, that image won't leave me so I write a short story. Still, that image continues to trouble me, or feels incomplete as if I haven't done it justice, and that's when I have to go to a novel.

MM: In your novels, you go to a great deal of trouble to detail place and the authentic material things of that place. Why is this important?

RR: Very often, for the reader to buy into the "big lie," which is what a novel is, the reader has to believe in the small things. As I say, we always miss something or get a few things wrong in our research. But if we can get enough things right, I think it allows the reader to stay in the dream. That's what reading a novel is like to me—entering a dream. Very specific, authentic details allow the reader to believe everything else that is being made up.

MM: Are you more focused on the character development or on how a place can shape the character of the person who lives there?

RR: Wow. I think both equally. One thing I'm fascinated with is how landscape affects our psychology. I have a line in my novel, *The World Made Straight*: "Landscape is destiny." I just have a sense that they're intertwined, they work equally. So I think for me, landscape is a character. I hope the reader feels that way, that the landscape is out there, has an influence and a kind of palpability.

MM: *Serena* has received high acclaim and national reviews. How is this attention affecting you personally? Does it have an effect on your writing?

RR: It's still just as hard to write, I still have the same frustrations; it doesn't make the next book any easier. However, I certainly worked harder on *Serena* than I have any other novel, and I feel like it's my best, so it is kind of nice that a few other people agree. I worked on *Serena* for three years, pretty much four to five hours a day, some days much longer, six days a week. It took a lot out of me so I think in some ways I'm in recovery mode, though I am working on a book of short stories that will be the next thing I'm putting out.

MM: Describe the transition from your introverted process of writing, to the public process of promotion.

RR: It's almost schizophrenic because I'm an introvert anyway. One thing that saves me is I'm a teacher so I'm used to getting in front of people and babbling. It's almost a type of performance. Maybe that's too strong a word, but you play the extrovert for a period of time, or try to, then you go back. It can be disconcerting, but at the same time I feel very lucky and fortunate that there are people who want to hear me at all.

MM: Some writers describe their writing as a rush of story, with a long revision process. Others write more slowly with less need for revision. How do you describe your process?

RR: I just throw it out on the page. To me a first draft is like being a potter—getting a big lump of clay is how I see a first draft. I don't worry too much about how vivid the language is. I just want to get something down to work with, to mold. It's when I go through the drafts—I did twelve full drafts on *Serena*—that I really start looking more and more at language, finding places I got lazy. I agree with Hemingway who said, "The only real writing is re-writing."

MM: Talk about endings. How do you know when your story is finished?

RR: That's always a problem, knowing when to stop. It just feels right. It's always intuitive, similar to everything I do in writing since I don't outline or plot.

MM: Your characters tend to be resilient, strong-willed, even stubborn, but this persona is often built over fragility (Serena, Travis, Billy). Do you recognize this in yourself? Does it uniquely reflect the Appalachian experience or just a general human condition?

RR: You're right. I think my characters very often tend to be wounded. To me, what's interesting is how someone in life responds to these wounds. Both Serena and Rachel respond in particular ways to what has happened in their lives. I guess somewhat because I've grown up in a rural, Western

North Carolina society where people are resilient and are expected to be I see, especially in my older Appalachian relatives, a kind of fatalism: that life is hard but that is just the way it is and you go on and endure. But I also think it's true of most people; all people have their wounds. One thing about being human is you're going to lose people you love, you are going to have bad things happen in your life, and I think most people do the best they can with the cards they've been dealt. The Appalachian region hasn't been prosperous. It's tough to live there and a harsh landscape to live in so I'm sure that has influenced me.

MM: How does teaching influence you as a novelist, and vice versa?
RR: I hope the fact that I'm struggling with my own work every day helps me to have a sense of what my own students are going through. They know I'm writing every day and working through problems, and I hope this encourages them. One of the best things is that sometimes I'll recognize something in my student's work that will help me realize something in my own. It helps me be more aware of my own writing. It's been a good experience for me; I enjoy teaching and hope to keep doing it.

MM: You often give new writers the advice to be patient and allow their skill to develop. How have you seen yourself evolve as a writer?
RR: It's been a very slow process. I look back on some of the things I wrote in my twenties and they're horrible. Anyone who saw my writing back then wouldn't have thought I could ever be a writer. There is just a certain amount of hard work to put in to learn how to write. The most underrated virtue for a writer is that ability to stick with it, a belief in yourself even when there seems to be no reason for it.

MM: Your first novel, *One Foot in Eden*, was published by the small, regional press of Novello. Now that you've also worked with larger publishers, speak to us about those different experiences.
RR: Sometimes that is how you have to break in. You start with a smaller press that believes in you; they get your book out there and you hope a few people notice it and go from there. Ironically, some of the New York houses that turned down *One Foot in Eden* when I was first trying to sell it bid on the paperback rights after Novello took it and it had gotten some good reviews.

MM: Is there something that came up during the interview, or anything else you'd like to discuss?

RR: No, I think we've covered plenty, thank you.

MM: Thanks very much for speaking with me, and best of luck.

Ron Rash:
Harmony Republic Interview

Justin Wade Tam / 2010

From *Harmony Republic*. Reprinted by permission.

After appearing on many "best of" lists for his work, this American writer has deservedly earned that honor after spending many years perfecting his craft. Poetry, short stories, as well as novels have all been part of Ron Rash's wide collection of work. After graduating from Gardner-Webb University and Clemson University, he dove headfirst into his love of writing. In 1994 he published his first book, *The Night the New Jesus Fell to Earth*, which was a collection of short stories. He has also written titles such as *Serena*, *Among the Believers*, and *Raising the Dead*. His work has garnered him several awards including the O. Henry Prize as well as being a finalist for the 2009 PEN/Faulkner Award. On top of his ongoing writing efforts, Rash has gone back to the classroom as a professor. He currently holds the John Parris Chair in Appalachian Studies at Western Carolina University.

Harmony Republic: It seems like the last year has been pretty fruitful with the new novel being out in the last few years and some pretty prestigious awards coming your direction.
Ron Rash: Yeah. I've been very fortunate of late.

HR: So you grew up in the Appalachian Mountain region?
RASH: Yeah. I grew up in Boiling Springs, North Carolina which is right in the foothills of the Appalachians.

HR: It seems like the Appalachians are a theme of your writing as well.
RASH: Yes, I spent so much of my childhood actually in Boone on my grandfather's farm and my mother's family and my father's family have been

in the region since the 1700s so there is obviously a deep sense of connection to the region.

HR: It's a beautiful area. I love the eastern Tennessee and western North Carolina area up there. Most of these stories you've written are based in the region. Is there purpose behind that or is that just kind of how you grew up and sort of infiltrated your writing?

RASH: Well, I think that Eudora Welty has a quote that I really love and it's, "One place understood helps us understand all other places better." And that has pretty much been my philosophy. I think that if you center on one particular place that it allows you to really get to the depths of that place and I think if you go far enough you're going to hit the universal. I think what a lot of Southern writers understand is that the best way to find the universal is through the particular, through a particular place.

HR: I think that's great.

RASH: Yeah. It's almost like a farmer drilling for water. You keep going deeper and deeper until you hit something or you hope you do. It's like it's going to resonate out wide and become more than just about one place. At least that's the hope. It's up to the reader to decide whether that's true or not.

HR: Well, it's definitely an area that is steeped in history to begin with it seems. I know it's fascinating to me. I'm from the west coast, but coming in to such an older mountain range with such a traditional folk history, it's gorgeous and you can feel it when you're there. How did you get involved in teaching in the area?

RASH: I went to graduate school, I love literature, and I thought teaching would be a good profession.

HR: Do you feel your students have an appreciation for the Appalachians or do you feel a burden to relay that to them?

RASH: I try to. And yes, I have actually taught an Appalachian literature class and I can remember after one semester an older student told me how . . . reading all these talented Appalachian writers such as Lee Smith and Fred Chappell really made her proud of the region in a way she never had been before. I think that's a very positive thing. The Appalachian region has been so behind in popular culture; I think that it's a good thing the students can take pride in being from there instead of being ashamed of it.

HR: I know you've written in multiple forms of literature. You've got some short story compilations out and some poetry compilations and then your novels as well. Is there a particular genre you prefer working in?

RASH: They all have their challenges, but they all have their rewards. I think the hardest to do well is the short story. I think that's the most challenging.

HR: Why do you think that?

RASH: I think because you have to bring so much of what you bring into poetry into it and then so much of what you bring into a novel. It's almost like you've got to do both simultaneously in a short story. You're working where every line matters because it's so short and yet, at the same time, you have to give the reader a sense of the full story, the sense of completeness that we look for in a novel.

HR: When you're coming up with a short story, then, do you tend to approach it differently than writing a novel?

RASH: Sometimes I don't know if it's going to be a novel, a poem, or a short story. Almost all my stories or poems or even novels begin with an image and I don't always know where that image is going to lead me. Sometimes I think it's going to lead me to a poem and I find out it's going to lead me to a novel ultimately.

HR: I was reading a few things on you and your writing and, to summarize, it suggested that being an athlete growing up has influenced your writing. Maybe you can speak a little bit about that. Is there a work ethic you try to stick to?

RASH: Sure. I think what athletics did was to give a certain degree of patience. For instance, knowing that you might have to train for a year to run a good race. Also the discipline to work and train every day was very good training for writing because there are so many days I would rather stab the pencils into my eyes than write another sentence. And I think that those are the days that make me a writer. It's the days that you don't want to write but do anyways that show you're serious about it.

HR: With the success of three novels, has there been something that makes you want to continue teaching or have you considered doing writing full time?

RASH: I enjoy teaching and I think it's good for me because there are a lot of days when the writing doesn't go well. The fact that I teach allows me to say I didn't write well today, but maybe I did some good in the classroom. It gives a sense of accomplishment at the end of the day. But it's beyond that. I truly enjoy teaching. I think I'm very fortunate to do something I truly love for a living.

HR: Do you have any suggestions for people who want to pursue a career in literature or the arts in general?

RASH: The main thing is to study the people who came before you.

Christophe Dupuis Interviews Ron Rash

Christophe Dupuis / 2010

Published on *Encore du Noir* Dec. 14, 2014. Translated by Frédérique Spill. Reprinted by permission.

This interview was conducted by Christophe Dupuis in Paris in 2010, right before the *Festival America* in Vincennes. Many thanks to Marie-Caroline Aubert, who translated simultaneously.

Christophe Dupuis: Your biography reveals that you published your first short story collection in 1994 (there are now three of them), your first collection of poems in 1998 (there are three now), and your first novel, *One Foot in Eden* (*Un Pied au paradis*), in 2002 (as of today, you have four published novels). What made you write novels and why did you pick the noir novel as a genre?

Ron Rash: The novel imposed itself upon me. I did not choose writing novels: the novel chose me. *One Foot in Eden* sprouted from an image, which became a poem.[1] It is the image of a farmer standing alone in a dry field facing his wasted crop. The vision of that man asked for a poem. But later the image demanded further expansion.

CD: Could the short story be considered your favorite medium?

RR: Yes, indeed, because of the conciseness it demands. Short stories allow me to work on the kind of writing resulting from the strong conciseness of the poem. There is also something of the novel in the short story: both genres are more narrative than poetry. The short story allows a sense of completion—the satisfaction of being done with your text—which is, by definition, absent from the poem. Therefore, it is between the novel and the poem that I feel best. There is also this impression of being challenged that I like.

CD: How would you account for this impression of being challenged? Does it have to do with the necessary briefness of the short story?

RR: In the short story, each single sentence has to be at the right place. If you put it elsewhere, if you shift it, things do not work anymore. Henry James said that Tolstoy's novels were "loose, baggy monsters" with pot-bellies, in the midst of a great mess. The short story cannot be messy. The advantage of the novel over the short story is that it allows for the creation of a wider, more complete world: the reader is brought into that world for a while, which the short story cannot do.

CD: Your biography also indicates that you are the John Parris Distinguished Professor of Appalachian Studies at Western Carolina University. What classes do you teach there?

RR: I give a few lectures and I work on the need for programs dealing with Appalachian culture at large. This includes music (bluegrass and country music come from Carolina). We are also concerned with the preservation of this culture—the environment, together with concrete cultural aspects. I teach literature and the elements that actually make up this culture. My teaching goes beyond literature, strictly speaking.

CD: The culture you are evoking is found in your books, whether they take place in the 1930s, in the 1950s or more recently . . . Your books read like an x-ray picture of Appalachia . . .

RR: It goes further back than the 1930s: for instance, *The World Made Straight* and a story associated with it go back to the Civil War. The times-pan is wider than that.

CD: The French readership has discovered you with the translation of *One Foot in Eden*. This novel takes place in Southern Appalachia, at the beginning of the 1950s. Where did you extract its substance (like Dismal Gorge, or the flooding of a valley in order to make a lake)? Family anecdotes? Oral tradition? . . . I have noted—and this has become rare in the case of American novels today—there are no thanks in the end . . .

RR: I cannot think of a particular source. My people have been living there for three centuries, they never moved; this is my culture. The book started with the fact that the power company built a dam that flooded the valley.

And that valley, which was right at the border between South and North Carolina—today the reservoir has banks in both states—was one of the most beautiful valleys. Its disappearance was a tragic event.

CD: At some point, you describe summer in a beautiful way, indicating how seasons can determine men: "A man who any other time would step around trouble, a man who, if his truth be known, might be a bit of a coward, will all of a sudden turn mean and crazy. He'll do something nobody, even himself, would reckon likely. He'll even kill a man."[2] Is summer that bad over there? Are the other seasons similarly powerful?
RR: Yes, seasons in Appalachia are very intense. Appalachia is a region where things are pretty extreme. In the summer very strange things can happen, as in the case of the snake that becomes blind, which I evoked in the novel. Dog days make people dizzy. I have not read Camus's *The Stranger* for a while, but I remember that heat dramatically perturbed the character's psyche . . .

CD: Your books offer a perfect illustration of Sardinian writer Giorgio Todde's notion that it is the earth that makes both men and stories . . . How does this sound to you?
RR: I completely agree. My own essential formula is "landscape is destiny," which means that who you are has to do with where you live. Where you live, your landscape, therefore conditions the way you see the world. You are who you are depending on where you live. If you live in the mountains, because of verticality, your feelings will not be the same as those of a person who lives by the sea, whose vision and perception will be entirely different. The mountains somehow dwarf people and characters, who have the feeling that they are controlled by something that is much bigger than them. I live in Appalachia, the world's oldest mountains. Facing these mountains, as a writer, I have the impression—and this is what I am trying to show in my writing—that human life is perfectly insignificant.

CD: Talking about human life being insignificant, and without wanting to spoil the reader's pleasure, how did you imagine the place Holland Winchester's corpse is hidden? Your reader is likely to conceive that if you made that up, you are a weird kind of man . . .
RR: I made that up [laughs], and my friends no longer want to take walks in the woods with me [laughs]! Actually, when I wrote the book, I started with Billy's version and with him hiding the corpse under his dead horse. Then,

as I was working on the novel, the sheriff came up. The sheriff is clever and much too smart not to check if there is anything under the dead horse; then I thought: this won't work; I need to find something else. So I went to take a walk in the woods and wondered: "I am Billy; how can I do this?" I tried to think as he would; I climbed trees, I started imagining things, and this is how it came. I remember telling this to a reader, who then told me that I would probably make much more money as a criminal than as a writer [laughs].

CD: *Serena* will be made available to French readers in 2011 (many thanks to Marie-Caroline Aubert for the sneak preview in French). It is an epic fresco staging an unmanageable woman who is at the head of a timber company in North Carolina after the 1929 crisis. I'm aware that you may have been asked this a thousand times, but I'll ask you anyway: where did Serena come from?

RR: She comes from my deranged mind [laughs]. As in the case of *One Foot in Eden*, Serena originates from a "real" vision: that of a woman sitting straight-backed on a horse, exuding energy and force. She was at the top of a cliff, facing the valley, as in a western movie: there was fog at the bottom and at the top this woman with sun in her radiating blond hair, forming something like a halo around her head . . . I saw her; Serena was there.

CD: And the writing of the book comes from there. Earlier we talked about the short story, where each sentence is at its proper place. In the case of *Serena*, considering how minutely you reconstitute a logging operation (you even evoke how the woodcutters looking for a job attempt to capture the attention of their would-be boss), the prevailing impression is that, though it is a novel, every sentence is at its proper place as well. I read on your publisher's website (HarperCollins, 2008) that you had never worked so hard and so long on a novel. So . . .?

RR: It was, indeed, a considerable job. When I started I worked a dozen hours a day for a whole month. I was in a kind of trance. Then, for a year, I worked on the book eight hours a day—I had never worked that hard in my life, I was totally immersed in it; there was nothing else I could do. My wife told me I spoke about the book in my sleep. It was a tough period for my family and for the people around me [laughs]. I wrote twelve successive drafts and in the last draft, I worked on every single comma, on every single sound to test how they sounded. When I was done with the novel, I was no longer the same, even physically. Different people told me I had changed.

CD: Could you imagine facing a similar trial for another novel or do you envision moving on to less time and energy-consuming things?

RR: No. When I was done, I told myself there would not be another novel; this is why I wrote this collection of short stories, *Burning Bright*.[3]

CD: Marie-Caroline Aubert and myself have the same heartfelt anguished reaction: "No more novels?"

RR: This is what I told myself when I was done with *Serena*, but there will be other novels. I'm currently finishing writing one.

CD: In *Serena*, the reader is made to witness the ravages of deforestation (wildlife is endangered, the polluted rivers have become fishless); there apparently was no ecological consciousness at the time though Serena and her man, Pemberton, fight against the project for a National Park. I had no idea that national parks were so old. Could you say a few words about this topic?

RR: It is really a miracle that at such a time, during the Great Depression— at a time when there was no money at all and when people were not concerned with the preservation of nature—there should have been visionary people like President Theodore Roosevelt who defended such a cause. John Muir also wrote about that topic. People became so fond of the idea of creating national parks that the Rockefellers ended up giving a lot of money, and many people did so, even in schools: kids donated their small change to contribute to the project. This is partly why I wrote this book: for people to be aware of this and remember it. At the time, it was very difficult to create national parks—people made special efforts—and it is so easy to lose a thing that was created with so much effort and generosity. The Bush administration was about to ruin it all since [George W. Bush] wanted, just like Serena and her husband, to put an end to national parks, the importance of which he did not see. At the time I was writing *Serena*, Bush appeared to be so determined to destroy it all that I was truly afraid he would do it. But, fortunately, people managed to stop his project. *Serena* works on two levels. I think it is convenient and efficient to set a plot in the past—in this case in the 1930s—for it is possible to make current issues emerge and to denounce certain things that are part of our present while situating them in the past.

CD: For greed is timeless . . .

RR: It is, indeed.

CD: We will conclude this interview with those "sad" words. Thank you, Ron Rash.

Notes

1. The original interview mistakenly mentions *Chemistry and Other Stories* as the book where this poem is to be found. Rash is actually talking about an eight-line poem that was never published and is now lost (note from the translator).

2. Ron Rash, *One Foot in Eden*. New York: Picador, 2002, 115 (note from the translator).

3. *Burning Bright* was translated into French by Isabelle Reinharez and published by The Seuil Editions as *Incandescences* in April 2015 (note from the translator).

Kill Your Darlings in Conversation with Ron Rash

Kill Your Darlings / 2011

From *Kill Your Darlings* no. 6 (August 2, 2011).

While his name might not be familiar to many Australians, Ron Rash has long been a critically acclaimed writer in the United States. Originally a poet, Rash published several collections of short stories before breaking new ground in 2002 with his first novel, *One Foot in Eden*, a work of Southern Gothic. *Serena*, an epic novel about a timber baroness with unwavering, brutal ambition, expanded Rash's celebrity internationally. The novel was nominated for the PEN/Faulkner Award for Fiction and was named Book of the Year in *The New York Times*, *Washington Post* and *Publishers Weekly*.

A Southern author writing in the tradition of William Faulkner, Flannery O'Connor and Cormac McCarthy, Rash's work finds its cornerstone in the mountains of Appalachia. *Burning Bright*, his most recent book of short stories, is a collection of dark love letters to the rugged people, language and landscape of rural Carolina. From construction workers plundering the graves of dead confederates to a boy who discovers a plane crash deep in the Smoky Mountains, *Burning Bright* contains the grace, purity and concision of language for which Rash is renowned.

Kill Your Darlings spoke with Ron Rash about *Burning Bright*, what it means to write out of a singular locale, and the mystery of inspiration.
– **Hannah Kent**

KYD: Thanks for agreeing to speak with me today, Ron. How are you, anyway?
RR: I'm doing fine. I've just finished up a new novel, so that's good news! I'm pretty happy about that.

KYD: Congratulations. I'd like to also congratulate you on the publication of your short story collection, *Burning Bright*, which is about to be released in Australia in August. I hear it won the Flannery O'Connor Award. What an achievement.

RR: Thank you. I love short stories, I love writing them, and it's nice to get some interest in them.

KYD: Well, as you may know, many Australians are not especially familiar with a lot of your work because your books have only started to be published over here. But what has been published has been met with outstanding reviews. So it's exciting to hear that you've got a new novel coming out.

RR: That means a lot to me. The great thing is that I love Australian literature so much. I've always felt a kinship with it.

KYD: Really? Any particular authors?

RR: Oh yeah, a million of them. [laughs] Patrick White—I loved *Voss*. Tim Winton, Kate Grenville, Janette Turner Hospital's *Oyster* is a wonderful novel. And Flanagan's *Gould's Book of Fish* is amazing.

KYD: Oh, that's great. It can be hard for the Australian voice to be heard overseas—we're so isolated, and the industry is comparatively small.

RR: Actually, I know Les Murray. Les did a blurb for my third book of poetry, which I was very grateful for. He's an amazing poet. *Fredy Neptune* is the best verse novel I've ever read.

KYD: Do you think you'd ever attempt a verse novel?

RR: [laughs] No, I don't think I could. I've actually got a new book of poetry coming out this fall, but I couldn't do what he did in that book. There's just no way. [laughs]

I enjoy Australian literature. I feel like the Australian sensibility is similar to my own. Landscape is very important to me, and also the natural world, and that's something Australian writers seem to have a similar interest in.

KYD: I can certainly see that focus on landscape appealing to you. One thing that struck me about this new collection of short stories is the extent to which they all evoked your chosen locale, which is, of course, the Appalachian Mountains. Now, some Australian readers might not be as familiar with this area as your US readers. Could you please tell me a little about this area, and what it means to you as a writer?

RR: Well, it's a big region distinct from the rest of the United States. The speech patterns are different. The country and bluegrass music that has come out of this region has had a worldwide impact. It's a mountainous region; it's populated with much more forest than many places in the United States. It's very important to me because my family lived here in the 1700s. I'm actually talking to you on land that my family lived on two hundred and thirty years ago.

KYD: Are you trying to bring this particular region to a broader audience, or is it something that you are inclined to explore for more personal reasons?
RR: Well, unfortunately there are a lot of stereotypes about this region, and one thing I hope my work does—while not sentimentalizing the people—is show readers that although these people are different in some ways, they are recognizably human and their fears and desires are like everyone else's. Only in a different landscape.

KYD: People are very, very quick to call you a Southern writer. You're often compared to Flannery O'Connor. Do you struggle with such labels?
RR: I have mixed feelings about it. I mean, certainly I'm proud to be part of that literary tradition, but it's problematic when people put a "just" in front of that: "just a Southern writer." [laughs] The great thing about Flannery O'Connor, and William Faulkner and Eudora Welty, is that even though they were very Southern and wrote about a very specific region, they were universal at the same time. You know, one of my favorite quotes is by Eudora Welty. She said: "One place understood helps us understand other places better."

KYD: You had written nine books before *Serena*, which was the novel that arguably catapulted you into Australian readers' lives and onto the international literary stage. You received a lot of attention for *Serena*. How has the attention affected your writing?
RR: Well, it's been gratifying. I've worked for a very long time. I'm fifty-seven now, and I really didn't start getting any recognition in the United States until about six or seven years ago. It's been really gratifying to get some recognition for what I've spent most of my life doing, and not only in the United States but also outside of it. I'm getting ready to go to France because *Serena* has done very well over there. I'm getting opportunities to travel and to see some countries I've never been to. I'm coming to Australia next year for the writers' festivals.

KYD: It would be great to have you here. One thing I wanted to ask you, regarding your experience as a writer, is concerned with your background in poetry. I know that you have published several collections, such as *Among the Believers* and *Raising the Dead*. To what extent does poetry—both your production of it and also your consumption of it—influence your prose?

RR: I think that, in many ways, the best training I have received as a prose writer is reading and writing poetry, because it demands vividness and concision. I was actually, earlier in my career, better known as a poet. Some people have chastised me for not writing much poetry now, but I hope when readers read my novels or stories that they sense that I am a poet writing prose. A lot of the poetry gets into the prose.

KYD: One thing that struck me about *Burning Bright*, as indeed it did in your novels *Serena* and *One Foot in Eden*, was the precision of your language. Can you tell me a little bit more about how you craft your sentences? Is it a very laborious process?

RR: It is. Actually, when I'm working on a story or a novel, during the last couple of drafts I'm just purely concerned with sound. I'm reading the words and the sentences and the paragraphs, and I'm listening to how they sound. And by that I mean I'm listening to which syllables are stressed, which are unstressed, and what type of rhythm each gives the paragraph. I'm very conscious of every word.

KYD: Does this mean that writing takes you much longer than it might an author who has written prose from the outset?

RR: I think so, because of what I tend to do . . . I think I wrote fourteen full drafts of *Serena*. And I'm talking about full drafts. I don't ever reread my novels because I always find places where I wish I could have done it better.

KYD: Just going back to the fact that you do, evidently, focus so closely on the words and the stress and the cadence of your prose—I read that your first novel, *One Foot in Eden*, actually began as a poem. How did it evolve into a novel?

RR: Actually, the poem/novel began with an image. Every novel I've written has come from a single image. For *One Foot in Eden*, the image was of a farmer standing in a field, and his crops were dying around him. That was all I had. I remember that image came to me essentially out of a dream. I woke up and kind of dredged it up, and that day I wrote a fourteen-line poem about a farmer in a field with his crops dying. But when I finished it I knew that . . . the image that I had in my head, that poem couldn't contain it. And then I wrote a short story and that didn't contain it. [laughs] And so I thought, well, looks like I might have to try and make this a novel.

KYD: Were you apprehensive about venturing into a new form?
RR: Oh yes. Very much so. Because I'd tried a few novels before and I'd never had any success, and I was fearful of that kind of commitment. Because I knew that it was going to be a commitment of a couple of years.

KYD: So, *One Foot in Eden* began with an image, which evolved into a poem, and then a short story and finally a novel. Do you generally get most of your ideas for both your short stories and the novels from an image and then write from there?
RR: Yes. Every novel or short story. When I wrote the title story "Burning Bright," I had an image of this woman looking out towards the mountains and I knew it was a time when fires were possible. The whole story started with this image of a woman looking out at the mountains. That's how it happens.

KYD: Once you receive an image, how exactly do you begin to build on that?
RR: The best way I can explain it is that when I get this kind of image, when I get a true, important image—and I know when it's important because I can't get it out of my head—the image nags at me. I don't know where the novel's going; I don't plot out my novels and I don't outline them. Very often I don't even know who the characters are. I just start with that image. What happens inevitably, with a novel at least, is that there comes a time after maybe six months, or a year, where the book just seems to die. It reaches a dead end and I can't seem to work out what to do next. Sometimes this will last several months, sometimes a few weeks. I think writers need particular beliefs, whether they're true or not doesn't matter. And the one I have to believe in, or that I make myself believe in, is some ways a little bit like what Michelangelo believed. You know, he would look at the untouched block of marble and he would believe that the statue was already in it; that it was just a matter of finding it. And what I believe is that if this image is so strong, if it haunts me day after day, if I can't get it out of my head, and I can't forget it, then I make myself believe that the whole novel is out there. It's just a matter of my discovering it.

KYD: I'd heard of Michelangelo's belief about his blocks of marble, but I've never heard a writer thinking of a novel in the same way. You often hear of writers speaking of how they don't know when their novel is going to end, or they're not particularly sure about their characters, but I've never heard of a writer thinking of the novel as fully formed before it is written. I think it could be enormously useful.

RR: It's very helpful to me, and it sounds crazy but it works. It's a great help in those bleak months of despair. You sit there thinking, "I've lost a year of my life writing this novel and now it's not working and I'll never complete it," and I make myself believe that that novel is out there somewhere.

The older I get, the more I write, the more mysterious writing becomes. Where does it come from? Say you write a short story—why is it that one day you think of an image or a character, and you've never thought of that before, and then one day it just comes. You know? Why is that? It's not something that I think can be easily explained.

KYD: Do you think there's a danger in questioning that too much?
RR: Of where it comes from?

KYD: In trying to analyze the intuitive, creative process.
RR: Yeah, I do. I think writers work best on intuition. Les Murray talks about writing as being very similar to a dream state. And I think he's right about that.

KYD: How do you feel then about the way in which creative writing is increasingly being taught at a very theoretical level in universities? Do you agree that creative writing and its processes ought to be taught and analyzed in an academic manner?
RR: Well, I have friends who have gone through Master of Fine Arts programs, and they've done fine. I do not have a MFA. What I did was actually get a traditional master's degree in literature and just read a lot. And I think ultimately the most important thing for any writer is to be reading a lot. You know, reading really good writers. And probably the best MFA programs incorporate a lot of reading of the great writers. It just depends on who you are and what works for you.

KYD: My next question is perhaps a little concerned with study. Many of the stories in *Burning Bright* are set in the past. *Serena* is set in 1929, and the events of *One Foot in Eden* begin in 1951. Your rendering of these times has a verisimilitude that suggests rigorous research: what lengths do you go to to achieve this historical exactitude and historical detail?

RR: I do a huge amount of research. I love to meet people who actually do what I'm writing about. For *Serena* I actually found one of twelve people in the United States who hunt with an eagle. He was very helpful in my understanding of how you would train an eagle to hunt rattlesnakes, the first person to say, "Yes, you could do that." Previously I didn't know if you could or not. I just thought it would be a really interesting idea if the character Serena could do that. I love to do that kind of thing. I love doing research. I'm curious. I love learning about things. But you always miss something. I mean, it's inevitable that you'll get something wrong, but you do the best you can.

The other reason I like to write about the past is because I think in some ways that it's a really good way to write about the present.

When I wrote *Serena* I was actually writing as much about what was happening in the United States five years ago as what was happening in the 1920s. About five years ago—and this is still a threat—there was an attempt to destroy some of the national parks by allowing logging.

KYD: I'm interested in how your fiction tends to revolve around the relationships people have with the landscape they inhabit. For instance, in *Serena* your protagonists have a very exploitative attitude towards the mountains, and this drives the narrative, but the other characters, oppositely, identify with and are connected with their surroundings in a very spiritual sense.

In *Burning Bright*, the short story "Into the Gorge" struck me as exploring the changing relationship people have with the land over generations. And "Hard Times" is of course a story of two families dependent on their landscape for survival.

What fascinates you as a writer about the connection between the natural world and humans, or the lack thereof?

RR: I'm fascinated with the way landscape affects human psychology. Actually, there's a bit of a phrase I tell myself. I can't articulate it as well as I want to, but it's that "landscape is destiny." How might someone who grows up amongst mountains be different from someone who grows up in the desert? I think there are differences. I've noticed them. The other thing is that it's not a matter of choosing whether the natural world matters to us. It has to! I mean, we're part of it. The idea that we cannot be connected to the land is ridiculous. If it stops working, we go with it.

KYD: In *Serena*, I thought it was especially significant that Serena herself is not from the Appalachians. She's from Colorado, and you can see the difference between her character and those that are from North Carolina.

The destruction of the natural world seems to be a continual theme in your work, as I've suggested. Do you consider your stories political in that they are environmentalist?

RR: Well, I've been concerned with environmental issues, but at the same time . . . One thing I try to be very careful about is to not let my books seem like propaganda. You know, I sign petitions and I do things like that, but I think for a work of art to do what it should . . . I don't think that's the right place for that kind of polemic. That's my view. What I hope to do, instead of telling my reader what to think, is to *show* the reader. I think my role is more that of a witness. I show what happened.

KYD: Has anyone ever accused you of didacticism?

RR: I'm sure someone has. One thing I hope I did in *Serena* was show the complexity of the situation. You know, you have men [loggers] who are starving. They need jobs and you have this terrible situation where they're destroying their very landscape, their very home, but they have to do it because their families are starving. The novel also shows the consequences of building a national park—there are people who are forced off their land. So I hope readers aren't going to say: "Oh yeah, he's just one of those tree-huggers." [laughs]

KYD: I'm reminded of the story from *Burning Bright*, "Into the Gorge." I thought that was a very interesting take on this issue of the natural world—especially after just having finished reading *Serena*. In this story, Jesse is stopped from collecting the ginseng that has been planted in the forest by his father and generations before him—he has a very close tie with that land—by the park rangers, and with dramatic consequences. Am I right in saying that?

RR: Oh yes, absolutely. And those grey areas in these "issues" are the most interesting to me.

KYD: Let's return to your creative process and your sense of locale and landscape. I think you have a particular gift for conveying the dialect of your region, particularly in the stories set in the past. How do you create the vernacular of your characters?

RR: I was very lucky growing up in that I spent a great deal of time with my grandmother on her farm. We didn't have a TV, or a truck or a car, and so we were pretty much just there. I got to spend a lot of time with my older relatives and got to hear their way of speech. A lot of the language I use is the language I heard as a child. You can still hear this kind of language in the region. I mean, it's disappearing, but what I hope to do as a writer is not allow it to completely disappear by recording it in a book.

KYD: I'm very fond of the way you present the vernacular of the region, particularly its unique similes and idioms. In the opening story "Hard Times," there's that wonderful phrase: "So damn dark a man has about to break light with a crowbar." Another one I liked in *Serena* was: "That fellow could hide from his own shadow." To many these phrases might seem a very alien manner of talking. Is this vernacular accurate? Do people actually talk in similes in the Appalachians?

RR: Very often. Yeah, they do. And one thing that I hope I do with my use of that vernacular . . . You know, for a long time these people have been seen as being not very well educated, but what I hope to do with my work is show that there's a real intelligence in their use of language, particularly in their use of simile. To me, the best kind of intelligence and complexity in language is the ability to create similes. Very often I use a lot of similes in my vernacular because I feel it's a way of showing the creativity and the intelligence of the character. They may not use an educated language, but there's a beauty and a poetry and an inventiveness in their language.

KYD: How do you remember these similes? Do you go around with a voice recorder or do you write them down in a notebook, or do you invent some of them? Or is it all from memory?

RR: Oh, I invent some. [laughs] Sometimes they're phrases I heard growing up, from my older relatives. I use anything I can. When I hear a good phrase I'll usually write it down. Actually, I heard one of my uncles say, "so dark you need a crowbar to break the light." That's actually something I heard growing up.

KYD: I think there really is a certain poetry to this manner of speaking which perhaps belies the stereotypes surrounding rural people. I think we have a very similar situation in country Australia. There are many city folk who think people out there are relatively uneducated. My father is from the country and I've grown up with him speaking a language of similes. Such as: "So windy it could blow a wombat out of its hole."

RR: [laughs] That's good.

KYD: Then there's: "So hungry I could eat the crotch out of a low-flying duck."

RR: Oh, I think that's great. [laughs] You know, one of the things I think is so useful about the similes rural people coin is that they use images of the natural world. It becomes the most universal language.

These similes translate better. Comparing something to a mountain is better than saying "like a blue-light special at Kmart." You might have no idea of what I'm talking about.

KYD: Nope.

RR: But if you say, "as swift as a flooding river," you have no problem with that.

KYD: These kinds of similes and phrases work beautifully in your own work because you do have that focus on the landscape, and explore that connection people have with the land. I found in *Serena*—where you have the loggers speaking in this vernacular and using a lot of these similes and a lot of these phrases—that it gives it some much-needed humor. The vernacular reflects the black humor that you find amongst rural people who are used to suffering hardship.

RR: Yeah, that was very, very important because it's such a dark book. It's funny, because I've had some people say they don't think there's any humor in the book, and I think I've written some of the best comic writing I've ever done in it!

KYD: The other things I think stem from the land—like this use of simile—are the superstitions and the folklore and witchery that are also explored in your writing. In *One Foot in Eden*, you have the widow woman who everyone believes is a witch, and then in *Serena* you have Galloway's mother who can see into the future. In *Burning Bright* there's a lot of folklore. Take "The Corpse Bird," for instance, which is about the old belief that if the titular bird calls out three nights in a row, someone in the next house will die. What interests you about these superstitions? What do you wish to achieve by exploring them?

RR: I include the folklore to convey a sense of wonder. I mean, to me this world is incredibly wondrous, and it's mysterious, and it's very striking to me that we seem to be oblivious to that. And also I hope that by using the folklore that, in a sense, it makes the world "bigger." Wider. I love that quote in *Hamlet*: "There are more things in heaven and earth . . ." I love the idea that the world is so much more mysterious than we ever realize.

KYD: Do you adhere to some of that folklore you grew up with, and are very familiar with?
RR: Oh, you know, not in the same sense as my characters do. But I always like to believe that the world is more mysterious than we think. I guess you would say that I'm someone who refuses not to believe.

I think writing about folklore is also a way of preserving something of that culture. One of the things about where I live is that it seems to be an overtly Christian culture, but there are many pagan elements in it which the people in the community don't realize. [laughs]

KYD: I was thinking about the re-occurring themes that come up in your work—like folklore—and one theme I continually noticed was the anxiety surrounding parenting and illegitimacy. Is this something you're aware of?
RR: I think part of it probably comes from the moral landscape that my parents lived in. It was such a big aspect of their lives. It was very important. So in a way this theme just reflects the obsessions of the times, because my stories are often set in the past and the idea of community and connectedness was very important.

KYD: One story I thought a particular standout from this collection was "Ascent." On the surface it seems very simple. There is a young boy who finds a recent light-plane crash in a forest and steals items from the victims inside to support his meth-addicted parents. But I thought it was beautifully nuanced, and it presented so many questions about what it is to be a parent, and also what it is to be a child, and who has the greater responsibility towards the other. When I read it I remembered *One Foot in Eden* and the child at the center of that narrative, and in *Serena* you have a child as a catalyst for the events that unfold. Are you particularly drawn to the idea of children and what they stand for, and our anxieties surrounding raising them?
RR: You know, that's interesting, because you're not the first person to point that out. It's not something I do consciously, but it's certainly there, and part

of it may just be from being a parent myself. I have two children. That may be in part just the anxiety of being a parent and always questioning your role and your child's role. But you're right; it's there.

KYD: Referring again to the fact that all of your work is set in one particular region, people are starting to call you the "voice" of the South. How do you feel about that? Do you feel a duty to continue writing about this region?
RR: Yeah, I would feel very uncomfortable being called the "voice" of the region. [laughs] I'm one voice in the region. We have a number of excellent writers in the region and I would never presume that I convey all of what my region is. I think any writer who did would be either incredibly vain or incredibly foolish. [laughs]

KYD: Do you see yourself writing out of a different locale in the future?
RR: Probably not. I have the example of Faulkner and O'Connor and also other writers as well. So much of Les Murray's writing is set in the rural area that was so important to him growing up. I think I've got enough here to last me a lifetime. There is a value in really knowing a place intimately. There are dangers, obviously, but . . . You know, I'm looking out of my window right now at the mountains and my ancestors did the same. I have people who lived on this ridge who are my DNA, looking out on it two hundred and thirty years ago. To be aware that you're in a place with that kind of connection—that's a gift for a writer.

KYD: You say that you plan to always write out of the Appalachians. How do you plan to challenge yourself as a writer in the future? Is this something you're concerned with?
RR: What I'll write about in the future?

KYD: I would presume that when you set out to write *One Foot in Eden* it was a challenge because you had never finished a novel before. *Serena* was a novel of epic proportions. Of course, there are always challenges inherent in the writing process, but I was wondering if you have a project in mind that you would like to attempt that you have not yet done.
RR: I just turned my new novel in two and a half weeks ago, so right now I'm just in a place between projects. I'm so tired from working on that novel for two and a half years that I've not been doing a lot lately. [laughs] But one thing I did in *Burning Bright* that I had not written about before was

the drug problem in the region. Particularly the meth. I think it's important that I don't just write about the past, but the present as well. For instance, the story "Into the Gorge" is the story of a people who had lived in a place for generations and were being displaced, because this region is changing. There are new stories that are emerging and I think they'll come to me. I think it's just a matter of keeping my antennae up and waiting for the stories to come.

KYD: Can you tell us a little bit about your new book?
RR: Yeah. It's actually set in 1918, but once again I think it's very much about the present. Part of it is historically true, and the part of it that is historically true is that in the western Carolina Mountains during World War I there was a German internment camp. Now, in the United States people know a lot about the Japanese internment camps. But it's pretty amazing to me how few people know about the German internment camps in the United States. I mean these were not prisoners of war. These were Germans who happened to be in America. They weren't soldiers or spies or anything. The novel deals with one of them who escapes, which is something that happened historically. And I have him meet a young mountain woman. It goes from there.

KYD: That sounds very interesting. And now, a final question for you. We've spoken about growing up within a particular vernacular and locale, and being immersed in this area, with all the stories that come from such an experience. Why do you think we need stories in our lives? What can fiction writers like you do that non-fiction writers cannot?
RR: Well, I think one thing we can do—and this is not my quote, it's Muriel Spark's, and actually Francis Bacon may have said it before her—is to deepen the mystery, to deepen the wonder of simply being alive. What does it mean to be a human being? What does it feel like? I think the best fiction does deepen that wonder better than anything else. It makes us pay attention to the mystery of being alive. I hope it also allows, through the imagination, a degree of empathy. I think it just gives us an incredible kind of pleasure that no other art form or popular-culture form gives us.

For a book or novel or story to work, there must be an act of communion between the reader and writer. I mean, if you think about it, what the writer gives the reader is splotches of ink on a piece of paper. It's up to the reader to read with intelligence and attentiveness to create those characters in his or her head and to respond to them, perhaps even become them. When a book makes someone laugh, or it makes someone cry, you have that incredible communion between reader and writer. And to me that's one of the great achievements of the human race.

KYD: Ron, it has been an absolute pleasure talking with you. Thank you for being interviewed by *Kill Your Darlings*. We wish you all the very best with your new novel.
RR: Thank you. I've enjoyed talking to you.

Interview with Ron Rash, 2011

Sylvia Bailey Shurbutt and David O. Hoffman / 2011

From *Anthology of Appalachian Writers*. Volume 4. Shepherd University, 2012. Reprinted by permission.

Sylvia Bailey Shurbutt & David O. Hoffman: You have spoken about the importance of "fathers" in your work—reconciling with fathers, finding fathers and father figures, reconnecting with fathers. You have also said that your own "father died pretty young, and there is a real sense of regret that I couldn't have spent more time with him" (Neufeld 10). When did you lose your father, and how do you believe that loss is evinced in your stories? Talk about your father and his impact on you and your writing.

Ron Rash: My father died when I was in my mid-twenties, and the greatest regret in my life is that he didn't live longer. His last decade was very difficult because of clinical depression and, had he lived a few more years, I believe the more recent drugs and therapies would have allowed him a much better life. He was a remarkable man—a mill-village kid who dropped out of high school at sixteen to work in the mill, then through incredible perseverance got his GED, went to college while working full-time, and eventually became a college art teacher. Except in the story "Chemistry," I've never consciously written about our relationship, but as you point out, father and son stories abound in my work. Perhaps on some level aspects of our relationship not resolved in life are being dealt with in my art.

S&H: Rather than following the MFA route toward authorship, you worked through the ranks as an English teacher—first as an instructor in a rural high school in Oconee County, South Carolina; then for seventeen years as a teacher in the Tri-County Technical College in Pendleton, South Carolina. For those of us who have traveled that route as scholars and writers, it is a busy road, to say the least. How have you managed to write and publish a steady stream of such quality poetry and fiction with such a schedule? What have been the advantages to your writing craft provided through your career as a teacher, and why do you think a degree in literature has been particularly beneficial to you as a writer?

RR: My years teaching high school and technical college made writing difficult, but I've always believed if writing is important enough to a person, he or she will make time. I got up early to write a couple of hours every weekday, wrote weekends and holidays. Many of my friends, all of whom are writers I admire, do have MFAs and found that experience what they needed. For me, however, a straight MA was better. I was a slow developing writer; I needed to immerse myself in literature during that period of my life. I do believe the best way to learn to write well is to read the best writers. All the really good writers I know, MFA or non-MFA, are voracious readers.

S&H: What contemporary writers do you read today and find particularly interesting? What writers are you teaching today in your Appalachian Literature course?

RR: This is always a frustrating question because I'll leave someone out and feel badly afterwards; so, except to say McCarthy is my favorite contemporary American novelist and Annie Proulx and William Gay my favorite short-story writers, I'll pass on the Americans. I've been reading a lot of Australian authors of late; I especially admire Richard Flanagan, Janette Hospital, Les Murray, and Tim Winton. I haven't taught my Appalachian Literature class in a couple of years, but the last time I did, I taught, among others, Lee Smith, Silas House, Robert Morgan, James Still, Kay Byer, Breece Pancake.

S&H: We really love the freshness and uniqueness of your poetry and marvel that you utilize, like Gerard Manley Hopkins and to some extent Dylan Thomas, some of the more ancient forms, which add to that freshness. Talk about how you discovered the Welsh *cynghanedd* form and the tales from *The Mabinogion*. What in particular interested you about the character Branwen who appeared in the *Among the Believers* volume?

RR: The Rash family came from Wales, so I've always been aware of that connection. *The Mabinogion*, the great Welsh epic, has been a rich source for me, and I've used its stories and images in a number of poems. Also, I've always loved poets whose work has a strong aural quality, poets such as Hopkins and Thomas. In my late twenties I did an intense study of traditional Welsh poetics and began to incorporate what I'd learned into my own work, but because I believe, as Brendan Galvin once said, "that in poetry clarity is the deepest mystery of all," I did not want the poetry's music to overwhelm meaning. I'm rather pleased when people don't realize (though I do believe their ears hear it) that I'm using *cynghanedd* and strict Welsh forms such as the *Awdyll Gwydd*.

S&H: Your *Raising the Dead, Eureka Mill,* and *Among the Believers* volumes are not only beautifully written but very accessible for your readers, often reading like an Appalachian *Spoon River Anthology.* You seem to have wonderfully wedded a lovely metrical expertise and vivid imagery with fascinating subject matter that is both grounded in place and, at the same time, transcendent of the region that breathes life into both your poetry and fiction. Talk about your latest volume of poetry—how does it continue to develop the ideas and style that you have evolved? Why have you waited so long to bring it out?

RR: The new poetry book is called *Waking.* The Welsh-influenced sound patterns are similar to my last two poetry volumes. The poems continue to focus on Appalachia, but a number of them are more overtly personal than in previous books, childhood moments of transcendence, what Wordsworth called "spots of time." I haven't written much poetry in the last decade because I've been immersed in novel and story writing. I cannot write poetry when I'm writing fiction. It's like being on two completely different frequencies. It is nice, though, to have another poetry book out. It assures my poet friends I've not gone completely over to the dark side.

S&H: As we read the many reviews and commentary on your 2008 book *Serena,* everyone, of course, is interested in and appreciative of the parallel between this beautifully written novel and Shakespeare's *Macbeth.* Some critics have brought up the Renaissance patriarchal fear of powerful women which Shakespeare reflects, suggesting there is some application as well in your book. We aren't necessarily sure that is the case, nor that Serena should be looked at as an explication of "the modern woman," as one critic asserted. We found Rachel a poignant and pointed balance to Serena, and, unlike Serena, Rachel is a character whom you portray as dynamic, growing more appealing to readers as she develops in the story. Since you were thinking strongly along the lines of Greek and Renaissance tragedy as you were writing this book, can you comment on what was going through your mind as you were beginning to write the character of Serena? Is she a metaphor for "the new woman," as one critic suggests?

RR: My hope was to create a character resonant enough to allow many interpretations of her, in the past as well as the present.

S&H: There is a wonderful connection between the poems, the short stories, and the novels, where your readers will find a story told in one genre and then in another. The effect is interesting in that the retellings always give us something new and different to appreciate about the tale. As teachers, we also appreciate being able to connect the stories from these different perspectives and points of view. What tells you that it is right to continue with a character or event for retelling in another genre? What commonalities do you find between poetry and fiction in your subjects and writing process?

RR: My goal has always been for the poems, stories, and novels to inform and enrich one another. I would hope that if someone read all of my work, he or she would think that it feels more like a quilt than mere pieces of different-angled cloth on completely different designs.

S&H: In one interview, you explained that your grandfather taught you that words can be magical. How has this childhood lesson impacted your writing? Further, do you credit your grandfather's "reading" to you as a child with instilling your interest in approaching stories from different vantage points and different genres?

RR: Yes, my illiterate grandfather making up stories did indeed make words magical for me, but I also credit my parents for making words magical. Both were voracious readers, and my mother would take my siblings and me to the library every week. My mother's mother had been a schoolteacher in the North Carolina mountains before marrying my grandfather and becoming a farm wife. As far as writing both prose and poetry, my childhood reading of Jesse Stuart, as well as the later example of Robert Morgan, James Still and Fred Chappell, showed me a writer need not be limited to one genre.

S&H: You've mentioned before, and it is quite apparent in your works, that compelling images often initiate and ultimately control your writing process. Talk about how these images develop for you and how they carry you through the development of your stories.

RR: The more I write, the more mysterious the process is to me. All of my novels have begun with images. For instance, *One Foot in Eden* began with an image of a man standing in his field, his crops dying around him. Writers need to believe certain things to keep going, and I make myself believe that if an image is so strong as to make me begin a novel, then the finished novel already exists; I just have to find it. In a way, it's similar to what Michelangelo said about the completed statue already being inside the block of marble.

S&H: What advice can you offer young writers who are reading your works and writing their own?

RR: That perseverance is the most underrated aspect of being a good writer. Read, read, and read some more.

Work Cited

Neufeld, Rob. "Interview with Ron Rash." *Together We Read*. Together We Read, Inc., 28 Mar. 2006. Web. Accessed by interviewers, n.d.

Ron Rash: Shaped by the Land, Torn Apart by Intolerance

Alden Mudge / 2012

From *Book Page* April 2012. Reprinted by permission.

Ron Rash believes that "almost all of the great books are regional books." What, he asks, "could be more regional than James Joyce's *Ulysses*," which unfolds during a twenty-four-hour ramble through Dublin, Ireland, on June 16, 1904?

So Rash bristles—in a modest, gentlemanly sort of way—when people use the word *regional* to pigeonhole, diminish or dismiss fiction like his, which roots itself in a particular place—Appalachia, and especially western North Carolina, where his family has lived since the 1700s.

"It's an important issue to me because I think there's a difference between *regional* and *local color*," Rash says during a call to his office at Western Carolina University (WCU) in Cullowhee, North Carolina. "Local color is writing that is only about difference—what makes this particular place exotic. Regional writing is writing that shows what is distinct about a place—its language, culture and all of that—yet at the same time says something universal. Eudora Welty says it better than I can. She says that one place understood helps us understand all other places better. That's been a credo for me. I think that if you go deep enough into one place, you hit the universal."

A point in his argument's favor? Ron Rash's novels, especially his recent bestseller *Serena,* are popular in France. He's been invited to read his fiction in places as far away as Australia and New Zealand. His books sell well in China. And his short stories and novels have been nominated for national, not just regional, awards.

Still, there is his sense of loyalty to his place of origin. On a ten-city book tour in France, for example, Rash, a charming storyteller with a strong regional accent, remembers that "they had me go to a local high school, I think partly [so students] could hear an American speaker. The first thing I told them was not to imitate me; they certainly would not be understood in New York City if they sounded like me!"

A regional setting and universal themes are definitely hallmarks of Rash's atmospheric new novel, *The Cove*. Set in the small western North Carolina town of Mars Hill at the end of the First World War, *The Cove* uses a little-known historical incident as a stepping-off point for a haunting narrative about intolerance and redemptive but illicit love.

"Obviously I love to read about the region's history," says Rash, who is the first person to hold the endowed Parris Distinguished Professor in Appalachian Cultural Studies Chair at WCU. "But a few years ago I was doing some research and I was amazed to find that [there had been] a German internment camp near where I live in western North Carolina during [World War I]. And this camp was not for POWs. It was for German civilians who happened to be marooned in the United States when the United States entered the war. That was fascinating to me. And it became even more fascinating to me when I started reading about the *Vaterland*, which was the biggest ship in the world at that time and was much more elegant than the *Titanic*, and these guys who ended up in Hot Springs [North Carolina] had been on the *Vaterland*."

Then Rash read an account of the internment camp that mentioned in passing the fact that one, and only one, German prisoner had ever escaped. "Wow! I thought, boy, what I can do with that. To me there was just this incredible story here that even a lot of people in the region did not know about. At the same time, because of some things that were happening in the United States, contemporary issues, I thought there were interesting connections."

But Rash, who customarily writes between twelve and fourteen drafts before completing a novel—usually while sitting in front of his fireplace with his two dogs at his feet—could not get his story of a German escapee to fly. Not, that is, until he realized that the real emotional center of his book was Laurel Shelton, a young woman who has lived all her life in a sheltered cove near Mars Hill and who longs to escape from a life blighted by the superstitious beliefs and confining scorn of most of her neighbors. Her dilemma threatens to split her apart from her brother Hank, who has returned to the family's hardscrabble farm in the deep shadows of the Appalachian mountains after being wounded in the war.

"To me," Rash says, explaining his intense interest in describing the ghostly place in which his characters rise and fall, "landscape is always a character. And I would say the cove itself, the landscape, is in some ways as dominant a character as any other character. . . . It's hard for me to completely articulate but to me it's like landscape is destiny. The environment you grow up in has to have some kind of effect on how you perceive the world. I would argue that *The Great Gatsby* could only have been written by a Midwesterner because the kind of expansiveness Gatsby could imagine fits a Midwestern sensibility; looking out on this endless expanse gives you a sense of endless possibility. The same might be true of someone who was born at the ocean. But if you live in mountains—I've seen this in my own family—two things can happen. One is that you feel protected by the mountains, almost like it's a womb that protects you from the outside world. But the other thing that can happen is that the lack of light does something physically to people who live in a cove. There's always a sense of your smallness, your puniness and insignificance compared to these mountains that have been here millions of years and loom over you. The result can be the kind of fatalism I saw even in my own family. I think *The Cove* is my strongest attempt to show that."

Though based on historical research and set almost one hundred years ago, *The Cove* is artfully layered with Rash's concerns about the present. One of his most persistent concerns is how easily we turn other people into enemies and go to war against them. In a remarkable way, *The Cove* dramatizes a hope that loving, reasonable sensibilities will prevail—and a fear of the tragic consequences if they do not.

"I don't want to be a propagandist, but I hope the reader senses that this is in the story. Certainly there are questions of what it really means to be patriotic, what it means to go to war. You kind of lay it out there and let the reader make the connections or not."

Then Rash returns the conversation to his interest in discovering the continuities of past, present and future. While researching his previous novel, he reports with delight, he discovered that the house he owns about three miles from the WCU campus had been in his family roughly two hundred and thirty years ago. And the future? Well, he says with some pride, like his wife and himself, his twenty-four-year-old daughter and twenty-two-year-old son have chosen to become teachers. "At least we didn't run them off from the profession."

Ron Rash, Redux

Robert Birnbaum / 2012

From *The Morning News*. Copyright Robert Birnbaum/Our Man in Boston. Reprinted by permission.

The fact that too many great writers live their lives in relative obscurity is, by now, an accepted though unpalatable facet of the literary world.

North Carolinian Ron Rash, despite having published four books of poetry, four books of short stories, and five novels, one of which was his stunning 2008 novel *Serena*, might suffer that fate but for the forthcoming adaptation of *Serena*, starring Jennifer Lawrence and Bradley Cooper. Of course, this circumstance only matters because, as with many fine writers, Rash's body of work deserves wider currency and greater attention.

Ron Rash's newest novel, *The Cove*, is set in backwoods North Carolina during the final stages of World War I, weaving a dark piece of local geography, obscure historical fact, an ornithological metaphor, and a love story into a riveting narrative exhibiting Rash's fluent and formidable prose.

Rash and I have chatted before. Here we discuss old dogs, Jim Harrison's popularity in France, reading reviews, this year's Pulitzer Prize kerfuffle (which was boiling at the time that we spoke), the American white underclass, young Southern writers and recently dead Southern writers, regional writing and, you know, other stuff.

So please read on, and discover for yourself another fine writer with a fine body of work and a major motion-picture adaptation under his belt.

Ron Rash: Is your dog still alive?
Robert Birnbaum: No, Rosie passed away.
RR: I remember your dog. I've got a couple of real old ones—I'm afraid they are going to die soon.

RB: How old?

RR: One's fifteen. Small dog. And the other one is ten. They're both mutts.

RB: I love big dogs but they don't live very long. Rosie's death was one of the worst days of my life. When she died her vet was incredibly compassionate.

RR: My experience is that vets tend to be amazingly decent people.

RB: Yeah, the money is not that great and it's a difficult task. It's not easy—you have to love those animals. Anyway, so here you are. The big news today is there is no Pulitzer Prize for fiction.

RR: That's wrong.

RB: What's wrong—that they didn't give an award, or that people are upset that there was no award?

RR: I don't know. That kind of struck me as just bizarre, that they couldn't have come up with a book. One of my hopes is—the only good thing that happened is that it caused such a furor that maybe it brought back the idea that books—it made books more visible. That's my most optimistic take on that.

RB: Why not just say that three books won? There were the darkest and gloomiest forecasts about literary fiction. Ann Patchett wrote in the *New York Times* an op-ed full of self-serving pretzel logic that I had difficulty reading. I want to know one reader that suffered. Please call me. Anyway, you live in western North Carolina—weren't you born in South Carolina?

RR: What happened was, my parents had come down from North Carolina to work in textile mills for a few years, and we went back up to where all my family was from. I think of myself as being from western North Carolina.

RB: And you teach there.

RR: Yeah, I've been there ten years now.

RB: Do you feel any sense of isolation? Do you travel much?

RR: I'd been on one overseas trip before I was fifty-five. I went to Britain when I was twenty-six and I had not been back overseas until I was fifty-five. Because of the writing I just got back last month from Australia and New Zealand, where the books are doing well. And I have been to France three times.

RB: Do they like you in France?

RR: Yeah, they do. They like Southern writers.

RB: They like Jim Harrison a lot.

RR: Yeah, Harrison's a god over there. That's been one of the great things, just getting the opportunity to travel. I never had that opportunity before—especially in the US.

RB: How much has that affected how you look at writing or what you write about?

RR: I don't know. I don't know that it's something conscious.

RB: In *The Cove* you chose to reference WWI POW camps, and things that are not commonly referred to in history texts—the seizure of the German liner *Vaterland*. How did you come to write that story?

RR: Well, just curiosity. I mean, once I started doing research on the Hot Springs camp I found out about the *Vaterland*. And I just thought that was amazing. I feel like I am reasonably well educated, but I had never heard about it. My editor in New York had never heard about it. I just thought it would make a good novel. Also, as I did in *Serena*, I think it's a good way to talk about the present by going back. I like that strategy of seeming to be writing about the past, but I hope the reader senses I am also writing about the present. I have used this quote a number of times; Emily Dickinson said, "Tell the truth but tell it slant." In a way, I kind of like the idea of sneaking up on the reader, that this is 1918 but then realizing that maybe something else is going on.

RB: *One Foot in Eden* was set around the Korean War. Or was the protagonist just a veteran?

RR: He was a veteran right at the time of the war.

RB: How much did you know about that war?

RR: I had several members of my family that were in Korea. They all survived. That's an interesting war, because it seems to be the forgotten war. Some of the stories that my relatives told me—what was the name of the reservoir?

RB: The Chosin Reservoir?

RR: Yeah, some of the most horrific fighting Americans had ever been in.

RB: When you think about it, what generation of veterans doesn't have a right to be pissed off—except for WWII vets? [both laugh]
RR: Yeah.

RB: Everybody has "Support Our Troops" bumper stickers—I guess you aren't a troop when you get back.
RR: I guess not.

RB: I skimmed some of the reviews of *The Cove* and at least one used *Serena* as a benchmark—is that fair? It's like criticizing you for the book you didn't write.
RR: Well, I tend not to read my reviews. Somebody just brought me up a copy of the *Boston Globe* [review] and wanted me to read it. I kind of scanned it. It was a very positive review and I was very happy about that. But I try to stay away from being too aware of them. I don't know that it's healthy in any way. 'Cause if you start believing what they say, the good stuff [laughs]—Colum McCann told me, "If you don't believe the good stuff, you don't believe the bad." [laughs]

RB: I'd read a review if I had experienced learning something from the writer of the review.
RR: I would say that *Serena* for me is the best novel I will ever write.

RB: Really? What's it like to have that feeling? Are you resigned?
RR: No, I just feel lucky that it just came together in a way that I had never had a novel come together. Part of it may be subject matter; it might have been the right age. It's interesting for me to see where a writer hits that—I think *Gatsby* is Fitzgerald's, or *Huckleberry Finn*—why is it that Twain hit a level that he never hit again? And part of it is just the timing and maybe the right subject. That's the book I am proudest of.

RB: In my experience, when asked their favorite book, authors will say the one they just wrote.
RR: Well, you're supposed to be promoting your book. I'm very pleased with *The Cove*. It's a very different kind of book. Sometimes something— it's almost as if you are writing better than you are. It's like grace. [laughs] Sometimes it happens—it happens with athletics. I was an athlete growing up. There are just those days when you can't miss a shot.

RB: Why do you call *The Cove* a different kind of book?

RR: It's a quieter book than my others. And I wanted it to have the feel of a dark fairy tale. I really wanted that sense. Even though a character like Chauncey, in other books I've written, would be much more nuanced—but in a fairy tale, the Big Bad Wolf, you don't find out that he's just having a bad day. [laughs]

RB: Both Janet Maslin and Ron Charles thought Chauncey was insufficient. But from your point of view he didn't have to be.

RR: Both those reviewers have been very fair to me over the years.

RB: I would not say those were bad reviews.

RR: They were very fair and honest reviews. I have no problem with that—from what people told me. You know, different people have different tastes.

RB: How are you received when you leave your home turf?

RR: It's been interesting—with each book it seems like there is a little more interest in me. After *Serena*, especially; that book was more popular by far than any of the others. And it's also brought people to some of the other books, including *One Foot in Eden*. It's also a book I feel very good about.

RB: Yeah, I love that book.

RR: I do too. So, yeah, it's been good. I get more invitations. And that's what you want to do as a writer. Last time we talked about the idea of regional literature. And I don't think either one of us wants to get into that, but one thing you do want is to know that your work is transcending your little place on the map.

RB: I get a sense that American white underclass is being more represented in stories than ever before.

RR: I agree with that.

RB: Daniel Woodrell, Donald Ray Pollock, Frank Bill, Bonnie Jo Campbell. And I don't know if you are familiar with this writer, Joe Bageant? He is devoted to telling that story, especially in *Rainbow Pie: A Redneck Memoir*. *Breaking Bad*, *Winter's Bone*, or *Justified*, an FX series that takes place in Harlan County, Kentucky. Suddenly we are getting these stories instead of *The Sopranos* or some other urban grit.

RR: I hadn't thought about that.

RB: One writer, talking to me about *Winter's Bone*, said, "They even made the trees look ugly."
RR: [both laugh] Daniel's a good friend of mine. He's a great writer. I love that book. He's got a Civil War book called *Woe to Live On*, which is really good. It's just being reissued.

RB: I've been reading Woodrell for years. I guess I shouldn't be surprised that it's taken a while for him to get recognized.
RR: What you hope for—Daniel and I have actually talked about this—we have both had some success these last couple of years. He said something like, "We were overnight successes but it took us thirty years." [laughs] We have both been writing seriously about thirty years.

RB: Like Edith Perlman, who is sixty-five-years-old, and some of the reviewers of her last collection asked why they had never heard of her, though she has been writing for years.
RR: Well, it happens. There is a writer I love, Donald Harington, who died a couple of years ago.

RB: An Arkansas writer.
RR: I kept thinking, book after book, somebody is going to recognize this guy. He's a genius.

RB: It was amazing that he continued to be published.
RR: Yeah—a lot of times it was a smaller press. But he did.

RB: A number of Southern artists have died this year.
RR: We're averaging one a week.

RB: William Gay, Lewis Nordan—
RR: Harry Crews. Another underrated writer, Doris Betts.

RB: I would include [musician] Levon Helm.
RR: Oh yeah.

RB: I wondered about the next generation of Southern writers, thirty-year-olds.
RR: I think there are some good writers coming up—a novelist named Mark

Powell out of South Carolina is good. And Wiley Cash has a new novel that's gotten some attention [*A Land More Kind Than Home*].

RB: I just came across his list of "11 Greatest Southern Novels." [laughs]
RR: Oh really?

RB: [laughs]
RR: But yeah, I see some younger writers that I think will do well—that young woman who won the National Book Award.

RB: Jesmyn Ward, *Salvage the Bones.*
RR: Yeah, that's a good book.

RB: I found it unreadable—I got one hundred pages into it and it got tiresome. I couldn't get a feel for the characters—I've liked books set in Louisiana.
RR: Have you read Tim Gautreaux?

RB: Yeah, I loved *The Clearing.*
RR: Yeah, that's my favorite book by him.

RB: His newest one, *The Missing,* was a good one. More complex than his previous stories.
RR: I love him and Tommy Franklin.

RB: He's one of those younger, up-and-coming writers.
RR: He's in his forties. Yeah, there are still a lot of good writers coming out of the region.

RB: Do the young ones think of themselves as Southern writers—part of a tradition? Are writers from the South still ghettoized?
RR: I think we have a sense we are really no different from any others. I think Richard Price is an incredible regional writer. I mean that in the best sense of the word, because I love his work.

RB: The region of five boroughs. [laughs]
RR: Yeah, but he just nails it, you know; he shows you so much of that world.

RB: I was reading Ishmael Reed's criticism of Price and *The Wire* and the new TV show he is producing, *NYC-22*. He offered the usual complaints of stereotyping. When I read *Samaritan* I didn't read any stereotyping—I found the characters to be vividly singular.

RR: And *Lush Life* was a wonderful book. That's my favorite by him. So I think we realize—I mean, as Southern writers, this is the world you have, and the world you know best. And you write about that, but always with the idea that ultimately if it doesn't touch what it means to be a human being, if it's not universal, then it's not any good. It just becomes local color, and quaint. You show how interesting and quaint these people are. That is something I am into.

RB: I don't know about the book, but the movie *Deliverance* was that: toothless mongoloids playing banjos in the trees. A cartoon.

RR: It's more about urban/rural. Jim Harrison is a writer who was very important to me growing up. I felt the world that he was writing about was so much my world.

RB: Growing up in Chicago, it's not my world, but I have always liked those stories. I was talking about urban stories with Hari Kunzru. He said, "Some writers think they are being risky if they have a character take a bump of cocaine."

RR: [laughs] When you read William Gay you are out there in some really dark ways.

RB: Isn't there a long-awaited novel?

RR: I don't know.

RB: You knew Gay?

RR: Yeah, he was a friend. Really a great guy and novelist. A great storywriter. I miss him. I don't think he ever really got his due in the United States. He was well known in Germany and France. It's interesting when I am overseas to see who is considered important.

RB: Are they reading people like Gay in English, or is it translated?

RR: Very often they read in English.

RB: I wonder how regional vernacular translates?

RR: At least in France they read a lot in English. I think you have to do that to get what William was doing—his language was so amazing.

RB: It doesn't seem to be translatable.
RR: Yeah, it's like trying to translate poetry—you just can't do it. You can give a sense of what's going on but you can never—

RB: I wonder how you can translate Chinese prose into English—there don't seem to be correlates.
RR: *Serena* has been translated into Chinese. And I have no idea. It had a really interesting cover. It looked like a western. What they made of that I couldn't imagine. [laughs]

RB: Apparently, Pablo Neruda is the most popular poet in the world. His poetry is translated into Chinese. How does that work, from Spanish to Chinese?
RR: One of my great regrets—I know some French and some Spanish. One of my favorite poets is Rilke, and you read the translations and you know you are missing everything. I actually have had a friend who knows German read it. I am kind of scanning along, and you hear it, you hear the music then.

RB: I wonder about people who translate using a dictionary, without really knowing the language.
RR: I don't know how you do that.

RB: Do you still write poetry?
RR: I do. I had a book come out last fall from a small press in South Carolina.

RB: Naturally.
RR: Yeah, poetry is not high on the radar. I love poetry. One of my hopes is that when people read my fiction that they know I am a poet. I mean, you can overdo that, but I hope that there's that sense.

RB: Jim Harrison has always considered himself a poet, though I don't think most readers see him that way. His poems are funny. And gentle.
RR: And there is a real clarity to them. Which, very often, is what I think distinguishes his prose—that kind of clarity.

RB: I don't get why he is not more present in the conversations about literature in the way that, for instance, Cormac McCarthy, Roth, or Updike are.

RR: I don't either. And there was a long time that McCarthy wasn't getting any attention. *All the Pretty Horses* was kind of his breakout book. He was just quietly doing his work. I think that's not a bad thing. When I talk to younger writers they don't want to hear this. I would not want to be a writer who had a lot of success early. To have a novel that got a lot of attention when I was twenty-five—that would not have been good for me, at least. So much of the other stuff starts getting in the way of the writing.

RB: Readings are still part of the publicity strategy. Public conversations seem to be preferred in Europe—do you do those?

RR: Oh, sure. It's always a little unsettling. I am not that quick. I am not one of those people that can come up with these, you know, like Samuel Johnson, and just say these memorable sentences. And when I get through I always think, "Well, why didn't I say this?" But you know, that's because I'm a writer. I write 12 or 143 drafts of something. Suddenly you are up there spouting nonsense.

RB: There is an expectation, after you have spent a long time alone creating a story, then you should go out for an extended period and be charming.

RR: I feel very lucky just because there are so many good writers not getting published, or who have been dropped by good houses. It's a weird experience. I make myself write on the road. That allows me to lock myself into a hotel room and not see people, just talking and doing a book signing. Writers tend to be introverts and I am certainly one. It takes a lot of energy. Because I teach, I am kind of used to getting up in front of people, but I find it draining. But at the same time I find it nice—for twenty years nobody cared.

RB: Want to speculate on what might happen if you hadn't finally enjoyed some success with *Serena*?

RR: *One Foot in Eden*—once you have a novel out, that gave me some—that kind of raised me to a little more visibility. To me, a healthy kind of building a readership and interest in the work. I just felt that I have written the books I want to write. I have written them at my own pace.

RB: You have been teaching as you have been writing?

RR: Yeah, I was teaching at community college—I was teaching five, six courses a semester for seventeen years. I taught two years of high school, and half of it composition. But you know, as I tell people, if it's important enough, you're going to find a way to write. What I do is just get up early and teach at night, so I can have a little time and energy in the mornings.

RB: That's some hard work—I wonder who is willing to do that these days?
RR: It is hard work.

RB: I'm thinking of young writers out of prestigious university writing programs getting their stories published in the *New Yorker* and being signed to half-million-dollar contracts.
RR: Well, I certainly was not part of that. Once again, it was probably a good thing for me as a writer that it was slow.

RB: There was the eighties brat pack—Bret Easton Ellis and Jay McInerney—they tasted early success and they haven't seemed to come close since then. Do you attend the conferences and festivals down South?
RR: I go to some. It's a good way to meet friends, and get to meet—I've been invited to festivals in Australia and France. That's been great. Actually I finally met Richard Russo in France.

RB: Russo's another writer who deals with white working-class characters—*Nobody's Fool*. He also writes movie scripts. Do you watch a lot of movies?
RR: Not a huge number.

RB: Have you been approached for movies of your books?
RR: Oh, they are doing *Serena* right now.

RB: I might have known that. Who's involved?
RR: Susanne Bier is directing. Jennifer Lawrence is Serena and Bradley Cooper is—

RB: You caught Lawrence at the right time.
RR: Yeah.

RB: She was great in *Winter's Bone* and in another obscure one called *The Burning Plain*.
RR: She's going to be good as Serena—she grew up riding horses and she's used to being outdoors. Serena, you know, hunts with an eagle and rides the horses. She's physical.

RB: And Brad Cooper is playing her husband?

RR: Yeah, and they have some other good people involved. Toby Jones, a great actor, plays the sheriff. Rhys Ifans is another good actor.

RB: Are you involved?

RR: No.

RB: The paperback reissue/tie-in will have Lawrence and Cooper on the cover. I remember talking with Russo when *Nobody's Fool* was made into a movie and how delighted he was that Paul Newman was on the cover of the reissued paperback. [laughs]

RR: Yeah, they're filming it now in the Czech Republic.

RB: That must look like North Carolina.

RR: I guess for all the timber-cutting scenes they unfortunately find them there.

RB: Are you on a schedule or pattern of writing—you just finished a novel and are on tour—have you already started another project?

RR: Oh yeah. Actually I am finishing up a book of short stories.

RB: Written specifically for this collection, or—

RR: Well, some of them are a little bit older, but actually when I finished *The Cove* about a year ago, I just started writing stories.

RB: Do you have to write all the time?

RR: Seems like it. I just don't feel right if I'm not. It's like exercising.

RB: What's the longest you can go?

RR: Oh, I can go a few days. [both laugh] Sometimes I have to. But I always start getting restless. I have done it so long, like I said, it's like not exercising that day—it just doesn't feel right.

RB: What does it feel like when you do? Do you go to another place?

RR: Oh yeah. To me, I'm pretty much oblivious to everything around me when I am writing. I need a quiet place—some people can write with music but I don't like distractions. Sometimes I write on my porch, which is very quiet. Actually where I do most of my writing is in my office, and I have a little photograph of Flannery O'Connor glaring down at me, keeping me honest.

RB: What does New England, Boston, look like to you after you step off the plane?

RR: I'm curious. I enjoy cities. I don't think I could ever live in one. That's just me. I wouldn't feel comfortable.

RB: Do you notice the noise?

RR: Yeah. The first time I went to New York, I could not sleep—I kept hearing the traffic, mainly. At the same time I love Indian food and I don't have a restaurant within forty miles of me that serves that. We have good bookstores, but—

RB: How close to Asheville are you?

RR: About fifty miles. Asheville has a lot of fine restaurants and a great bookstore.

RB: Warren Wilson [College] is there.

RR: Right outside it.

RB: It seems that Vermont and North Carolina seem to have the most writers per capita in the U.S.

RR: I think North Carolina right now—it just seems like there is one over every fence. It's pretty amazing—just a lot of really good writers.

RB: Do you have any worries about books disappearing?

RR: Yeah, it may be generational, but for me there is something so wonderful—I like the fact that it's tangible. And very often it has a beautiful cover, the aesthetic, so that I just find wonderful. I have trouble reading off of a screen—a novel at least. Like I say, it may be generational, but it doesn't feel quite right for me.

RB: Any novel in the works? Do you have a master plan? You want to write a bookshelf full of novels and X amount of stories and X amount of poems?

RR: I like a kind of symmetry. For a while I had four books of poetry, four books of stories, and four novels. Now I have five novels, I'll have five books of stories—that means I'll owe another book of poems. I kind of like that. Novels are so horrible to write. It takes me three years. Very often I'd rather stick pencils in my eyes. But when you finish them, it's wonderful. Right now I can't even think about writing one.

RB: Having written five novels, do you have doubts that you can write another one?

RR: Well, no, not in that sense. Just whether I want to do that to myself. [laughs] I mean, I was pretty miserable for about a year, year and a half, just because it kept going the wrong way. I would throw away fifty, sixty pages. And it was good writing. The writing was good, I felt. It was like pulling out organs.

RB: Do you actually throw it away, or do you store it somewhere?

RR: I throw it away. Occasionally there might be a description that I feel like, *Maybe this can go somewhere else.* I did a huge amount of research for *The Cove* on jazz because I was going to have the character Walter join a jazz band those three years the ship was in the harbor. I probably read twenty books on jazz—I figured out who would have come from New Orleans, how quickly they could have gotten to New York, all those kinds of things. I ended up writing about forty pages where Walter actually hangs with those guys. He's learning this exotic kind of music he's never heard before.

RB: I didn't think they used flutes in early jazz.

RR: Well, to me that's what would make it interesting—I think they did occasionally, I mean, Herbie Mann—

RB: That's much later.

RR: I thought it would be interesting for him to try—it is fiction. Maybe nobody else ever heard of it. But you know, it wasn't working with the book, and I had to get rid of it.

RB: What's the interchange after you submit the manuscript to your editor [Lee Boudreaux]?

RR: She reads it carefully. She's a great editor, she really is, and we discuss it, and very often she is dead-on right. I sensed the jazz scenes were slowing the story down and she concurred. And I want that.

RB: Has she been your editor all along?

RR: I was with Holt for my first three books and they didn't want *Serena*—Ecco did. I just feel lucky that someone in New York picked it up. I was afraid I wouldn't have a New York publisher.

RB: It's not like you turn your copy in and that's it?

RR: No, no. She reads it carefully and, as I say, makes a lot of good suggestions. Sometimes we disagree, and she is very open when I feel strongly that something needs to stay the way it is. That's what you hope for from an editor. I always feel the book is better because of her.

RB: Those are very special relationships.
RR: Yeah.

RB: What do you do besides write?
RR: Oh gosh—not a lot.

RB: Sports—pay attention to sports?
RR: I love sports. I ran track in college. I love basketball. I love watching NBA basketball. So I am excited about the playoffs. I fish some. I like to spend some time outdoors.

RB: What have you been reading?
RR: Let's see—I went back and reread *Light in August*, and I have been reading some Australian writers that I like. The problem with writing novels is, after spending six hours writing I am so burned out at night I just want to sit and watch a ball game. It's hard to have the energy to read. I mean, I do—maybe thirty minutes.

RB: Random House is reissuing some Faulkner and I started rereading the Snopes trilogy. I was amazed—mostly by whole passages that I don't think I understood, but I continued to read it.
RR: Oh yeah. He's just amazing. *Light in August*, it'd been about twenty years since I read it. I had forgotten how great a book that is.

RB: I remember being introduced to Faulkner and Melville and James in high school—I didn't get any of them. I wonder if that discourages people from becoming readers?
RR: What is initially important is if students have bad experiences with reading, reading a book that that person can't connect to or [is] over their heads. When I look back on what I read—I was reading the Hardy Boys. I'd read some Poe and things like that, but I was developing that love.

RB: I remember the first book to really excite me, the first real literary work I read, was Thomas Pynchon's *V.* Funny, complicated, and engaging. From there I jumped into all sorts of stuff. I don't think we foster real literary appreciation.

RR: What I try to do is be optimistic about it. One of the great things is I'll have a kid who is not a reader—one of the books that has done well especially with male high school students is *The World Made Straight*. It's about somebody their age getting into serious trouble—they find that interesting. I just can't imagine living a life without reading. I mean, I just can't. It's not even being judgmental. To me it's something that would be missing. Missing one of the best things about life. I mean, really—a really good book is like communion. The reader is taking these splotches of ink and making them real, and being affected by them. But the reader has to bring a lot. A good reader is an artist. You have to have that kind of ability. I feel sad that they are missing out on it.

RB: It seems to be a failure to teach appreciation for what a story is. Same problem in teaching history. We teach a lot of details and leave out the good stories.

RR: Randall Jarrell said, "Man is the narrative animal." That may be changing. We are becoming the visual animal. There is something about story that continues to resonate with us as human beings.

RB: I was reading an essay by Lewis Lapham that argued that language today is not used to tell stories but to encourage us to buy stuff. It's about transactions.

RR: What I sense from overseas is more readers. Australia and New Zealand, there are a lot of readers there, I would think percentage-wise much more than the United States.

RB: That there were 300,000 titles published last year must be a good sign—in aggregate the money is there.

RR: That's amazing.

RB: Well thanks.

RR: Yeah, good to see you again.

Encounter with Ron Rash: Hell in Eden

Clémentine Thiebault and Mikaël Demets / 2012

From *L'Accoudoir*, 21 September 2012. Translated by Frédérique Spill. Copyright Mikaël Demets and Clémentine Thiebault/*L'Accoudoir*. Reprinted by permission.

"Every last one of you hillbillies is going to be flushed out of this valley like shit down a commode."[1] With *One Foot in Eden*, a dazzling debut novel that captures the end of a world, Ron Rash opened a haunted world—places with "vowel-heavy"[2] names in ancient Cherokee territory, a kind of hell in the clawed mountains, in the triumphant heat, in the bare lands, in a valley threatened by flooding, where even men are rough. *One Foot in Eden* is a choral drama, a chronicle hanging from a piece of nature that is about to become "a place for the lost"[3] and where it has become difficult to tell what started the vicious circle that unrelentingly unravels the relationships between men (who are often cruel) or between men and their environment. Then *Serena* was published, midway between the detective novel and the historical epic. The novel goes back to the origins of modern America, to the dark days of the Great Depression, the bitter years in the course of which workers stood in lines in order to find a job, any kind of job, and whom Rash describes with the sharpness of Dorothea Lange's photographs and the violence of *Grapes of Wrath*. The sawmill, massive deforestation, the terrible everyday life of woodcutters, the imprisoning valleys, the stifling forests, the massacred mountain, the relentless accumulation of deaths; and change, forever looming.

With *The World Made Straight*, a rite-of-passage novel situated in the heart of a world of rivers full of fish—a world fraught with despair—Ron Rash carries on with his impressive exploration of men's darkness, men that risk being chased away from a place where they have one foot only: Eden. Beauty, harshness, and landscapes that are destiny, the Appalachian Mountains always, and "[a] voice capable of transforming sorrow and regret into something beautiful,"[4] conjuring up that of Johnny Cash.

Clémentine Thiebault and Mikaël Demets: *One Foot in Eden*, *Serena* and *The World Made Straight* all take place in Appalachia, in North and South Carolina. Why do your novels display such a unity of place?

Ron Rash: As Eudora Welty put it, "One place understood helps us understand all places better." I am part of this tradition of writers seeking to tell a universal story through a local story. William Faulkner and James Joyce were part of the same tradition: *Ulysses* is one of the most regional books I can think of. When I write I try to reconstruct Appalachia as intimately as possible, trying to grasp not only the essence of that particular territory, but also the essence of all territories.

T&D: Nature is omnipresent in your books. The nature you describe is strong, beautiful and majestic; at the same time, it is likely to turn into a diabolical trap. How do you account for this duality?

RR: In my region, nature can be protective and healing, but it also turns out to be stifling and oppressive, ensnaring people. Many Appalachians were born in misery and were denied access to education. They ended up being trapped, physically and psychologically. It is a sublime country, but there are numerous remote villages that have been stuck at the bottom of dark coves for generations. As I often say, our destiny depends on where we live. If I were to get a motto tattooed on my body, this would be it. I've met young women like Lori, one of the female characters in *The World Made Straight*, who came from underprivileged social backgrounds and had understood that the only way for them to escape their destiny was education. They focused on their goal: to go to college, not to fall pregnant, to remain free, not to end like their mothers. But beyond their determination, there was also a great deal of bitterness.

T&D: The relationship that you describe between man and his place can take other forms: attempts to tame nature, for example by cutting trees (in *Serena*) or by building dams (in *One Foot in Eden*).

RR: My task as a novelist is not merely to tell stories; it is also to describe places by giving specific details about their fauna, flora, a rock or a river, in order to reveal nature, its complexity, its beauty, and to examine the interaction between man and his milieu. I must first make it possible for readers to see the beauty of a region; then they can be made aware of what man does to nature.

T&D: Ecology is henceforth a recurring topic in your books. In *Serena*, for instance, you evoke the burgeoning ecological consciousness at the beginning of the 1930s.

RR: I wrote *Serena* as a direct response to what was going on under the George W. Bush administration, which wanted to ruin protected forests in order to make money. Republicans today still announce that they want to tamper with how national parks protect nature in order to exploit oil and natural gas. *Serena* relates the beginning of the struggle between exploitation and ecology.

T&D: Does it seem to you that Carolina is representative of the US?

RR: I believe it is. Most Americans live like the characters of Jim Harrison, Daniel Woodrell or Annie Proulx, not like Bret Easton Ellis's New Yorkers. New York or Los Angeles are almost another world that is disconnected from the United States. When you read Bret Easton Ellis, you observe a very small portion of the country that is not necessarily representative. Authors like Richard Price manage to do so more truthfully when they describe several layers of society at the same time.

T&D: So when you write you do not exclusively have your region in mind?

RR: I never do. I do not want to write solely about Appalachia. For instance I consider *Serena* as a typically American novel, with a deeply American character, comparable to Scott Fitzgerald's Gatsby or Thomas Sutpen, the main character in Faulkner's *Absalom, Absalom!* Serena is a woman that never looks back, but systematically projects herself in the future. The Americans' great illusion is to believe that they will never have to face the consequences of their acts. So they move on, thinking things will be all right. Once all the world's rivers are destroyed, they will keep going. This "American innocence" is certainly not our best feature . . .

T&D: History pervades all your novels. You describe Carolina like a haunted place. How do you account for this haunting presence of the past?

RR: In my region, memory is crucial. Most Southern writers have a special interest in the past. In big cities and in regions like California, people seem to be more uprooted; they sometimes are unaware of what happened ten years earlier. The South is very much concerned with history. Part of this is related to the Civil War since most great battles took place there, but also because people have been living there for generations. My family has not moved for two hundred years! This is a short time from a European perspective, but it is a long time in America. Southerners do not move, very often because they cannot move.

T&D: Each of your three novels is anchored in a key period of American history: *One Foot in Eden* takes place in the 1950s and focuses on the arrival of modernity and rural exodus; *Serena* is set right after the 1929 crisis and evokes the birth of ecological consciousness; *The World Made Straight* returns to the Civil War. How do you pick such moments?

RR: I voluntarily choose very significant periods, crucial moments. In a novel I try to make different historical periods interconnect in order to make the narrative livelier, more colorful and more complete for the reader. I do my best to depict a place by putting its history in perspective. For instance, *The World Made Straight* takes place in the 1970s, at a time when small farmers became archaic: a traditional way of life, according to which whole communities had lived for dozens, sometimes hundreds, of years, then disappeared. I describe a world in transition, with people that have no clue what is going on and what their future will be. This raises questions that do not only have to do with Appalachia, but with all farmers or workers replaced by machines: what happens to people that witness the disappearance of their way of life? What can be done to help them?

T&D: This sadly echoes a sentence that is to be found in your latest novel: "The worst thing the nineteen sixties did to this country was introduce drugs to rednecks."[5] This highlights the misery and boredom of lives turned upside down by modernity.

RR: If you are young and uneducated, there are not many alternatives. Either you join the army and go fighting in Iraq, or you sink in drugs, become a dealer or grow marijuana. The situation has lately become worse because of chemical drugs like methamphetamine, which is cheap and even more addictive than heroin. It is a drug that kills. Young people now make it themselves and there are more and more walking dead.

T&D: The Internet did not help to open up populations?

RR: People are now connected to the World Wide Web and they could leave if they wanted. But where would they go? They fear what they don't know. This is the only place where they have ever lived, which is often the land of their ancestors. So, in the end, most of them stay.

T&D: To come back to history and *The World Made Straight*, why did you choose to evoke the Civil War through the Shelton Laurel Massacre? Did you regard this bloody episode—the execution of thirteen Union sympathizers by a Confederate regiment in January 1863—as the epitome of the American Civil War?

RR: My family fought during the Civil War and, as was the case of many other families, they sided with the Union, the Northerners, while they were Southerners. Many Europeans do not realize that a lot of people in North Carolina or Eastern Tennessee did not fight with the Confederacy, but with the Union. The two sides were not as distinct as people believe. What happened in Shelton Laurel does not only epitomize the Civil War, it also says something about what went on in Rwanda, Kosovo, Cambodia or today in Syria: people have known and lived peacefully together for generations and, all of a sudden, they start fighting violently. This says something about the human soul, something about what men do and will never stop doing.

T&D: It is not quite easy to determine precisely when *The World Made Straight* takes place: it could take place anytime between the 1950s and the 1990s . . .

RR: This is what I wanted. I like the idea that a novel should be rooted in a specific period, but at the same time I try to convey a universal, almost biblical, sense of blurring.

T&D: Reading you one has the impression that events that are a century and a half old are still palpable in the region. Is this so?

RR: Despite technology and the Internet, there is the persisting awareness that something happened in that place. One day, I got this phone call from a woman who had just finished reading *The World Made Straight*; she asked me whether I knew where the story came from. I told her that writers never really know how the things they write come to them. She then told me: *"These are stories the dead want us to tell, stories they would have liked to tell."* She gave me the creeps . . . I'm not saying I believe this is true, but I sometimes have the impression that it is the landscape that inspired that story.

Notes

1. Ron Rash, *One Foot in Eden*. New York: Picador, 2002, 184 (note from the translator).

2. *Ibid.*, 23 (note from the translator).

3. *Ibid.*, 214 (note from the translator).

4. Rash, *The World Made Straight*. New York: Picador, 2006, 109 (note from the translator).

5. Rash, *The World Made Straight*, 31 (note from the translator).

"Nothing Gold" Stays Long in Appalachia

Scott Simon / 2013

Scott Simon, Host: Traveling soon? You know, you can put less time into reading a short story in Ron Rash's new book, *Nothing Gold Can Stay*, than you do into a quick game of "Angry Birds." And if you do read Ron Rash you might meet characters whose stories will stay with you for life. Ron Rash is considered a master of the form and Appalachian ballad writer of a kind who writes pointed, fierce, funny and tightly packed stories about people on the run, betting their all, trying to get through lonely nights. Ron Rash is also author of bestselling novels, including *The Cove*, and winner of the Frank O'Connor International Short Story Award. He teaches at Western Carolina University. He joins us from the studios of Clemson University. Thanks so much for being with us.
Ron Rash: Glad to be here today.

SIMON: How does a short story idea come into you?
RASH: Very often, they're not ideas at all. I actually start sometimes with a voice, usually an image, an image that won't leave me alone and I have to find out where that image will lead me.

SIMON: Can you give us a for instance?
RASH: Well, in "The Trusty," the first story in the book, I had an image of a trusty, a prisoner, in the nineteenth . . . it was early twentieth century, who

was walking down the road with a bucket in his hand. I didn't know where he was going or who he would meet but I knew I wanted to follow him.

SIMON: He's a guy in a chain gang sent ahead to get water and he sees a young farmer's wife. And I love this exchange. She asks him: Have you ever considered trying to escape? And he says . . .
RASH: Have you?[laughter]

SIMON: So, these are two seemingly lost souls but . . .
RASH: Seemingly.

SIMON: Yeah, exactly. I guess the lesson of that story is don't kid a kidder.
RASH: Very true.

SIMON: When you're writing a story like "The Trusty," how do you put yourself back in another time?
RASH: I think that's what I love about writing is the ability to try to, in a sense, take a vacation from yourself and try to enter the sensibility of another time, another character, another place. But very often I will do research. Certainly, I will try to find out just the little things, because one thing I found about writing fiction is that if you don't get the small things right the reader won't believe the big lie.

SIMON: You grew up in a small North Carolina town, I gather.
RASH: I did. The same town as Earl Scruggs. That's our most famous citizen.

SIMON: Did you grow up thinking you'd be a writer?
RASH: I didn't, but I think I showed all the symptoms. I was very comfortable being by myself. I spent a lot of time alone and particularly out in the natural world. I think I had a particular moment when I was fifteen years old. I read *Crime and Punishment,* and that book just, I think, more than any other book made me want to be a writer, because it was the first time that I hadn't just entered a book, but a book had entered me. I can remember exactly where I was. I was in a biology class. I was supposed to be listening to the teacher but I was on the back row. And I can just remember so vividly just never having that kind of feeling, that kind of intensity from a book. And, obviously, at fifteen I didn't understand exactly what was going on with Raskolnikov. But there was a particular scene early in that book

where the pawnbroker was murdered that I will never forget. It's one of the most vivid memories in my life—not just my reading life.

SIMON: This book is set in Appalachia, and I gather you've written a lot about the area in which you live. Have you ever thought about going to Paris or New Zealand?
RASH: Well, I've been there.[laughter]

SIMON: Well, I didn't mean as a visitor.
RASH: Well, I decided early in my writing life that I would adhere to what the writers I love most have been able to find, the universal in the particular. That included James Joyce, William Faulkner, writers such as Eudora Welty. Eudora Welty once said one place understood helps us understand all other places better. And I chose to be that kind of writer.

SIMON: Want to ask you about one of these stories in the book toward the end called "Nighthawks." Ginny is a former middle-school teacher whose story you tell. She becomes a late-night DJ. But as you go deeper into her story, you realize this is a character who, if I can put it this way, wants to hide in plain sight.
RASH: Absolutely. And her problems in the story I think go back to childhood. And she's someone, I think, in many ways a very tragic character. But she has a kind of integrity and flawed beauty beyond the physical that I found very interesting.

SIMON: We should explain as a middle-school teacher, there's a terrible tragedy that befalls one of her students. She holds herself responsible. It does raise the question as to what powers there are in the universe that make us steer our lives one direction or another.
RASH: Absolutely. And one aspect of that I'm fascinated by is how landscape is very often destiny, that the landscape a human being grows up in has an incredible impact on the way he or she perceives reality. I always argue that Gatsby could only be written by a Midwesterner. He's such a Midwestern character in the sense of possibility. My character . . .

SIMON: This is F. Scott Fitzgerald from Minnesota coming east to Long Island.
RASH: Right. And Gatsby just strikes me as that optimism, that belief that he can undo the past is very Midwestern. And the openness, the

expansiveness of that landscape . . . I'm more interested in what happens in the Appalachian landscape because we see very often a sense of people who grew up in the region being intimidated because the mountains are always reminding us of how fleeting our lives are, our smallness. It can also work in a more positive way in the sense of almost a womb-like protectiveness. But that's one aspect of literature of landscape I'm fascinated with.

SIMON: I want to take an unusual step here and end our interview with a reading, 'cause I find a graph you have in there just about the loveliest thing I've read for a while. I wonder if you can set the scene and read that for us.

RASH: This is at the very end. Ginny has gone back to the radio station. It's a snowy day. She's broken up with the man who loves her, and she's preparing for the night. And she knows what awaits her. [reading] "At the radio station she would unlock the door, and soon enough Buddy Harper would end his broadcast and leave. She would say, This is the Nighthawk, and play 'After Midnight.' Ginny would speak to people in bedrooms, to clerks drenched in the fluorescent light of convenience stores, to millworkers driving back roads home after graveyard shifts. She would speak to the drunk and sober, the godly and the godless. All the while high above where she sat, the station's red beacon would pulse like a heart, as if giving bearings to all those in the dark adrift and alone."

SIMON: That's utterly beautiful. I can't thank you enough.

RASH: Thank you for having me.

SIMON: Ron Rash. His new book of short stories, *Nothing Gold Can Stay*.

An Interview with Author Ron Rash

Joshua Christopher Jones / 2013

From *MFA Blog*. Reprinted by permission.

Ron Rash is the author of five novels, five books of short stories, and four collections of poetry. His work dwells in the Carolinian Appalachians, delving into its cultural myth, past, and present. He teaches as a professor of Appalachian studies at Western Carolina University. This interview was conducted over the phone in November of 2013 and recorded with the author's permission.

Joshua Christopher Jones: When I was researching your work, I came across quite a few interviews you've done about your fiction, and I wondered if you had done interviews for your poetry and the difference between how you write your fiction and your poetry.
Ron Rash: I think I've done some in the past. I went over to the "dark side" of fiction in the last decade, and as you know, unfortunately, it's not fair but fiction gets more attention. I've talked some about it. I can't remember all the details. You know Matt (Boyleston) has done an article on me and Seamus Heaney and I'm sure I've done some; I'm just not sure where.

JONES: So what is your composition process?
RASH: It's very different. I think the difference between poetry and fiction for me is that I think in lines for poetry. Just the individual line. I really may move out of this, but I really like that tight syllabic line I've been using in the past few books. So I tend to just—it's a matter of the line as opposed to the paragraph or sentence.

JONES: You mentioned the syllabic line, and I assume you mean the seven syllable line.
RASH: Yeah.

JONES: So how did you come across that, and how do you think it works in the poems?

RASH: Well, I've always been interested in Welsh poetry because some of my heritage is Welsh, and I've always loved Hopkins, and—so you know—I just kind of started, because he'd been influenced by Welsh poetry, studying it and those old forms. I can't remember how to say it but the "cynghanedd."

I just got really interested in that, and, you know, because I'm mostly a narrative poet, I wanted something that really could keep my work from being broken-lined anecdotes or stories, and I think it's always the danger if you are a narrative poet. So I wanted the lyric intensity even though I was working in narrative, and I felt like that did it for me. And, I wanted that sound intense line and Welsh poetry does that.

JONES: Yes it does. One of the things I've noticed, reading through your work chronologically, in your first book, *Eureka Mill*, you've got a very centered narrative on that mill and how it all goes down. But, you move away from that in your other books. I wanted to know whether it was just a conscious project, and you never came across another worthy project or how the decision to make a book comes together.

RASH: You know, I hope that book had the feel of a novel. I wanted the reader to come away feeling he had been immersed in that world and in a sense the narratives are not necessarily connected. They give an overall sense of that world. Part of that was just personal because that world was disappearing and nobody seemed to notice that so many lives had been spent there, and I felt it was just something to acknowledge—the passing of the lives that'd been lived that way—and honor them. And, so yeah, I think in a way I haven't written fiction about the mill experience because I think I used that book to pretty much have my say about it. Or at least as best I could.

JONES: So here and in a few other interviews you've mentioned Seamus Heaney as an influence, and obviously Matt's essay about the similarity between your work and his work. I also noticed that *Eureka Mill* actually has a poem "Invocation"—I think it's the last poem in the book—and when I read it through the first time, I couldn't help but think of "Digging," and I wanted to know if that was a conscious move in that poem, particularly, and on another note how and whether you have been affected by or what you think about his recent passing?

RASH: Yeah I think, in a way, I felt like "Digging" is an important poem for me, especially a sense of being connected. It wasn't that kind of obvious consciousness, but I'm sure that somewhere along the line I was thinking of that. I actually got to have lunch with him in April at one of the last public events he did, and I went to his reading. I was in Ireland doing a reading at the same festival myself, and that was a great honor, but, yeah, I'm very sad. I mean I'm sad for poetry because I think he was that kind of poet who had a broad audience that transcended the usual people that read poetry which I think was very important. But, yeah, he was a great poet who was still writing very fine poems. It wasn't as if he didn't have much more to offer; so I felt he was still producing really, really wonderful poems. So very sad.

JONES: On a different note, in a lot of the books and poems and short stories—as well as interviews—you talk about your Christian faith and its relation to your work, and a lot of your symbolism is straight out of the Bible to an extent. How would you consider yourself a Christian in relation to literature and whether that is stifling? Because I know you read Flannery O'Connor's essays and she thinks it's liberating to be a Christian, in her case a Catholic. How do you work inside that Christian worldview?

RASH: Well, that's always a tricky question. Not tricky in a sense, but I think the best thing you can say is that certainly has influenced me—growing up Christian, and, yeah, it's just part of my sensibility, and I think part of it is just coming out of an environment where those things were seen as being as real as anything else. So I think certainly that that background influenced my work.

JONES: Here's a different sort of question; what are you reading now, and what do you think of it? And what are you working on now generally?

RASH: Well I'm working on a new novel now, but I am doing something that's—I've got a new narrator who feels that Hopkins has saved her life, and she survived a school shooting as a child and she feels he taught her how to see the world again. So she's almost autistic but maybe not quite—I'm rambling here—but her language is very much Hopkins-influenced. Her internal monologue, her thoughts, that's kind of what I'm working on now. A kind of intense language—well here I'll just read you a bit I'm working on here. "Gerald," this older man she's seeing, "takes the kitchen match places it under the andirons. The fire streams around kindling thickens and pools swirls upward. Sparks crackle and splash. The applewood catches and sprouts feathers red yellow green the lost parakeet phoenixed in herculean fire."

JONES: That's beautiful.

RASH: So, that's gonna be fun to run with that kind of voice and sensibility.

JONES: That'll be a fun poetic take on novel writing. I really enjoy that aspect to your work generally, but that's exciting that it will be a major part of the novel. Just one more question. So as I read through your work, the symbol of the hunting of the panther—the Carolina panther—is all over the place, and sometimes I feel it's a symbol for a lost sense of place, and other times it's a religion that's been killed off. I don't want to say "What does it mean" but "What does it mean?"

RASH: Well, all of it kind of ties together a sense of loss of a sense of wonder and wildness, but at the same time that need for us to believe in unseen things, to believe that the world holds more than we can see, that the world holds its mysteries at least for my characters—and wanting to believe. The world can still hide secrets from us. I think it ties in the metaphysical and ecological—just a sense that we want wonder in the world. That's what this novel I'm writing is about—just wanting to find wonder in a world where technology is against that.

JONES: Well, thank you so much for talking with me, and thank you for such great books. I've really enjoyed your work and talking to you. It's been great.

RASH: Well, thank you and good luck with your work. And, tell Matt hello next time you get to talk to him.

An Interview with Ron Rash

Frédérique Spill / 2014

Originally published in *Transatlantica* 1/2014, *http://transatlantica.revues.org*. Reprinted by permission.

Ron Rash (born in Chester, South Carolina, in 1953) is the author of five novels, five collections of short stories and four collections of poems. He is currently completing his sixth novel, *Above the Waterfall*. He probably owes the international attention he now enjoys to the publication of *Serena* (the novel was a 2009 PEN/Faulkner Award Finalist), whose plot retraces the fate of a Lady Macbeth-like figure at the head of a timber industry in the Appalachian Mountains in North Carolina at the beginning of the 1930s. But when *Serena* was published in 2008, Rash had been writing for most of his life. He has been translated into fourteen languages: most of his novels are now available in their French translations, and soon so will some of his short stories. Rash lives in the North Carolina mountains. He is the Parris Distinguished Professor in Appalachian Cultural Studies at Western Carolina University in Cullowhee, North Carolina.

We met in Paris, rue Delambre in the 14th arrondissement on the afternoon of June 6, 2014. A guest at the Saint-Malo *Festival des Étonnants Voyageurs*, he had flown into Paris the very same morning. Before we started the interview he showed me the old, much read yet new-looking edition of Faulkner's *Absalom, Absalom!* that he had started rereading on the plane. We had a look at the map of Yoknapatawpha County that is included at the end of that volume and I marveled at his unlikely reading choice for travelling. For about an hour, we talked about his tastes, literature, cinema, the South, the mountains and their people, but mostly about his approach to writing and the tensions that underlie his work. A spoiler alert might be necessary for those who have not read the books evoked in our conversation.

Frédérique Spill: Do you know what you'll be doing and whom you'll be meeting at the *Festival des Étonnants Voyageurs* in Saint-Malo?

Ron Rash: I will meet several writers whom I already know. Colum McCann is a friend of mine. I'm acquainted with Chris Womersley from Australia and Alan Hollinghurst, but it's mainly going to be writers I haven't met. I'm glad it's so international. I think I'm the only American this year.

FS: I would like to start this interview by submitting to you a few selected (and adapted) items from the Proust questionnaire. Would you agree to start that way?

RR: Yes.

FS: Your favorite color?

RR: Blue.

FS: Your favorite flower?

RR: Let's see . . . There's a very rare flower called the Oconee Bell; it's a very beautiful white flower and the only place in the world where it's found is in the South Carolina and North Carolina Mountains.

FS: Your favorite flavor?

RR: Chocolate.

FS: Your chief characteristic?

RR: Driven.

FS: Your idea of happiness?

RR: . . . Probably when the writing's going well.

FS: Your idea of misery?

RR: When the writing is not going well.

FS: Your favorite prose authors?

RR: Dostoyevsky, Faulkner, Melville, Hardy, Giono.

FS: Your favorite heroes in fiction?

RR: Ishmael in *Moby-Dick*; Faulkner's Caddy[1] in *The Sound and the Fury*; Raskolnikov in *Crime and Punishment*; the Judge in Cormac McCarthy's *Blood Meridian*.

FS: What is the book you re-read most frequently?
RR: Probably *Macbeth*. I dip into *Moby-Dick* often.

FS: What's the best book that you have read recently?
RR: I read a book by Giono I had never read, *Joy of Man's Desiring* (*Que ma joie demeure*). I think that's a remarkable novel.

FS: You come to France quite regularly and obviously enjoy a much deserved visibility and success that keep increasing thanks to the excellent translations of your novels by Les Éditions du Masque and Le Seuil. How is your work received in other countries?
RR: It's been doing very well; it's been translated in fourteen languages now. It's done particularly well in Ireland, England, Denmark, Netherlands, China, and Australia. Translations are just coming out in Italy and Brazil.

FS: Will there be French translations of your collections of poems and short stories?
RR: There will be a translation of my short stories in December or January—a book called *Burning Bright*.[2]

FS: Do you have any clue how they will translate that title? It's a beautiful title, but a tough one.
RR: No; actually my translator was saying it was a tough title to translate in French.

FS: What about your place in American literature in the US?
RR: Well, that's hard to know. Sometimes there is a sensibility in the United States that Southern writers are apart from the rest of the country's literature, which I find absurd. But I've done fairly well. I've published in *The New Yorker* and won or have been a finalist for some major awards and prizes.

FS: Is the label "Southern literature" still much in use?
RR: It's still used a lot. I'm very proud of this tradition. I think an inordinate number of the best American writers have come out of the South; the best music, too, for that matter. But sometimes I fear that the term is used in a limiting sense: he's *just* a Southern writer. But I think *Serena* is as American a novel as any. She's an American character, not even a Southerner at that.

FS: You live in the Appalachian Mountains, the territory that feeds your writing. Could you imagine living anywhere else?

RR: I've thought about it and I may some time. The way things are going in the United States politically, I sometimes want to leave because I'm so frustrated. But to get back where I live it's pretty isolated so I'm pretty much left alone. I don't know. Some of my region's writers have had the feeling that they had to leave the South: Carson McCullers felt she had to leave, Truman Capote, Tennessee Williams. But Eudora Welty, Flannery O'Connor, Faulkner—they felt they had to stay and I think I'm one of those that feel they have to stay in touch with their landscape.

FS: It seems that your titles' inscription in the topography of Appalachia is more and more obvious (I'm thinking of *The Cove*[3] and of the novel that we're looking forward to reading—*Above the Waterfall*). Is this deliberate?

RR: Yes, it is. One thing I want to do is for landscape and my characters to be inextricably bound together. I believe the landscape people live in has to affect their psychology.

FS: Likewise, I have the feeling that the tone of your writing is becoming graver and graver, or somberer and somberer (it seems to me that the constant darkness of *The Cove* is emblematic of this evolution)—is this just a personal impression or does it make sense to you?

RR: I think it's true. Part of it is, especially with *Serena* and *The Cove*, caused by the political situation in the United States. Often the best way to talk about the present is through the past. This is not a good time for my country. But actually this new novel[4] is a book more about wonder, about how nature might sustain us. I wanted to look at the world a little more hopefully.

FS: I was actually amazed to discover that the list of your published books starts with an instance of comedy with *The Night The New Jesus Fell to Earth* (1994). Some of the situations you created in that collection are just hilarious. Could you imagine returning to comedy?

RR: I may; I like comic writing. The writers I admire most are able to be both tragic and comic: Shakespeare, Melville, Faulkner—Faulkner can be hilarious—O'Connor. To see both the tragic and the comic is to hold a mirror up to life. Usually in my short story collections I have at least one story that is comic. *Burning Bright* has one about the guitar player[5] that is supposed to be funny. It's sad in a way, but it's funny too.

FS: How do you come up with the titles of your books?

RR: They usually emerge when I'm deep into the book, sometimes toward the end. I had a really tough time with *The Cove*. I just could not find a title that gave me what I wanted. I wanted to call it *Shadowland* but that title had been used for a couple of books. But I think *The Cove* works.

FS: You often evoked how the idea for a plot first came to you in the form of an image. Would it be correct to assume that it first comes to you in the form of a poem, likely to develop into a short story that, if the initial image is haunting enough, may transform into a novel?

RR: That's pretty much it. It's a scary way to work because I don't outline. I just have faith that the image is enough. When I wrote *Serena* all I had was an image of her on horseback.

FS: You are a full time poet, short story writer and novelist. Or shall I formulate things in a different order?

RR: No, I hope I've done worthwhile work in all three. When I started writing I first wrote a few short stories and a few poems; then I pretty much just wrote poetry for six or seven years. Then I wrote short stories for a couple of years. Yes, it is kind of a movement toward the novel.

FS: What happened to your creative mind between the short story entitled "Pemberton's Bride" (published in *Chemistry and Other Stories* in 2007) and *Serena* (2008)? The genitive form in the title of the short story somehow presents Serena as her husband's better half (but only a half), while in the novel she obviously takes precedence over him. How come?

RR: I think Serena simply became more and more interesting to me, particularly because in American fiction I don't think we have women quite like her. We have female characters who have power within a family, but to have a woman, particularly in 1928–1929, that has that kind of will to go out and have control over hundreds of men goes beyond that. She was so strong she somehow pushed me aside as well and put herself at the center of this world. That was a strange experience writing that book. I went into a deep, dark place and I've never been that consumed by a book before or since. People said they could tell a difference after I finished it, even physically.

FS: Why did you decide to alleviate the denouement of Rachel's story in the novel's version of it (in the short story, she is sacrificed; in the novel, she manages to escape)?

RR: I believe Serena changes some during the novel, more so than most readers seem to recognize. But I thought I needed a character who made a larger transformation. And I also felt I had to be true to the world. There are always Serenas out there, but there are always people who will fight them and people who will find their power from love instead of the desire for power.

FS: So, paradoxically, you somehow became more hopeful with the novel and your decision to save Rachel, showing she could fight?
RR: Yes. One thing I did very deliberately: in the opening scene of *Serena*, I wanted the novel to open more like a play than a novel. All the main characters are on the train station's wooden platform. And Rachel does not move; in that whole scene, she doesn't move. Then, from being completely immobile, she evolves into a woman who is strong enough to triumph over Galloway and Serena.

FS: Now comes a fishy question: what about the overwhelming presence of trout in Southern writing? Trout have a strong symbolical dimension in Faulkner's *The Sound and the Fury* (in Quentin's monologue); the same can be said of the finale of Cormac McCarthy's *The Road*, where the appearance of trout in the river seems to suggest the plausible return of life. In your work, trout reoccur whatever form of writing you pick up as, it seems to me, a metaphor of resilience.
RR: Trout have to live in a pure environment unlike human beings; they can't live in filth! And so I think there is a kind of wonder; to me, they're incredibly beautiful creatures. I can remember being only four or five and staring for long periods at them, just watching them swimming in the water. But also, like Faulkner in "The Bear," the idea that when such creatures disappear, we have lost something that cannot be brought back. And I think this is what McCarthy is getting at, at the end of *The Road*. They mean many things: beauty, wonder, and fragility, in the sense that they can be easily destroyed. In *The World Made Straight*[6] I felt that Travis's response to the trout showed his maturity: first he's just catching them without even caring about killing them, but then he has that moment when he is in the field and sees the beauty of them and he never has before. To me, that's a sign of maturation and wisdom on his part.

FS: I believe you are an amazing choreographer of scenes of drowning. Would it be too personal to ask you where your fascination with drowning comes from?

RR: No, it wouldn't be. I have always been fascinated by water, that's one thing. And I think part of that was probably my religious upbringing. I was brought up in the Baptist Church and in the Baptist Church they totally immerse you. That is an experience that you don't forget because it's somewhat terrifying. I have always been attracted to water. Concerning drowning, I guess it is that whole idea of water being able to destroy and to give life—that paradox. Part of my ancestry is Welsh and in Welsh folklore water is seen as a conduit between the living and the dead. In *Saints at the River*[7] I hoped to evoke that idea. But it's a strange obsession and not something I tend to do consciously. People started pointing it out in my work and, yes, it is there; it is all over the place.

FS: Your admirers have been impatiently looking forward to the release of the film adaptation of *Serena* next fall. What's your perception of Susan Bier's adaptation? Of the cast? Is Jennifer Lawrence's acting the part of Serena somehow faithful to your first idea of your character?
RR: Well, I don't know. I haven't seen the movie or read the script; I have deliberately stayed out of the process. So I don't know much about the film except that I do like Susanne Bier's movies. Have you seen any?

FS: I saw *Brothers*[8] and I liked it a lot.
RR: I think she is a serious director and Jennifer Lawrence is a very good actress. Her performance in *Winter's Bone*[9] was extraordinary.

FS: What about the coming release of the movie adaptation of *The World Made Straight* (2006)? The film is David Burris's first film as a director. The attention you get from the movies is quite remarkable, isn't it?
RR: It's been surprising. It's something I never expected.

FS: What happens in the mind of a writer whose most successful novels are adapted into movies?
RR: It's a bit unsettling, but it brings people to the books who might normally not read them. There's some money that comes into it, which is nice.

FS: I know it took time, but it seems you're getting a great deal of attention all of a sudden.
RR: Yes, but I believe it was good that I had to wait a long time. If the recognition had happened earlier, it might not have been a good thing for me.

I've been able to concentrate solely on the writing most of my career. Being ignored can be a blessing for a young writer.

FS: Are you still teaching?
RR: Yes, I am.

FS: Most of your writings are characterized by a rather sharp contrast between the restriction, distance and suggestiveness (I'm still looking for the word that may encompass such impressions—maybe "delicacy?") of your writing style and the extreme violence of some of the scenes you describe. Could this be considered one of the main tenets of your aesthetics as a writer?
RR: I think very often that's what makes particularly tragic writing bearable to us. That's why we can respond to Shakespeare. If the language were not so beautiful and sublime, particularly in a play such as *King Lear*, the experience would be unbearable. What I'm trying for in my work—it's up to the reader to decide if I do—is the sublime. I want my work to take the reader to that place. And I think you can do that with that juxtaposition of language and violence. Violence allows revelation of character; that's what O'Connor believed and I think she's right. You don't use it to titillate; you use it to get to the essence of who a character is.

FS: In the writing process is the plausible cathartic dimension of your work foremost in your mind?
RR: I'm very conscious that I'm often taking the reader into a deep place, sometimes a very dark place. By entering that place, I hope the reader might find something cathartic.

FS: I'm probably not the first person that tells you that the denouement of *The World Made Straight* is particularly heart-rending. Did Leonard really have to die?
RR: I hated for him to die; I really did. Writing that scene was hard emotionally for me, particularly as he was thinking of his child as he was dying. But I think that he had to die because there was this historical balance with the Civil War killings. For his sacrifice to matter in an ultimate way, Leonard had to offer up his life. Interestingly, I actually wrote a short story where Travis was going to be killed; I felt so bad about killing a teenager that I revived him, but then I ended up killing Leonard. But I have had a lot of

complaints about his death from readers, which I take as a compliment. It means that I succeeded in creating a character that they cared deeply about.

FS: Another common feature of your writing is the reappearance of maimed or mutilated characters, either literally (for instance Galloway, his mother, Dr. Cheney in *Serena*; Hank in *The Cove*) or symbolically (Laurel or Walter in *The Cove*, but it seems to me there are many more). Aren't they somehow all avatars or variations of the figure of Tiresias, the blind seer whose very blindness qualifies him as a seer?

RR: Yes, I'm very fond of mythology, as is obvious in *The Cove* where I evoke the Orpheus myth, and in *Serena* Galloway's mother is definitely a seer in the sense you describe. I think I tend to use maimed characters with the idea that the world they inhabit is wounded. In *One Foot in Eden*, I wanted Billy to evoke the Fisher King in Grail mythology; he is wounded and the land is dying. Yes, I love to integrate those aspects into my work; I don't want it to be heavy-handed, but I want it to be there.

FS: Would it make sense to say that the characters I mentioned are somehow part of the gallery of grotesques started by O'Connor?

RR: Yes, you could certainly date it back to her. I don't know, there's something about the South: maybe it's partly our heritage, partly the region's Christian sensibility. Original sin argues we are flawed/grotesque from birth. O'Connor, a devout Christian, certainly believed that. Her characters' physical flaws are indicative of spiritual flaws.

FS: Would it be exaggerated to consider the return of figures of loss in your work as rewritings of the South's failure?

RR: I think there is something to that. The South has always been the part of the United States that's the poorest, the least educated. The part of the upper South I focus on has certainly had its share of hardship, of a failure to achieve the prosperity of the rest of America, though that failure is in large part due to the fact that more has been taken from the region, from coal and timber to soldiers for our wars, than given back. But this hardship has also produced an incredible outpouring of art—jazz, bluegrass, country music, blues, rock and roll, as well as a huge number of exceptional writers. There's a great quote in Carol Reed's movie *The Third Man*—a character says the Swiss have had four hundred years of peace and prosperity and all they've given us is the cuckoo clock. Art seems so often to come out of turmoil.

FS: I believe that one of the main forces of your short story collections is the ambiguity of their timeframe as, from one story to the next, you take your readers back and forth in time. In that way, in your last three collections— *Chemistry, Burning Bright, Nothing Gold Can Stay* (2013)— the Civil War is likely to cohabit with the Great Depression or with Modern America, while it is for your readers to pick up clues in order to determine when events are occurring. My impression is that there are at least two very divergent ways in which this changelessness can be interpreted: while such seclusion from the wider world is likely to appear as frightening, at the same time it is very reassuring to observe that some things, in keeping with the land you describe, may resist change and remain true to themselves.

RR: I believe so. I think there is something reassuring in that belief and also that other people have also endured challenges, because there never was an edenic time. In a sense, I'm writing a current that runs through time in those stories. And, also, paradoxically time is a kind of geography as well. It is also a way of showing people in much different cultural mindsets, even within a specific culture, and thus another way to probe for the universal within a specific cultural landscape. Faulkner does this obviously, as does Seamus Heaney in his poetry. In the story collections, I want the reader to be, at times, uncertain of the era. That uncertainty creates an effect that I want.

FS: You obviously do quite a lot of research before you write. Was the idea of Doctor Candler's ledgers in *The World Made Straight* directly inspired by your research on the Shelton Laurel Massacre?

RR: It was. I actually had a relative at that time who was a doctor in the area. I didn't have access to his ledgers. But my family had very deep roots in that region and from what I've been able to find out I'm pretty sure I had relatives on both sides of that massacre. So I just thought it would be interesting to have this man who had saved this boy's life to be there at the massacre. What would this mean to Leonard? What is our responsibility to the past? I did a lot of research on nineteenth-century medicine; so everything in the journal is what a doctor would have done. I enjoy research.

FS: I am forever trying to put words on the forcefulness of your writing and I would like to suggest that, though they could not be more different, *Saints at the River* and *Serena* are very representative of what you are doing when you write: my assumption is that a great part of the force of your writing essentially rests on its subtlety. You manage to picture characters and

situations that are often extreme because they are either particularly polemical (as when you expose the conflict opposing the mourners in search of the lost corpse of their daughter and the environmentalists in *Saints*) or tragically violent (indeed, nothing can stop Serena's ambition) without passing judgment. Yet I do not want to suggest that you are stuck in the grey zone of "either . . . or" or "neither . . . nor" because this is absolutely not true. You locate your narrative stance right in the middle of the crisis and I think you are particularly good at exposing the complexities of a situation.
RR: That's my hope.

FS: The effect this has on your readers is that they're encouraged to think before they flare up. Does this make sense to you?
RR: Exactly, that's what I want. Black and white is for politicians; they give the easy answers, the simplifications. For me, this is a matter of respecting the reader—that the reader doesn't have to be preached to or told how to feel. To me, that's insulting the reader's intelligence. I believe that a novel is an act of communion between the author and the reader; it's a shared consciousness, very intimate. The reader is taking these blotches of ink I've written and bringing them to life.

FS: Most of your works are suggestive of a dramatic contrast between the extreme violence of human exchanges and the almost imperturbable serenity and beauty of nature. The mountains' rock-hard permanence almost indirectly reads as a commentary on the triviality of men, while constantly highlighting their finitude.
RR: Yes, I would agree. I think the psychological makeup of mountain people is very interesting. A person has to be influenced at seeing these things that have been there for millions of years, blocking any long gaze, reminding oneself of one's small life, perhaps its insignificance? Yet sometimes the mountains can also be like a womb, protective from the outside world. That duality is very interesting to me.

FS: How is the writing of *Above the Waterfall* progressing?
RR: It's going; I'm doing something really different. I've got a narrator who is attempting to create her own language. It has been a difficult book and I've come close to giving up on it several times.

FS: Is there a specific timeframe?
RR: Yes, the present.

FS: May I ask you whether one of your own books is your "heart's darling"?
RR: Yes; two of them. But if I had to pick one it would be *Serena*. I feel that's the one that is the most ambitious. But I also love *One Foot in Eden*; maybe that's because it's the first novel I published, but also for what I did in that book with the vernacular.
FS: Thank you, very much.

Notes

1. Caddy is the only sister in the Compson family in Faulkner's *The Sound and the Fury* (1929).

2. A collection of twelve short stories, *Burning Bright*, was first published in 2010.

3. Ron Rash's fifth novel, *The Cove*, was first published in 2012. It was translated by Le Seuil as *Une terre d'ombre* (2014).

4. Rash is evoking his novel in progress, *Above the Waterfall*, which will probably come out in 2015.

5. That story, entitled "Waiting for the End of the World," is a first-person narrative told by an ex-teacher become guitar player who makes ends meet by playing all night long in a seedy joint. At the patrons' request, he keeps playing Lynyrd Skynyrd's "Free Bird" and obviously is sick and tired of having to do so.

6. *The World Made Straight* was first published in 2006; it was translated in French as *Le Monde à l'endroit* (Seuil, 2012).

7. *Saints at the River* is Rash's second novel, published in 2004. It relates the aftermath of a twelve-year-old girl's drowning in the Tamassee River in South Carolina, as decisions have to be made in order to rescue her body. The novel has not yet been translated into French.

8. *Brothers* is a 2004 Danish film written and directed by Susanne Bier.

9. *Winter's Bone* is a 2011 film directed by Debra Granik; it was adapted from Daniel Woodrell's 2006 novel of the same title.

Interview with Ron Rash

Rob Neufeld / 2014

From *The Read on WNC* Apr. 9, 2015. Edited version published in the *Asheville Citizen-Times* Nov. 2, 2014. Reprinted by permission of Rob Neufeld, author; producer; book and local history feature writer, *Asheville Citizen-Times*.

Rob Neufeld: My head is now so full of Ron Rash characters.
Ron Rash: There's a load of them.

RN: Did you have to reread everything in order to put *Something Rich and Strange* together?
RR: I had to reread every story. That's pretty much thirty five years of writing.

RN: What was that experience like?
RR: I could see changes in my style and my voice. I guess I have a hundred short stories. What I did was pick the thirty four I thought were the best.

RN: I bet there were some you left out you were sorry you couldn't put in.
RR: There were, several that were in *Chemistry*. I could only take four from that because of copyright problems.

RN: Oh—so that's why "Not Waving but Drowning" didn't get in.
RR: Yeah, and "Overtime," the one about the basketball players. I hate that, but I couldn't do anything about it.

RN: I loved you starting out the collection with the story "Hard Times."
RR: I thought that was the one to start off with. I thought it set a tone and put the reader into I'd guess you'd say my psychic landscape [laughs]. I put in "3 A.M." second. I wanted to do that because that first story is a tough one

to read because of the sadness and the darkness of it. "3 A.M.," I hope, is a story that gives the reader a little bit of a recovery.

RN: Do you think about the various ways of getting out of grim situations and finding redemption, solace, or grace?
RR: It comes from trying to be true to the world. There are hard times for people, and there is humor, courage, grace, and goodness. In the story "Hard Times," you see people trying to do the best they can. A story like that, in some ways, might hearten us through our own hard times . . . It's interesting that you bring that up because I'm finishing up *Above the Waterfall* right now, my new novel . . . It's a book about finding wonder in the world. To be true to the world, I have to acknowledge that as well.

RN: The first indelible image in "Hard Times" is Hartley killing his dog in response to the insult from Edna, the farm woman. Do you find that insulting someone's intelligence and integrity is a particularly high crime?
RR: Yeah, particularly with someone who has little else. Hartley has nothing, essentially, but his pride and honor. And she's accusing him of letting his dog go out and cause damage, and that's such an affront to him because he has so little. Doing that to people with less power is a horrible thing.

RN: How have you become familiar with people like your characters?
RR: Probably a lot of what I learned came early, because of my family and because of differences I saw in education and income . . . For almost seventeen years, I taught at a community college. In that environment, you see so many people from tough situations. I was getting adults who had been out of school twenty years, who'd been suddenly divorced or laid off from their jobs. I found them for the most part heroic. It was very difficult for them to come back. They were intimidated at times. It was tough financially to be able to do it. I saw a lot of people that I wouldn't have seen if I had been at a university all my life. I taught English for seventeen years at a community college, and for two years at a high school in a rural, poor area. It was very rewarding, and in some ways troubling because I could say the wrong thing. Something that I said that I wasn't thinking about might discourage a student, who had worked so hard to come back. I was aware very often of their situations.

RN: It sounds like you were the kind of teacher who took a real interest in each individual student.

RR: I tried. I tried not to judge them too quickly. Say a student is out a week. It might be that their power had been shut off. I'd had that happen. They had all sorts of stresses on them. Something might happen at their job, the kinds of things that a lot of people have the luxury of not worrying about. I wouldn't pry, but I would let them know I was open to what was happening, and try to encourage them. One of the joys of my life has been meeting some of these students years later, sometimes at readings, and them telling me that my class had been valuable to them.

RN: Let's see, who are the teachers in your stories? There's Ginny, who let the girl go to the classroom window during that hurricane, and then became the Night Hawk on the radio.
RR: Well, I think Leonard in *The World Made Straight*—that was really a book about a man for whom teaching was his calling; and when he tried to deny it, he couldn't.

RN: Are there some characters that you put yourself into more than others?
RR: I think sometimes there are characters I feel a deeper connection to. Actually, Ginny's one. I'm not an overtly autobiographical writer. "Chemistry"—that story—I'd certainly identify with that. That one is one of the few that has autobiographical elements.

RN: How do you feel when you write about a bad guy?
RR: One of the secrets that writers know is that very often writing about the bad guys, or bad girls, is more fun than writing about good people. It's empathy and trying to imagine that kind of darkness. The goal is to deepen the mystery of what it means to be human . . . The bad guys I write about, I think you can find plenty of people who fit the mold.

RN: What is that mold?
RR: I think it's different molds. When I'm writing Chauncey Fife in *The Cove*, it's that rah-rah patriot who never goes to war, but sends other people's children . . . The name Chauncey is Cheney and Hannity. Cheney got deferments, and he's a big hawk to send other people and other people's children to war. I think part of an artist's responsibility is to bring those people into the literary world because they're in the real world; and also to expose them.

RN: Do you think it's more effective to do that through fiction rather than through journalism?

RR: I wouldn't know about that. One thing I feel as a fiction writer, I have a little more freedom. I can create characters that are archetypes of these people. You want them to be distinctive characters. I don't want my work to be didactic. For instance, if I write an op-ed about fracking, I'm going to be more overt than I'd be in a novel because part of what I want to do in a novel is not so much answer the questions, but respect the reader enough to present the questions, and have enough faith in leaving things up to the reader. When a reader reads *Serena*, I don't tell the reader that this kind of logging is bad. Actually, I show people who desperately need it—not just the entrepreneurs, but also the people around the area, the loggers, these people who desperately needed these jobs. When I talk about National Parks, I don't avoid the fact that people who lived in the Smokies were run out of their homes and off their land. Those are important questions. What is the price? I don't need to preach to my audience. That's not my role.

RN: But you would very much want people to be able to read your stories and come up with questions for themselves such as "What is the price?" You want them to have clear questions that come out of it.

RR: I see the writer's role as more as witness. When I write *The Cove*, the question readers ask is, "What is patriotism?" Can it be abused with a person like Chauncey, who uses it for his own ends, and hides behind these words—"patriot," "Hun"?

RN: I was looking at your author photo on your book, *The Night the New Jesus Fell to Earth*. You look like Madison Bumgarner, someone who would wrangle horses. You don't look like Truman Capote.

RR: No, you're right. I haven't got an ascot on.

RN: What is it like being a physically strong person and a sensitive poet person?

RR: It's a way of blending in, of being like a chameleon. I don't want to sound dramatic, but I've always sensed that I was seeing the world a little bit different than most of the people around me, even growing up. I was also conscious that this is something that I didn't want people to know necessarily. I think you keep that to yourself. For a long time I wrote with nobody knowing I was doing it. One reason was I just wasn't sure that I was any good at it. The other reason was it seemed a little bit strange. Why is he doing this? And then when my friends found out, they started calling me Ron Boy, like John Boy on *The Waltons*. I think as a writer or any kind of artist, you're always aware that you're seeing the world, or feeling the world, in a different way. I mean, you have to; otherwise, everybody would write. What is it that would make someone want to write anyway? It's kind of bizarre. Particularly fiction—to make up stories, to tell three hundred-page lies? That's pretty strange.

RN: It's the lucky person who discovers what his or her aptitudes are early.
RR: I think I always did have empathy. I can remember even when I was very small, I would see somebody who was in a wheelchair or something like that, and it would really affect me. Maybe it was affecting everyone else, I don't know, but I remember those kinds of things I could get emotional about.

RN: How much control did you have over *Something Rich and Strange*—which stories to include, the order, how to title it?
RR: I had total control. And I thought that was the right title. It comes from *The Tempest*. Ariel is telling Ferdinand that his father has drowned, but he's become something rich and strange. It's about transformation. That's what art does. Even when writing a very dark story that maybe doesn't even have a sense of grace, you hope there's a kind of beauty in the language, in the art, that is able to transform that into more than mere sadness.

RN: And that story, "Something Rich and Strange," is probably the best example of that.
RR: Yeah.

RN: It was used to create the novel, *Saints at the River*, which took such different turns from the story.
RR: Yeah, very different.

RN: What are your feelings about the differences between those two works, the story and the novel?
RR: It's almost like a musician with different riffs. With every poem, story, and novel, I'm trying to create a kind of quilt. There's an interconnectedness, taking stories, images, and themes and putting them in a different patch, different color, hue. One aspect of my work that I've been conscious of early on is that it's all connected.

RN: Do you find the connections happening in more ways than theme?

RR: I've got stories set on the same road in Boone in 1865 and early 20th century, and during World War II and in contemporary times. All these journeys are going on. Blending time is important to me. One thing that's important in terms of placement of stories in books, I want the reader to sometimes feel unmoored from time. The reader might think, this is a contemporary story and then might realize two pages in, it's 1930. I want that.

RN: Why is that?

RR: This is hard for me to articulate. I think it does something as far as taking the reader into another place, a mental space, a kind of uncertainty. What did it do for you? Did it confuse you, or is there a fluidity of time? One thing it does is add a kind of depth in that there's a repetition through the generations of these things, and there are variations. Time is a kind of geography as well. It allows us to go into different mindsets, different cultures.

RN: In your story, "The Corpse Bird," the main character, who's connected to a past time, has read about the Hmong, so there's a connection between traditional Appalachian thinking and pre-modern thinking. Is that right?

RR: Yeah, in that story. And I'm fascinated with the idea of what we have lost as human beings. There are tribes that can see things in the heavens that we can't. I have had this kind of vision when I have spent a lot of time outdoors. I had a situation when I knew that there was a snake on the other side of a log. Something in me knew, though I couldn't see it. It's almost as if something jerked my leg back. I've talked with a number of people who have spent a lot of time outdoors, and they sense the same thing. Hunters tell me they know the deer's about to appear.

RN: Is there a story that contains the kind of character that has that kind of sense?

RR: I'm just finishing up a novel that has exactly that sense.

RN: Wow!

RR: My new novel, *Above the Waterfall*, is about a woman who has this incredible connection to nature, and that's the way she has to survive. She's actually gone to the point of where she is creating a new language of the world out of nature. She's a park ranger, and she brings children into the park and has them do things such as, "What do you see in this field? And what else?" She shows them a trout and asks, "If you had a friend that had never seen a fish before, how would you describe it?" Making them see the world. The whole book is about that. This is my most optimistic book. Nobody drowns. Nobody dies. It ends happy. People are going to be immensely disappointed, probably. [laughs] No, I think they will be relieved, actually.

RN: I think it will be a sensation.
RR: It's my most poetic book.

RN: So, what took you so long to write this kind of thing?
RR: That's a good question. My writing reflects the state of the country. Our country has been a darker place than it has been in a very long time. There are things that worry me politically. It affects my perception of the world, and even when I'm writing about the past, I'm writing about the present. I've wanted to do this because to be true to the world, and to be true to life, there's an incredible wonder. Maybe I think because I'm getting older now, I think that only when you sense you're going to lose something can you really value it. As I get older, I'm more and more aware of the wonder of being alive, of the natural world, of the mystery of it. It was time for me to write this book. The other thing I would say about that, hoping not to be grandiose, is that part of what writers do is we want to give hope and talk about what is good, what is there to celebrate.

RN: Do you confront the issue of climate change?
RR: That's what this woman's so concerned about. The first thing she has to do in this new novel is show children that they're connected to the world. You have to know that nature exists before you can care about it. I think we live in a world now where everything's seen through a screen, and we have this illusion that we're outside the natural world. And we're not. We think we're not connected to the natural world, and we can do anything to it.

RN: There's an interesting variety in your stories. You have that story, "Waiting for the End of the World." In it, you refer to the pent-up Appalachian soul. What gifts or wisdom does the Appalachian soul have for the world?
RR: Oh, man. We have so many good writers coming out of the region now, having had the opportunity to go to college. There's a kind of energy that's similar to what happened in the lower South in the twenties and thirties.

RN: So, you're saying that the pent-up Appalachian soul is being released now?

RR: Yes, I think in the stories, and in the beautiful, rich language of the region. At the same time, we have these serious issues, such as fracking, that need to be dealt with and thought about very seriously.

RN: It seems to me that your use of the mountain language, and mountain poetry, and colloquial sayings increased as your writing went along.

RR: Yeah, I think I've tried to go deeper and deeper into my past. Who am I? Where did I come from? What shaped me? The first poem in *Among the Believers* is set on the border between Scotland and England. Those things helped shape me, too. One thing I've tried to do as a writer who writes about a particular place is to explore that world as deeply and intimately as I can.

RN: You've answered the question about how you look over your career very well. But is there anything else you'd like to say?

RR: It is interesting to go back and look at the stories. I never re-read my novels; and I rarely re-read a story. The only time I'll do that is when I'm reading for an audience. It was interesting to go back [for the collection]. The stories in *The New Jesus*—one thing I was glad to see was that I don't think I was condescending to the people. That's easy for a young writer to do—you know, I left this hick town and I'm so glad to get out of there. I went back and I read those stories, and obviously some of those stories are satirical, and you have characters like Larry, but I think that I showed a love of that place.

RN: So I looked up Ron Rash online, and there isn't a Ron Rash website. But then again, there is. There's Ron Rash, the tattoo artist.

RR: Somebody told me about that.

RN: You don't have a tattoo, do you?

RR: No, no.

RN: Would you ever have a tattoo?

RR: If I did one, it would be a Carolina parakeet. That bird is like a talisman for me.

RN: That story that includes it mentions that they flock together when they're shot at.

RR: That image, when I first read it, I was in tears.

RN: You have achieved a life dream with your career. Have you ever received a great gift?

RR: I did a reading recently, and a woman, the host, gave me a magazine made of wormy chestnut. Her father had made it. I've talked about the chestnuts, and the chestnuts had been so much a part of Appalachian forests.

Above the Waterfall by Ron Rash, and Talk with Author

Rob Neufeld / 2015

From *The Read on WNC* Aug. 30, 2015. Published in the *Asheville Citizen-Times* Aug. 29, 2015. Reprinted by permission of Rob Neufeld, author; producer; book and local history feature writer, *Asheville Citizen-Times*.

Ron Rash's new novel, *Above the Waterfall*, weds a contemporary thriller with a portrayal of people tapping an ancient way of being.

A fish kill precipitates the story involving fishing rights, a crystal meth epidemic, and two reeling characters: Les, the county sheriff, who's sick of human depravity and preparing to retire; and Becky, a park ranger, who has lived in a dream of words and animals ever since she'd witnessed her schoolteacher being shot by an intruder.

Nature watch

"I like to go up above that waterfall and look at them specks," Gerald Black-welder, a mountain hold-out, responds when questioned about poaching on what has become private resort property.

"That water's so clear you can see every dot on them."

Watching is the first step toward getting to be nature-smart, Rash observed in an interview Monday.

Becky's aptitude for that kind of "old awareness" grew from the muteness that afflicted her after the shooting and from her time on her grandparents' farm, to which she'd been sent by exasperated parents.

"Word and wonder and world could be one," Becky writes.

Two voices

Becky takes turns narrating the novel with Les. In her opening chapter, she establishes her voice.

"I watch last light lift off level land," she murmurs, walking in her park. "Ground shadows seep and thicken . . . The meadow itself becomes a pond filling."

In the meantime, Les stages a meth bust in a trailer and finds a destroyed woman who points to the microwave when asked where her infant is.

"For a few moments no one breathed," Les recounts. "It was like we believed if we were still enough that her words and their meaning might slide right past us and evaporate."

As his characters seek ways out of their hurts, Rash arranges themes like flowers and hooks it all to a thriller plot, featuring clues and solutions. The result is an original product that has you thinking about it afterward.
The following interview took place on August 24, 2015.

Rob Neufeld: It was great looking into your poetic state of mind with your character, Becky.
Ron Rash: I wanted to do something a little bit different this time. The voice of that woman, I just wanted to see what I could do with it, so I ran with it.

Rob: How much did you go into your own practice of writing poetry in order to create Becky?
Ron: I hoped to be able to use all that I've learned over the years writing poetry in a voice that speaks in prose, conveys information. I particularly used [Gerard Manley] Hopkins. I did the best I could to make every syllable count . . . Hopkins has that kind of intensity that Becky has to see the world in. She has to put herself this deeply into the natural world to survive.

Rob: It's compelling when she says she wants sight, sense, sound, words, and the world all come together. Could you talk about that some?
Ron: This was a book in which I was trying to reach a place that is almost beyond words . . . Part of what Becky is trying to do is close up the gap as much as possible between language and vision. Also, she had a horrific experience one time when she'd spoken. She believes she caused her teacher's death by being afraid and speaking out loud. It's almost as if the whole idea of language is corrupted by that. She can't get past the destructiveness of her utterance. She's trying to restore a language that she can survive with,

a language that will restore the world, restore beauty and hope. She's grasping for it almost like a lifeboat, and not just the language, but also the ability to experience nature so deeply she can transcend into it, get as close into it as she can. The language is stretching and straining to get there as well.

Rob: How do you figure out a voice like that?

Ron: She is feeling or seeing the world in a way that maybe nobody else was. I think that's where I was thinking not just of Hopkins, but also a little bit of Emily Dickinson. Emily Dickinson, she does these beautiful lines, she makes you see the world in a way you haven't before. But also you just get the sense that no one's ever thought quite this way before . . . That's the hope, that somebody can think this way, or make these connections; to see just the outline of a fish and think how would that sound.

Rob: Can you give me a fitting Emily Dickinson poem to look at?

Ron: Look at "A Narrow Fellow in the Grass."

Rob: Let's talk about Les, a character who has to deal with his former cowardice. How did his character develop for you in this novel?

Ron: Oh, this book changed so much. When I first started it, Becky didn't even have a voice.

Rob: Wow.

Ron: It was all told from Les' point of view. I knew he was connected to her. As I got into the drafts and he started developing, she did, too. I think they're both trying to find a way to survive. Because of this human but horrific thing that Les had done, telling his wife, "Well, just go ahead and kill yourself"—and she almost did—that since then, he's tried to look for the worst in the world because in a way it lets him off the hook . . . I see Becky at the same time—and it's words that are so destructive for both of them—Becky has to find the good and see the beauty to survive.

Rob: How did she come into your head?

Ron: I knew there was going to be a crime—or a fishkill—because I always start with images, and the image that started this one was a fishkill. I could see the dead trout in the stream. And I knew that Les was going to be working with her. I also knew that they both were scared of any kind of commitment to another human being.

Rob: Why is that?

Ron: For her, it was not only the shooting, but then when she had finally fallen in love with someone, and trusted someone, he turned out to be an [eco-] terrorist. Les, I think, is afraid of what he could do to another person. I knew that these were two loners. I just thought of [the painter, Edward] Hopper. As different as his landscapes are, there was something about what he does that these characters are also doing—that separateness.

Rob: That's great. So, Becky was a major character but not a narrator in the first drafts.

Ron: Right. And it was really more of a plot-driven book, a whodunit, and I brought in SBI agents, and made it into an eco-terrorist story, and I thought, "This is horrible." And it was. So I asked myself, "What is this book really about? What is the core of this thing?" And it's that there are these two people who have been severely wounded by language and who are trying in some way to find a way back into the world. They're both exiles in different ways. They're people who have been drawn to loneliness.

Rob: Despite the human suffering and the loss of animal species, the book, because of the characters, is not a downer.

Ron: I think this is my most optimistic book, which is not raising the bar too high.

Rob: [laughs] How does one effectively communicate the urgency regarding ecological disaster?

Ron: I think I do that in this book. Becky has that vision later in the book . . . where she's able to imagine a world when there's not anything left alive. I think the last line is: "wind and water pass past unheard." A lot of this book is about the need to protect the natural world, or revere it. But I think people have to first see the world before they can even care about it.

Additional Resources

Aiken, Elisabeth C. "Capitalizing on Appalachia: Resisting Colonization and Exploitation in the Works of Ron Rash and Fred Chappell." *Dissertation Abstracts International* 75.8 (2015): n. pag. *MLA International Bibliography*. Web. 6 Aug. 2015.

Baldwin, Kara. "'Incredible Eloquence': How Ron Rash's Novels Keep the Celtic Literary Tradition Alive. *South Carolina Review* 39.1 (2006): 37–45. *MLA International Bibliography*. Web. 6 Aug. 2015.

Bjerre, Thomas Ærvold. "Ron Rash: *One Foot in Eden.*" *Still in Print: The Southern Novel Today*. 233–247. Columbia, SC: U of South Carolina P, 2010. *MLA International Bibliography*. Web. 6 Aug. 2015.

Boyleston, Matthew. "Wild Boar in These Woods: The Influence of Seamus Heaney on the Poetry of Ron Rash." *South Carolina Review* 41.2 (2009): 11–17. *MLA International Bibliography*. Web. 6 Aug. 2015.

Brinkmeyer, Robert H., Jr. "Discovering Gold in the Back of Beyond: The Fiction of Ron Rash." *Virginia Quarterly Review* 89.3 (2013): 219–223. *Academic Search Complete*. Web. 6 Aug. 2015.

Brown, Joyce Compton. "The Dark and Clear Vision of Ron Rash." *Appalachian Heritage* 30.4 (2002): 15–24. *MLA International Bibliography*. Web. 6 Aug. 2015.

Brown, Joyce Compton, and Mark Powell. "Ron Rash's *Serena* and the 'Blank and Pitiless Gaze' of Exploitation in Appalachia." *North Carolina Literary Review* 19 (2010): 70–89. *MLA International Bibliography*. Web. 6 Aug. 2015.

Foxofbama. "My January Interview with Ron Rash." *Asfoxseesit*. Blogspot, 10 September 2010. Web. 6 Aug. 2015.

Graves, Jesse. "Lattice Work: Formal Tendencies in the Poetry of Robert Morgan and Ron Rash." *Southern Quarterly* 45.1 (2007): 78–86. *Academic Search Complete*. Web. 6 Aug. 2015.

Hecht, Anthony. "A Gift Matched with Skills of the First Order." *Among the Believers*. By Ron Rash. Oak Ridge: Iris, 2000. xi–xv. Print.

Higgins, Anna Dunlap. "'Anything but Surrender': Preserving Southern Appalachia in the Works of Ron Rash." *North Carolina Literary Review* 13 (2004): 49–58. *MLA International Bibliography*. Web. 6 Aug. 2015.

House, Silas. "Making Himself Heard." *Appalachian Heritage* 30.4 (2002): 11–14. *MLA International Bibliography*. Web. 6 Aug. 2015.

———. "A Matter of Life and Death: Old and New Appalachia Meet in *One Foot in Eden*." *Iron Mountain Review* 20 (2004): 21–25. *MLA International Bibliography*. Web. 6 Aug. 2015.

Hovis, George. "The Legacy of Thomas Wolfe in Contemporary Appalachian Fiction: Four Recent North Carolina Novels." *Thomas Wolfe Review* 36.1–2 (2012): 70–91. *MLA International Bibliography*. Web. 6 Aug. 2015.

Lane, John. "The Girl in the River: The Wild & Scenic Chattooga, Ron Rash's *Saints at the River*, and the Drowning of Rachel Trois." *South Carolina Review* 41.1 (2008): 162–167. *MLA International Bibliography*. Web. 6 Aug. 2015.

Lang, John. *Understanding Ron Rash*. Columbia: U of South Carolina P, 2014.

Lee, Joshua. "The Pembertons and Corporate Greed: An Ecocritical Look at Ron Rash's *Serena*." *James Dickey Review* 29.2 (2013): 44–60. *Literary Reference Center Plus*. Web. 2 Sept. 2015.

Lee, Maureen, and John Lee. "Ron Rash Bibliography." *South Carolina Review* 39.1(2006): 46–56. *MLA International Bibliography*. Web. 6 Aug. 2015.

Lefler, Susan M. "Inside the Prism: Themes that Flow Throughout Ron Rash's Works." *Appalachian Heritage* 32.4 (2004): 72–77. *MLA International Bibliography*. Web. 6 Aug. 2015.

Miller, Mindy Beth. "Long Remember, Long Recall: The Preservation of Appalachian Regional Heritage in Ron Rash's *One Foot in Eden*." *Journal of Kentucky Studies* 26 (2009): 198–209. *MLA International Bibliography*. Web. 6 Aug. 2015.

Morrow, Christopher L. "Acknowledgment, Adaptation and Shakespeare in Ron Rash's *Serena*." *South Central Review: The Journal of the South Central Modern Language Association* 30.2 (2013): 136–161. *MLA International Bibliography*. Web. 6 Aug. 2015.

Peeler, Tim. "Resting on the Gift of Their Labors: The Poetry of Ron Rash." *Iron Mountain Review* 20 (2004): 7–12. *MLA International Bibliography*. Web. 6 Aug. 2015.

Rueda, Carmen. "Transience and Change in Appalachia: Ron Rash's *Nothing Gold Can Stay*." *Appalachian Journal* 42.1/2 (2014): 82–89. *America: History & Life*. Web. 6 Aug. 2015.

Satterwhite, Emily. "'The Longing for Home,' Appalachian Fiction, and Ron Rash." *Appalachian Journal* 42.1/2 (2014): 24–35. *America: History & Life*. Web. 6 Aug. 2015.

Shurbutt, Sylvia Bailey. "'*Burning Bright*': Language, Place, and Storytelling in the Poetry and Prose of Ron Rash." *Anthology of Appalachian Writers*. Ron Rash Volume IV. Shepherd University: Edward Brothers Printing, 2012. 18–56. Print.

Smith, Jimmy Dean. "Spirit Country: The Voice of the Earth and Ron Rash's Southern Appalachia." *North Carolina Literary Review* 20 (2011): 111–120. *MLA International Bibliography*. Web. 6 Aug. 2015.

Smith, Newton. "Words to Raise the Dead: The Poetry of Ron Rash." *Iron Mountain Review* 20 (2004): 13–20. *MLA International Bibliography*. Web. 6 Aug. 2015.

Vernon, Zackary. "Commemorating vs. Commodifying: Ron Rash and the Search for an Appalachian Literary Identity." *Appalachian Journal* 41.1/2 (2013): 104–124. *Literary Reference Center Plus.* Web. 2 Sept. 2015.

——."The Role of Witness: Ron Rash's Peculiarly Historical Consciousness." *South Carolina Review* 42.2 (2010): 19–24. *Literary Reference Center Plus.* Web. 6 Aug. 2015.

Warren, Karen Wheeler. "Loosening the Bible Belt: The Search for Alternative Spiritual Narratives in the Fiction of Randall Kenan, Lee Smith, and Ron Rash." *Dissertation Abstracts International, Section A: The Humanities and Social Sciences* 71.6 (2010): 2056. *MLA International Bibliography.* Web. 6 Aug. 2015.

Wilhelm, Randall. "Ghostly Bodies and Worker Voices: Power and Resistance in Ron Rash's *Eureka Mill." South Carolina Review* 42.2 (2010): 25–36. *Literary Reference Center Plus.* Web. 2 Sept. 2015.

——.*The Ron Rash Reader.* Columbia: U of South Carolina P, 2014. Print.

Willis, Rachel. "Masculinities and Murder: George Pemberton in Ron Rash's *Serena." James Dickey Review* 29.2 (2013): 13–34. *Literary Reference Center Plus.* Web. 2 Sept. 2015.

The World Made Straight. Dir. David Burris. Bifrost Pictures, 2015. Film.

Index

www.ingramcontent.com/pod-product-compliance
Lightning Source LLC
Chambersburg PA
CBHW020655030726
47498CB00002B/520